JAVA 3D™

API *Jump-Start*

ISBN 0-13-034076-6

9 780130 340764

Prentice Hall PTR Jump-Start Series

JAVA 3D API JUMP-START
Aaron E. Walsh and Doug Gehringer

MPEG-4 JUMP-START
Aaron E. Walsh and Mikaël Bourges-Sévenier

OTHER BOOKS BY AARON E. WALSH

XHTML EXAMPLE BY EXAMPLE
with Dave Raggett

CORE WEB3D
with Mikaël Bourges-Sévenier

JAVA 3D™

API *Jump-Start*

AARON E. WALSH • DOUG GEHRINGER

Prentice Hall PTR, Upper Saddle River, NJ 07458
www.phptr.com

Library of Congress Cataloging-in-Publication Data

Walsh, Aaron E.
Java 3D API jump-start / Aaron E. Walsh, Doug Gehringer.
p. cm.
Includes index.
ISBN 0-13-034076-6
1. Java (Computer program language) 2. Computer graphics. I. Gehringer, Doug.
II. Title.
QA76.73.J38 W35 2001
006.6'93—dc21

2001033945

Editorial/Production Supervision: Faye Gemmellaro
Acquisitions Editor: Tim Moore
Editorial Assistant: Allyson Kloss
Development Editor: Jim Markham
Manufacturing Manager: Maura Zaldivar
Marketing Manager: Debby van Dijk
Cover Design: Talar Agasyan
Cover Design Direction: Jerry Votta
Interior Design: Pine Tree Composition

Prentice-Hall, Inc.
Upper Saddle River, NJ 07458

Prentice Hall books are widely used by corporations and government agencies for training, marketing, and resale.

The publisher offers discounts on this book when ordered in bulk quantities.
For more information, contact Corporate Sales Department, phone: 800-382-3419; fax: 201-236-7141; e-mail: corpsales@prenhall.com
or write: Prentice Hall PTR
Corporate Sales Department
One Lake Street
Upper Saddle River, NJ 07458

Printed in the United States of America

10 9 8 7 6 5 4 3 2 1

0-13-034076-6

Pearson Education LTD.
Pearson Education Australia PTY, Limited
Pearson Education Singapore, Pte. Ltd.
Pearson Education North Asia Ltd.
Pearson Education Canada, Ltd.
Pearson Educación de Mexico, S.A. de C.V.
Pearson Education—Japan
Pearson Education Malaysia, Pte. Ltd.

Contents

Foreword

In March 1997, at the annual JavaOne developers conference, Henry Sowizral and I gave the world its first look the new Java 3D™ API. This demonstration mixed 3D animation, background music, and 3D spatialized sound—in an application written entirely in Java. Prior to seeing the demo of Java 3D, Java programmers were united in their unquestioning belief that Java was necessarily slow. Java 3D has helped to alter that perception. In the talk that accompanied the demo at JavaOne, we unveiled our plans for a high-level, 3D graphics API that would be easy to program without sacrificing performance. Developers were naturally excited by this new technology, and were anxious to realize the promise of creating and animating 3D content quickly and easily. No longer would they have to rely on low-level, platform-specific APIs to deliver their 3D content.

Fast forward four years: Java 3D is now a full-featured API in its second revision. Thousands of Java 3D programmers have sprung up eager to put their ideas onto a three-dimensional canvas. These developers have already realized many of the benefits of Java 3D. Java 3D does make it easier to develop 3D content. However, there are several challenges that an application writer has to overcome. Chief among them is the sheer size of the API. The 1.2 revision of the Java 3D API defines 159 public classes, 4 public interfaces, and over 2000 public methods, constructors, and fields. And that doesn't include the vector math classes in the javax.vecmath package or any of the utilities in the com.sun.j3d.* packages.

Navigating the classes in the Java 3D API is a daunting task. Where is a programmer to start? As of this writing, the only general purpose Java 3D book is the formal API specification, which is meant as a reference, not as a means to learn how to program in Java 3D. Further, Java 3D has many subtle, and often complex, interactions among its various classes that are difficult to describe within the confines of a specification. Java 3D programmers have been patiently waiting for a programming resource to help them get over the initial hurdle of programming in Java 3D.

Java 3D API Jump-Start fills this void with an easy-to-understand format that will have you writing your own Java 3D applications in no time. Its chapters are organized around key concepts, for which all of the pieces needed to understand a particular feature are discussed. The source code for the example programs shown in this book can be downloaded from the web, and are useful both as an aid in understanding the concepts and as a starting point for developing your own applications. Together, they will help you unlock the mysteries of Java 3D.

The authors of *Java 3D API Jump-Start* are uniquely qualified to write this book. Doug Gehringer was an early Java 3D user at Sun, where he worked on the implementation of the VRML97 loader for Java 3D. Doug also spent many hours helping application developers who were trying to decipher Java 3D from the API specification. Aaron Walsh has written several books on web-based 3D graphics and Java, including *Core Web3D* and *Java for Dummies*.

I believe that the Java 3D API is the future of 3D graphics on the web and in other environments where cross-platform applications are essential and programmer productivity is key. Its rich feature set and high-level constructs make it the API of choice among developers. Let this book be your guide in taking the first steps toward this future.

Kevin Rushforth
Java 3D Team
Sun Microsystems

Introductory Note

Although Java 3D has been available for several years, today it is truly poised to make a tremendous impact in the world of interactive 3D development. In much the same way that Java itself grew significantly in the years that have passed since it was first unveiled, the latest version of Java 3D is clearly ready for prime time. This is especially true when Java 3D is deployed over the Internet. As I wrote in *Core Web3D* (the book that led to the *Java 3D API Jump-Start* you are now reading), Java 3D is a power keg of potential just waiting to explode. The match is in your hands; all you have to do is strike it, one page at a time.

I suspect that *Java 3D API Jump-Start* will light the way for a new class of 3D applications. Led by Java 3D expert Doug Gehringer, this book is designed to get you up and running with Java 3D immediately. It teaches you, the professional Java developer, exactly what you need to know to jump headlong into Java 3D today.

As a Staff Engineer at Sun Microsystems, the company behind Java 3D, and a member of the Java 3D Engineering Team, Doug was uniquely qualified to drive *Java 3D API Jump-Start*. After working with Doug on *Core Web3D*, for which he was my Java 3D technical editor, it was clear to me that he was the person in whose hands the budding *Java 3D API Jump-Start* should be placed. This book was originally planned to be a simple enhancement and update to the Java 3D section featured in *Core Web3D*, and today, thanks to Doug, it's a comprehensive introduction to Java 3D that I believe you'll find an invaluable companion on your journey to mastering this exciting 3D extension to Java.

Doug has spent the past 14 years of his career at Sun working on graphics software, and as a result he has extensive experience programming for all of Sun's graphics APIs, including GKS, PHIGS, PEX, OpenGL, and, naturally, Java 3D. He's an expert on graphics performance tuning for large-scale applications, and he has worked on a number of the world's largest Java 3D projects. He was one of the first developers on the planet to use Java 3D, for which he co-authored the original Virtual Reality Modeling Language (VRML) loader that was maintained by the Web3D Consortium, and he is a respected member of the Java 3D community that he contributes to regularly.

In addition to all of his daily responsibilities, Doug took the time to develop a Java 3D Explorer application exclusively for you, the *Java 3D API Jump-Start* reader, while simultaneously writing new and improved material for this book. He also arranged for key members of Sun's Java 3D team to review the manuscript, which in turn made the material that you're about to read even stronger. I hope that you enjoy *Java 3D API Jump-Start*, and with it strike a flame that contributes to the explosion of interactive 3D for the Internet and beyond.

Aaron E. Walsh

Preface

Welcome to *Java 3D API Jump-Start*. This book was designed to enable Java programmers to jump directly into the exciting and powerful world of 3D. Written by professional Java 3D developers, this book covers everything you need to know to get up and running with Sun Microsystems Java 3D application programming interface (API) in no time flat.

About This Book

Java 3D API Jump-Start was written for Java programmers by Java programmers. Assuming that you're already comfortable with the basics of Java development, this book walks you start-to-finish through the most important and useful aspects of programming with the Java 3D API. To this end, *Java 3D API Jump-Start* is organized into the following six chapters:

Chapter 1, "Java 3D Overview"

Chapter 2, "Scene Graph Basics"

Chapter 3, "Creating and Loading Geometry"

Chapter 4, "Appearances"

Chapter 5, "Environment Nodes"

Chapter 6, "Tools: Transforms, Viewing, and Picking"

The first two chapters form an introduction to Java 3D. Chapter 1 gives examples of Java 3D applications and describes the basic features; Chapter 2 describes the basic structure of Java 3D programs. Chapter 3, 4 and 5 describe the three basic "building blocks" of Java 3D programs. Chapter 6 covers three tools that most Java 3D programs use.

Upon completing each chapter, you'll have gained valuable knowledge and hands-on experience related to a specific area of Java 3D capabilities and features, enabling you to explore that topic in more detail on your own as you see fit. By the time you finish all six chapters you'll be experienced with the most important aspects of Java 3D necessary to create your very own interactive 3D applications.

Style Conventions

Throughout this book specific font styles and faces have been used to make it easy for you to distinguish between normal text and source code. The main text of the book is 10-point Palatino, while source code is `9-point Courier`. The text that you are reading this very moment, for example, is formatted using the style applied to the main text throughout the remainder of this book. The following snippet of source code, on the other hand, appears in the style applied to all code listings in this book:

Example of formatted Java code

```
// The following allows AppearanceExplorer to be run
// as an application as well as an applet
public static void main(String[] args) {
new MainFrame(new AppearanceExplorer(), 650, 1001);
}
```

Java source code that appears alongside normal text (such as code that appears directly inside a paragraph of text) is formatted using the following combination of styles to further help you distinguish among the various types of Java language elements that appear in this book:

- Methods appear in `10-point Courier`. For example: `main()`
- Class and objects appear in **`10-point Courier bold`**. For example: **`Transform3D`**
- Fields appear in `10-point Courier`, and all characters in the field name are capitalized. For example: `CAP_BIT_HERE`
- Variables appear in `10-point Courier`. For example: `myvar`

Special Elements

In addition to the normal text, source code, and figures that appear in this book you'll find a number of special elements designed to grab your attention. Following is a brief summary of each of these elements:

The Javadoc element calls your attention to information found in Sun's official Java 3D API Java documentation ("javadoc"). Javadoc contains detailed API-level documentation for all Java 3D classes, methods, and fields. You can refer to the Java 3D Javadoc online through the Java 3D homepage at http://java.sun.com/products/java-media/3D/. Alternately, you can download the entire Java 3D Javadoc archive to your local computer for off-line browsing.

The Note icon calls your attention to information that supplements the current discussion.

The Online icon directs you to Internet sites related to the current discussion.

The Tip icon provides you with useful information that can save you time, money, or frustration.

Web3D Series

Java 3D Jump-Start is part of a new "Web3D" series of books produced by Prentice Hall, and dedicated to 3D and the Internet. To get your hands on additional resources related to *Java 3D Jump-Start* (such as the freely available Java 3D Explorer application used extensively throughout this book), or to learn more about related 3D technologies, visit the Web3DBooks.com Web site at web3dbooks.com/.

Author Acknowledgments

Doug Gehringer:

Thanks to Aaron for inviting me to work on *Java 3D API Jump-Start* and supporting me through the many stages of writing. Thanks to my manager, Linda Fellingham, for letting me take on this project and supporting me as the weeks stretched into months. Thanks to our reviewers: Andrea Tartaro, Paul Pantara, Kevin Rushforth, Bruce Bartlett, Louis Chow, and Christine Kerschbaum. Thanks to Michael Shulman for help finding the applications and images, and to the companies for giving us the images. Thanks to Shawn Kendall at FullSail for his help. Thanks to the many people at Sun who answered questions and provided encouragement, including Dan Petersen, Travis Bryson, Roger Day, Paul Byrne, Rick Goldberg, Jon Cooke, and Brian Burkhalter. Thanks to the entire Java 3D team, for putting together such a powerful, high quality product. Thinking of you, Bob. Finally, and most importantly, thanks to my wife, Kate, and my boys, Drew and Luke, for their patience and support during this project.

Aaron E. Walsh:

With special thanks to Doug, my *Java 3D API Jump-Start* co-author, for his extensive and expert work on this book. To Sun Microsystems, and the entire Java 3D team in particular, for producing Java 3D, without which *Java 3D API Jump-Start* wouldn't exist, and for technically reviewing this book as it wound its way from start to finish. With thanks, also, to Tim Moore, Jim Markham, and Faye Gemmellaro of Prentice Hall, for making this book possible in the first place. And, finally, to my family, friends, and colleagues, for your enduring patience and support.

CHAPTER 1

Java 3D Overview

TOPICS IN THIS CHAPTER

- A 30,000-FOOT LOOK AT JAVA 3D
- A LOOK AT JAVA 3D IN ACTION
- UNDERSTANDING THE DESIGN GOALS BEHIND JAVA 3D
- COMPARING JAVA 3D TO OTHER GRAPHICS OPTIONS
- EXPLORING JAVA 3D FEATURES
- JAVA 3D AND THE JAVA PLATFORM

If you listen carefully you'll hear the rumblings of a true revolution in the making. Startling advances in computer graphics hardware are making it possible for owners of ordinary desktop computers to produce film-quality interactive graphics rivaling those of Hollywood studios and special effects houses. Graphics processors and accelerators that were once available to a relatively small and specialized group have broken out of their high-end niche and are now surfacing in consumer-level machines. For the first time in our digital history the power to create broadcast quality graphics is in the hands of the masses as illustrated by Figure 1–1.

At the same time Java has swept over the planet to become the language of choice for object-oriented, platform-independent application development and is today considered the de facto standard for developing Internet applications. Java 3D, the subject of this book and the center of great excitement in its own right, stands at the crossroads of these trends. Java 3D is the Java interface for interactive 3D graphics. As a standard extension to the base Java technology, Java 3D allows developers to construct comprehensive, platform-independent applets and applications that feature interactive 3D graphics and sound capabilities.

In this chapter we'll give you a top-level overview of how Java 3D relates to Java, and how the two combine to form a powerful 3D development platform. During our blitzkrieg tour you'll see that Java 3D is part of the Java Media family of applications programming interfaces (APIs), making it a sibling of many other media-centric Java extensions. Along the way we'll introduce you to essential Java 3D jargon as we explore the fundamental structure common to all Java 3D programs.

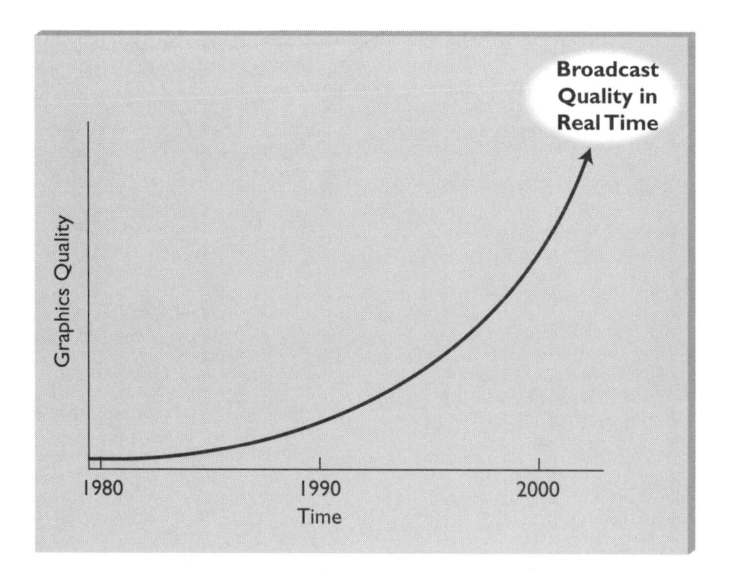

FIGURE 1–1 As of the year 2000, a revolution in consumer-level desktop graphics is in full swing thanks to dramatic advances in computing power and 3D graphics acceleration chips and boards.

Digging into Java 3D

Java 3D is a full-featured 3D graphics API. It employs a scene-graph programming model in which the application program describes a scene; Java 3D then manages the display of that scene. Java 3D's scene graph allows your program to focus on what happens to the objects in your scene, while the Java 3D runtime and rendering engines do the hard work of figuring out how to draw your scene on the display as fast as possible.

Java 3D includes the most essential features found in other popular 3D graphics APIs such as OpenGL and Direct3D (the 3D component of Microsoft's DirectX suite of graphics APIs). Because it is based on Java, however, Java 3D offers higher-level programming constructs when compared to these low-level APIs. As a result, programmers familiar with Java can create sophisticated 3D applications in a shorter amount of time than they could expect to with lower-level graphics APIs. In other words, Java 3D allows developers to focus on *what* to draw, not *how* to draw.

With Java 3D it is easy to create virtual worlds with lighting, texture mapping, behaviors, and other features that immerse users in a rich visual and interactive experience. But that's just the beginning. Java 3D allows you to create virtual worlds complete with objects that move automatically and with fully spatialized sound. In addition, Java 3D makes it simple to create programs that operate consistently across a variety of output devices—from a single monitor to stereo glasses to room-sized, multiscreen immersive "caves."

Extremely large, yet crisp and responsive, virtual worlds can be created in Java 3D thanks to its ability to maximize both the CPU and graphics display resources. In short, Java 3D supports the features required for today's most demanding 3D applications while offering plenty of "headroom" to accommodate tomorrow's applications.

Java 3D in Action

Java 3D is designed to support a wide range of applications, from traditional graphics applications such as mechanical computer-aided design (MCAD) to scientific visualization, product visualization, collaborative engineering, eCommerce solutions, and games. If the current trend in 3D graphics progress continues, we'll be able to interact with impressive Toy Story-quality Java 3D content delivered over broadband Internet connections in just a few years.

To appreciate what the future holds for Java 3D we must consider the types of applications developers have created today. In the following sections we'll explore just a few of the many ways in which developers are pushing the envelope with Java 3D.

Fun and Games with Java 3D Entertainment Applications

Entertainment is arguably the most common way in which people today are exposed to 3D graphics. Even as you read this book, high-powered desktop computers and console games are flooding into the home market, bringing interactive 3D content to the masses. Fun and games with 3D is fast becoming the norm; only a few years ago compelling 3D entertainment was relatively hard to come by.

Millions of home computers and console devices such as Sony PlayStation and Microsoft XBox are whirring around the world. This very moment cutting-edge games such as Quake, Tomb Raider, Tekken Tag, Soul Reaver, Madden NFL,

Oddworld: Munch's Oddysee, Final Fantasy, and countless others are further priming the market for an emerging class of Java 3D entertainment applications.

Likewise, many movies today take advantage of 3D in order to add a dash of realism to otherwise entirely fabricated characters, props, and locations. Past box-office smashes *Toy Story*, *Antz*, and *A Bug's Life* were all created using sophisticated 3D technology developed exclusively for the movie industry. This technology is now being used in live action movies and television shows.

Note

Nearly every movie that rolls out of Hollywood these days is produced using some form of 3D technology. If you've seen a motion picture in the past decade you've almost certainly been exposed to 3D. From virtual sets and environments, to digital creatures and synthetic human actors, 3D touches almost every aspect of the broadcast film and television industry. The blockbuster movie *Gladiator*, for instance, made extensive use of 3D technology to create virtual sets and combat scenes. 3D also allowed the studio to construct a completely synthetic face and body for an actor that passed away before the filming of *Gladiator* was complete, creating, in effect, an utterly realistic yet entirely digital human being.

Although relatively new to the industry, Java 3D is proving to be well suited to developing commercial entertainment applications. Specifically, the combination of Java 3D's powerful yet easily mastered graphics capabilities and the portability and networking provided by the ubiquitous Java platform result in a compelling development platform for entertainment content.

At Boston's Museum of Science (www.mos.org/), for example, children interact with a Virtual FishTank™ created with Java 3D (see Figure 1–2). Developed by Nearlife, Inc., this unique interactive exhibit offers visitors the ability to construct their very own digital fish. By configuring options using a touch-sensitive computer screen, visitors create their own fish by hand. After selecting the physical attributes for their fish, users next specify rules for how it will interact in its environment and with other fish, and finally release their virtual creation into a digital "tank" that consists of jumbo computer monitors mounted on the museum walls. Visitors can then interact with their fish in the real world museum exhibit using data captured from motion sensitive cameras or online through a Web browser front end at www.VirtualFishTank.com/.

Online

Even if you're not in Boston you can create your own Virtual FishTank™ fish online at www.VirtualFishTank.com/. Using a combination of Shockwave and Java, this online version of the application allows users to create fish that interact with the Virtual FishTank™ exhibit currently installed at the Boston Museum of Science.

FIGURE 1–2 Nearlife's Virtual FishTank™ Java 3D application allows exhibit visitors to create and release their very own digital fish into a "tank" that consists of jumbo computer monitors mounted to the museum walls. (This figure also appears in the color plate section at the center of this book.) Image courtesy of Nearlife, Inc. Used by permission.

Cosm is an online 3D fantasy game being developed using Java3D. In Cosm (www.cosm-game.com), players use magic and swordplay and take on the role of a character that can interact with players from across the room or across the world. Players can develop their character from humble beginnings to become a mighty warrior, powerful wizard, wealthy merchant, or virtually anything they want in this dynamic society. Figure 1–3 shows an image from Cosm.

Another online Java3D game being developed by Liquid Edge Games is called Roboforge (www.roboforge.com/). Using Java 3D, Roboforge players create and train their own digital robots. Players then enter their robots into tournaments, a shared online space where their creations battle in a large arena. Figure 1–4 is a

FIGURE 1–3 Cosm is an online fantasy world developed in Java3D. (To see this figure in color, turn to the color plate section at the center of this book.) Image courtesy of NavTools.com. Used by permission.

screen capture from the game in which we see the lab where new robots are constructed, while Figure 1–5 shows a pair of fully constructed robots battling in the "Gigadrome."

Linear versus Interactive Content

When we watch a traditional movie or television broadcast we simply look at the frames of film as they speed by, which results in the illusion of movement. Because traditional movies aren't interactive, however, it is difficult to truly compare them to games and entertainment applications created with Java 3D.

Although they can be visually impressive and extremely compelling, movies and TV shows are shot entirely from one viewpoint. We have no control whatsoever over what we see, nor can we navigate or explore linear content such as this; we can only watch what the director wants us to see. We are, in effect, passive observers of a linear production. Interactive Java 3D content, on the other hand, puts us in the driver's seat.

The Java 3D entertainment applications discussed here allow you to interactively explore the scene and change viewpoints and perspective at will. Although it will be a few more years before graphics hardware acceleration enables Java 3D content to match the realism of motion pictures, we can still enjoy a level of interactivity that traditional film and television broadcasts can't touch.

FIGURE 1–4 In the Java 3D game Roboforge (www.roboforge.com/), players create and train their own digital robots for online battle (see Figure 1–5). Image courtesy of Liquid Edge Games Limited. Used by permission.

FIGURE 1–5 Roboforge robots battle to the death in the online "Gigadrome." Image courtesy of Liquid Edge Games Limited. Used by permission. (Both images on this page appear in the color plate section at the center of this book.)

Conducting Business Online with Product Visualization and Electronic Commerce (eCommerce)

Product visualization and data visualization are two areas where three dimensions truly outshine two. Without the benefit of interactive 3D, products sold over the Internet are typically presented to the viewer in the form of 2D images on a Web page accompanied by a paragraph or more of descriptive text, or a combination of both images and text. While a photograph or illustration can go a long way towards accurately describing a product, especially when accompanied by a text description, traditional 2D images and text lack the expressive power of interactive Java 3D content.

Whereas images and text are static and can only be experienced from a single perspective, Java 3D allows products to be visualized from whatever angle the end user desires and in many ways that images and text simply do not allow. The Nokia mobile phone seen in Figure 1–6, for example, is an example of a product visualization designed to give the end user complete control over the viewing experience. Rather than merely looking at a photo or illustration of this product, this interactive Java 3D application gives us the ability to thoroughly examine it from any angle and actually give the device a test drive. While interacting with the 3D visualization of this product, users can press buttons on the phone, examine menu options, change ring tones, and so forth.

Created by Asenza Corporation, a startup company from Palo Alto California, the Nokia mobile phone is one of many eProducts offered by the firm. Using Java 3D, Asenza can develop and deploy fully functional, interactive 3D eProduct visualizations for standard Web browsers. Asenza creates eProducts directly from computer-aided design (CAD) data for an actual product. The process employed by Asenza emulates the product's behavior and uses Java 3D to create an efficient 3D representation such as the one for the cellular phone.

The Xtivia Reality Server (XRS) is another example of Java 3D hard at work in the digital business arena. Created by Xtivia, XRS is an eCommerce server that can be configured to host business applications such as virtual shopping environments, online galleries, and electronic customer relationship management (CRM). Figure 1–7 shows an example XRS application that allows users to shop online using nothing more than their Web browser. As you can see from this figure, shoppers select items to purchase from shelves in a virtual store. Java 3D is used to draw the animated shopping cart as the user meanders about the store picking items for purchase. When the shopper selects an item from the store shelf, a detailed product description appears in the lower section of the Web page. The left side of the page, meanwhile, shows the current contents of the shopper's cart.

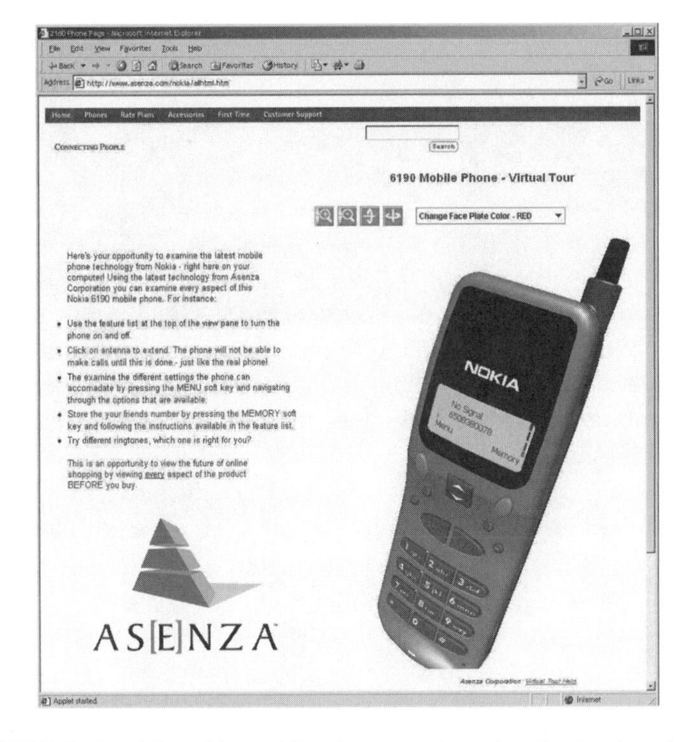

FIGURE 1–6 This Nokia mobile phone product visualization is only one of many Java 3D visualizations developed by Asenza Corporation as part of their eProducts electronic commerce application. Image courtesy of Asenza Corporation. Used by permission.

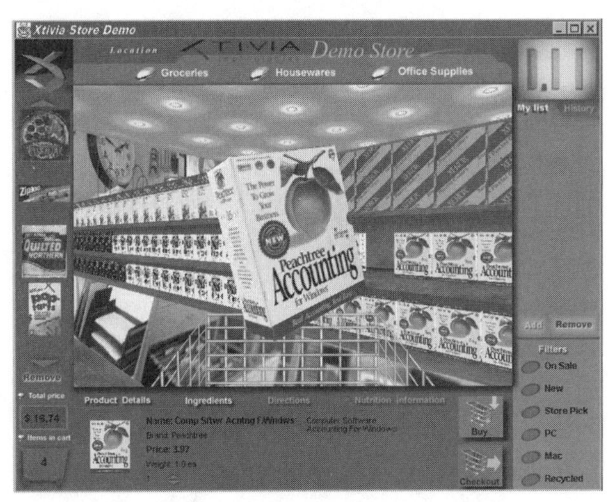

FIGURE 1–7 Using Java 3D, Xtivia is able to represent a store using a 3D interactive view rather than simple 2D images or animations (www.xtivia.com/). Turn to the color plate section at the center of this book to see this figure in color. Image courtesy of Xtivia Technologies. Used by permission.

Tip

Interactive 3D content typically increases the "stickiness" of Web sites, meaning end users stick around longer than they otherwise might if presented non-3D content. In other words, interactive 3D content tends to suck Web surfers into an involved experience that lasts much longer than that of viewing static content such as text or images.

Seeing the Invisible with Data Visualization

Product visualization revolves around real-world products or product concepts; data visualization revolves around information. Specifically, data visualization is a specialized field dedicated to rendering and interacting with information that isn't otherwise tangible. In simpler terms, data visualization lets us see structures and patterns in data that aren't visible to the naked eye (who among us can actually "see" information without the aid of simulation or visualization tools, after all?).

Data visualization isn't new. Scientists have relied on it for years to help them make sense of extremely complex information sets such as global weather patterns, seismic activity, human gene mapping, and other types of highly sophisticated data that would be impossible to comprehend in raw form. Today, however, data visualization has escaped from research labs and found a new home on the desktop and Internet.

Java 3D uses an object-oriented, portable approach that is a powerful combination for creating visualization toolkits for scientific, medical, and business data. To date, several developers have created Java 3D toolkits for data visualization.

VisAD, for example, is a distributed component architecture for interactive and collaborative analysis and visualization of numerical data. It uses Java and Java 3D as the foundation for a portable, networked visualization framework. Using VisAD instead of stand-alone applications, scientists can use their Web browser to connect new display and user interface components to an existing network of data and computations (see Figure 1–8).

The Surgical Planning Labratory of Brigham and Women's Hospital and Harvard Medical School has developed SPLViz, a Java 3D visualization tool for viewing diagnostic medical data. SPLViz is a simple, portable, easy-to-learn, and easy-to-use viewing tool for medical data sets generated by a more complex product called the 3D Slicer. Because it offers a larger suite of capabilities and features, 3D Slicer is considerably more complex to use. Figure 1–9 shows the tool in action. Here, we see the visualization of a brain tumor shrouded in blood vessels and the surrounding brain structure alongside traditional computer-aided tomography (CAT) scan data.

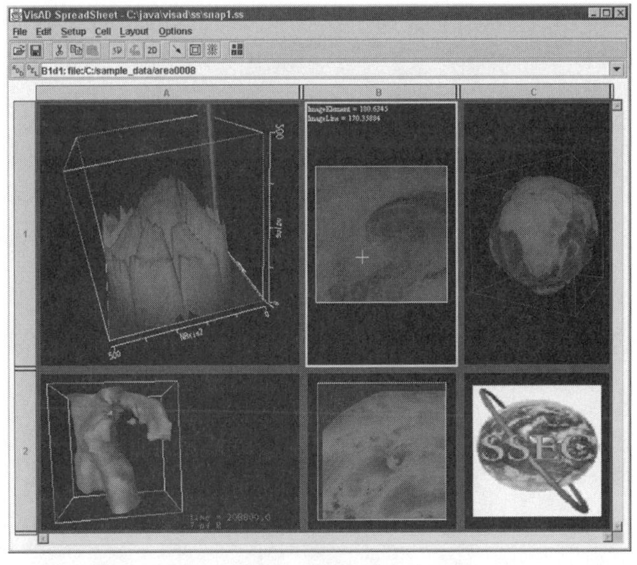

a

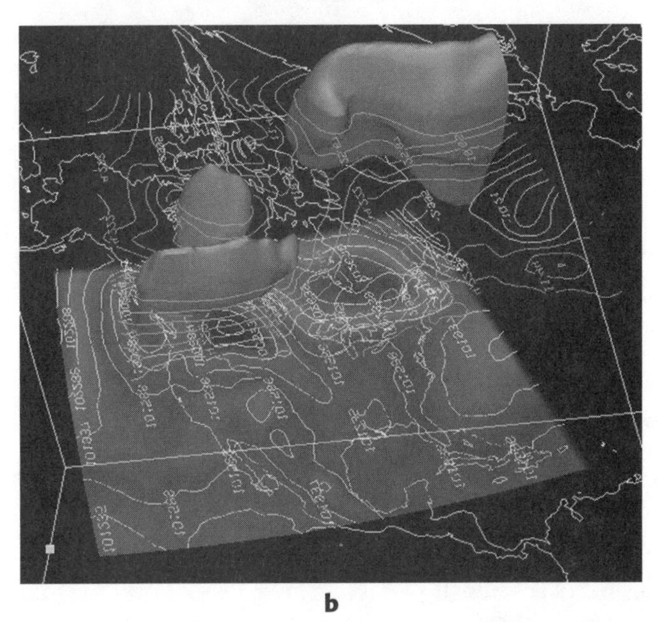

b

FIGURE 1–8 These screenshots show two different VisAD applications. The first is of the VisAD SpreadSheet (a), a fully collaborative spreadsheet that can be used to visualize a wide variety of numerical data. The second is from the Unidata Program Center's 3-D (b) gridded data viewer for visualizing numerical weather simulations. For more information, visit VisAD online at www.ssec.wisc.edu/~billh/visad.html. (These images appear in the color plate section at the center of this book.) Images courtesy of VisAD. Used by permission.

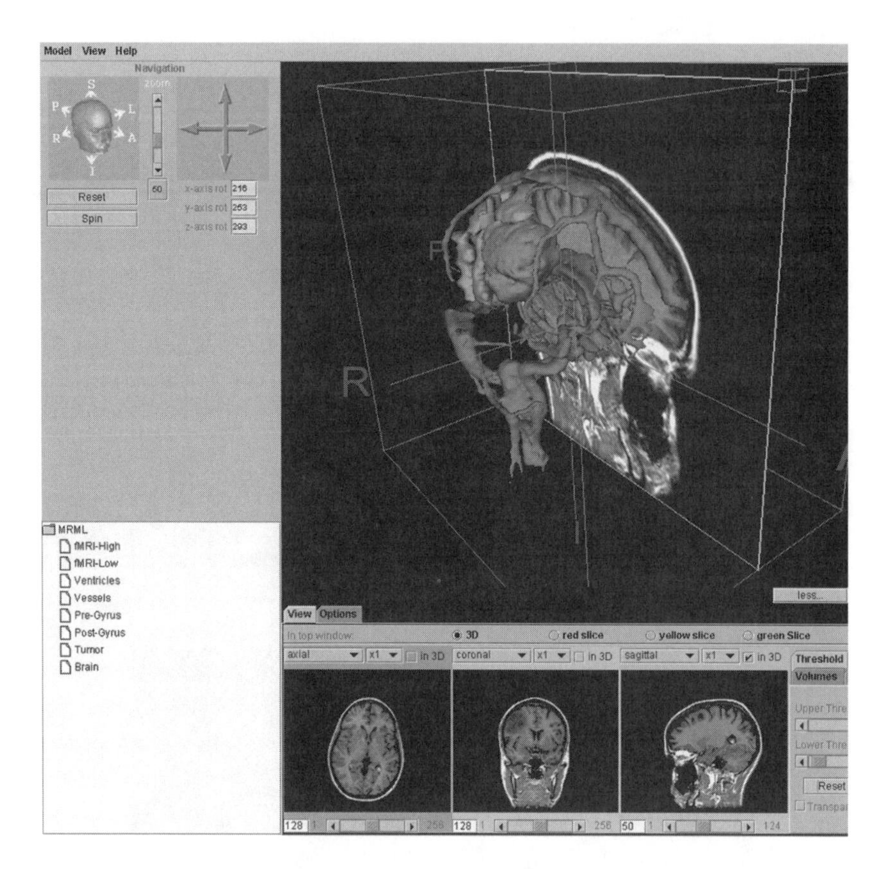

FIGURE 1–9 The brain tumor shown here is visualized with SPLViz, a Java 3D visulization toolkit developed by Brigham and Women's Hospital and Harvard Medical School. SPLViz visualizes data produced by the more complex 3D Slicer program (www.slicer.org/). (This image also appears in the color plate section at the center of this book.) Image courtesy of Surgical Planning Laboratory, Brigham and Women's Hospital/Harvard Medical School. Used by permission.

Figure 1–10 captures another example of Java 3D data visualization in action. Here we see a product screenshot of INT's Java 3D toolkit for visualizing business and seismic data. Using J/View3Dpro, users can quickly display datasets to manipulate, annotate, and edit complex 3D scenes. Figure 1–10 shows two kinds of data supported by INT. The first is a financial data display that demonstrates the product's ability to visualize detailed analysis and performance of investment portfolios. The second data set example is a 3D geologic display of well information and subsurface geometry, information that a geologist might use to help develop drilling strategies and monitor reservoir performance.

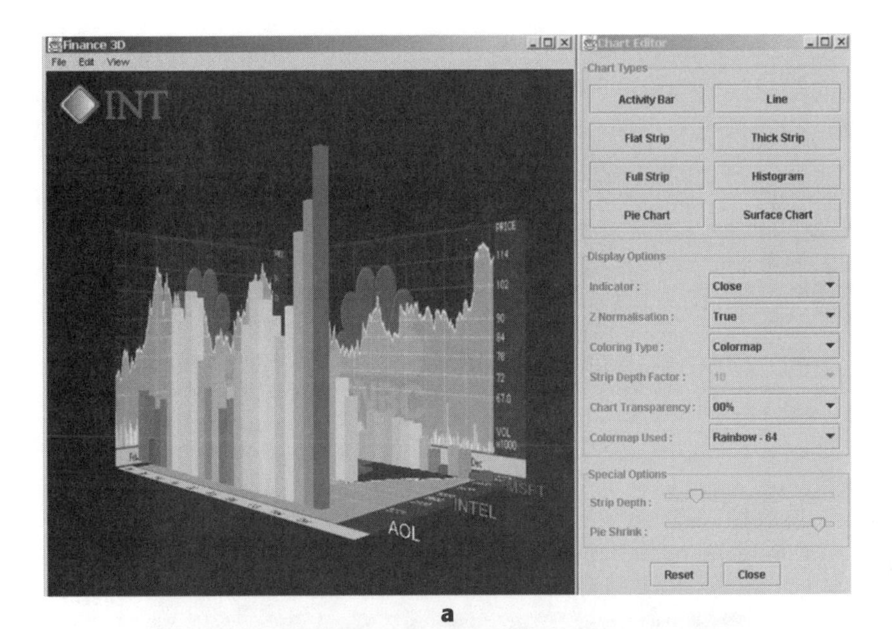

a

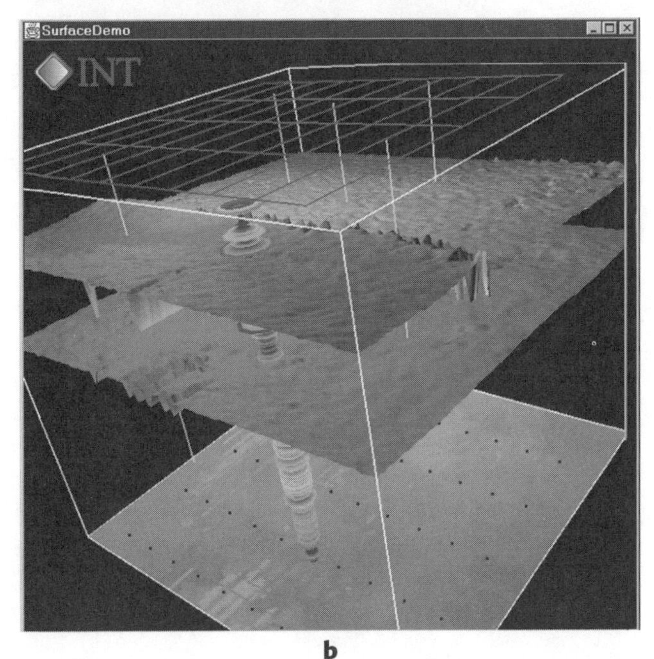

b

FIGURE 1–10 INT's J/View3Dpro product supports 3D visualization of various data types, including financial data (a) and geological data (b). Visit INT online at www.int.com/ to learn more about this company's Java 3D visualization toolkit. (Turn to the color plate section at the center of this book to see this figure in color.) Images courtesy of INT, Inc. Used by permission.

Building Better Products with Collaborative Engineering

In addition to its ability to enable entertainment, business, and visualization applications, Java 3D is also well suited for computer-aided design (CAD) products. Java 3D supports the graphics features needed for high quality data display, such as lighting, antialiasing, and depth cueing. Combined with the Java platform's power and flexibility, Java 3D is an excellent vehicle for creating portable, networked applications for collaborative engineering. Users of such applications can, for example, view design data in a manner that compares to the design application while simultaneously interacting with other users for annotation, design reviews, and product reference.

Consider, for example, Structural Dynamics Research Corporation (SDRC). SDRC is a premier provider of mechanical design automation, product data management, and collaborative engineering software. When SDRC needed a platform to support their Web-based design viewer, they turned to Java and Java 3D, which in turn enabled them to create the I-DEAS Viewer product. With the

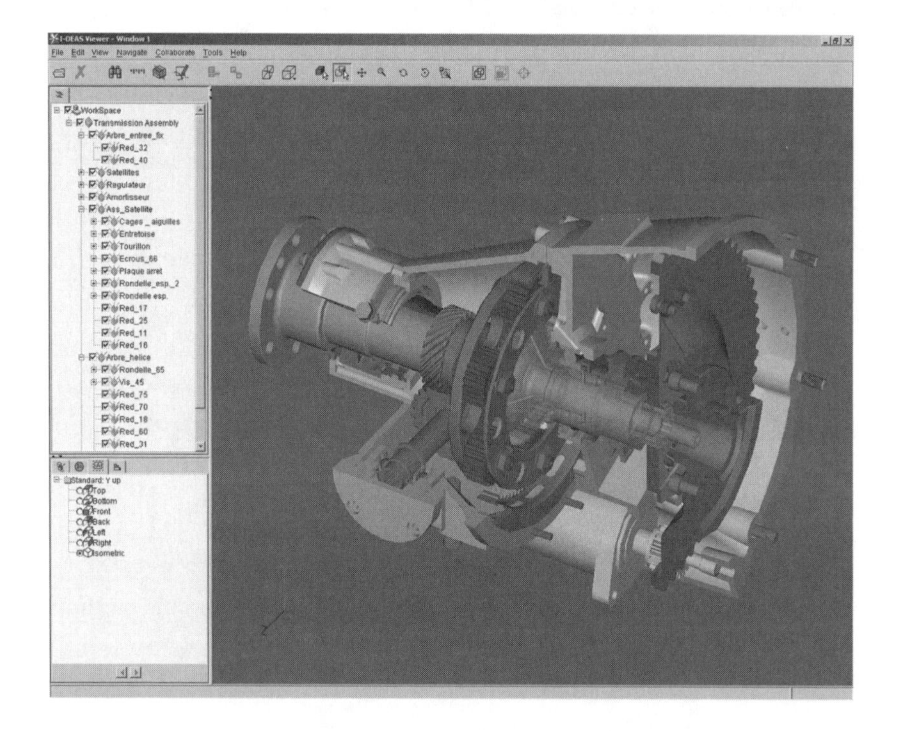

FIGURE 1–11 Here we see an assembly loaded into SDRC's I-DEAS Viewer collaborative engineering product. Users can view product dimensions, bill of materials, and other design data. Visit www.sdrc.com/ideas/ideas-viewer/features.shtml for details. (To see this figure in color, turn to the color plate section at the center of this book.) Image courtesy of SDRC. Used by permission.

viewer, users can exchange fully annotated product designs that can be viewed at a level of detail and performance that compares to the full I-DEAS design product (see Figure 1–11).

Webscope is another example of Java 3D enabling collaborative engineering. Webscope is a system for Web-based, secure, real-time product collaboration. Using Webscope, engineers can view data from many different design and analysis applications. With secure connections, users can share a view to exchange annotations and design ideas, as seen in Figure 1–12. This figure shows an interactive discussion involving a part under development taking place through Webscope. Each Webscope user involved with this project session can interact with the 3D model and make design comments during this activity.

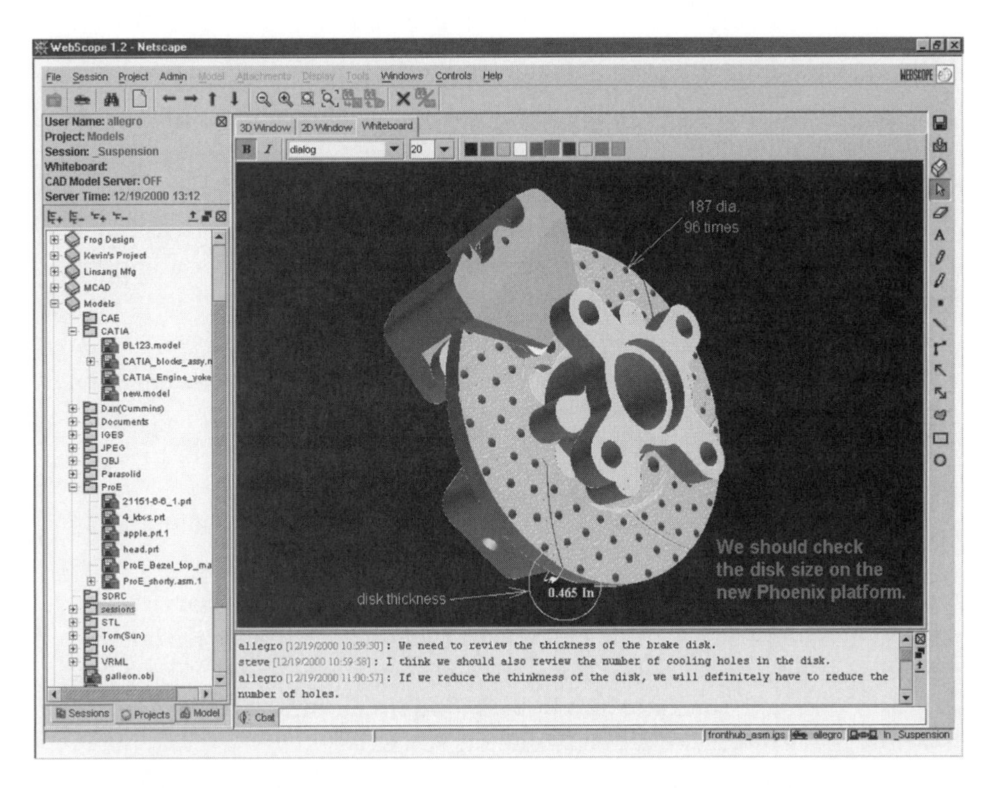

FIGURE 1–12 The Webscope collaborative engineering system allows engineers to view data from many different design and analysis applications. Here we see an interactive discussion involving a part under development, during which participants can interact with the 3D part model and contribute their comments to the group discussion. Visit www.webscopeinc.com/ for details. (Turn to the color plate section at the center of this book to see this figure in color.) Image courtesy of Webscope Inc. Used by permission.

Java 3D Design Goals

Java 3D was designed to support a wide variety of applications, including the types that we just explored. The Java 3D specification was developed as a collaborative effort between Sun, SGI, Intel, and Apple. Several major design goals drove the development of the specification, including:

- **Java integration**. Java 3D is built with the goals and advantages of Java in mind. A Java 3D applet or application will run unmodified on computers running different operating systems, using different low-level graphics APIs, or different graphics hardware. It provides a platform-independent mechanism for developing 3D graphics.
- **High performance.** Java 3D was designed from the onset with high performance and scalability in mind. Specifically, Java 3D was designed to layer on top of low-level graphics APIs (such as OpenGL and Direct3D) to take advantage of hardware acceleration. In addition, the Java 3D scene graph structure supports high levels of optimization and multiprocessor rendering.
- **Support for a rich suite of critical capabilities**. Java 3D incorporates a complete range of 3D graphics features from the low-level graphics APIs it is built on. Java 3D provides a consistent interface for lighting, shading, texture mapping, and other basic computer graphics features.
- **Industrial strength**. Java 3D was built to do more than add a spinning 3D object to Web pages. Java 3D was built from the ground up to support large, complex datasets.

Digging Deeper: Comparing Java 3D to Other Graphics Options

One of the most commonly asked questions regarding Java 3D is how it compares with existing 3D graphics APIs. On one side of the fence are the established rendering APIs such as OpenGL and Direct3D; on the other are 3D file formats such as DXF and, to some extent, VRML (VRML isn't merely a 3D file format, although it isn't a full blown 3D programming API either).

In short, Java 3D falls somewhere in the middle, with capabilities more like those of rendering APIs than file formats. Although Java 3D offers a high-level, scene graph programming model that shields programmers from low-level rendering details, it also permits low-level control similar to that of OpenGL and Direct3D. Like VRML, Java 3D allows developers to focus on scene composition rather than rendering (*what* to draw, not how to *draw*), although Java 3D also offers low-level rendering control that VRML does not provide.

Java 3D versus Low-Level Rendering APIs

Java 3D is a 3D programming API that is similar to OpenGL and Direct3D. In fact, Java 3D implementations are layered on top of native low-level rendering APIs like OpenGL and Direct3D, making Java 3D a high-level, cross-platform 3D API, as illustrated in Figure 1–13.

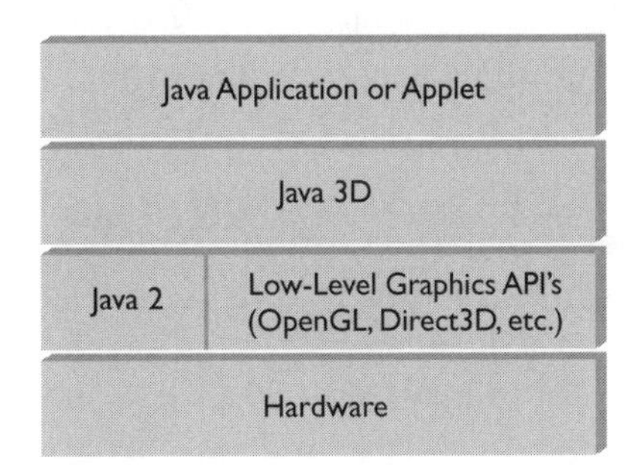

FIGURE 1–13 Java 3D is layered on top of Java, extending Java's core capabilities to include support for interactive 3D graphics.

Java 3D differs from low-level 3D graphics APIs in its general approach to 3D programming and the facilities it offers. Like low-level APIs, Java 3D allows the programmer to get down to the raw triangles used in rendering if necessary. While such low-level rendering control can be useful in some cases, most of the time it is an unnecessary burden. 3D developers are typically more concerned with the overall design and implementation of their program than they are in rendering control. Java 3D uses a high-level interface where the programmer describes the scene to be drawn, and Java 3D manages the rendering. This allows the programmer to focus on more general aspects of development, such as user input (mouse, joystick, or keyboard input) and interactive behaviors. Using Java 3D, you focus on your virtual world, not triangles.

Java 3D also differs from OpenGL and Direct3D in the simplicity with which it integrates with other programming facilities. To display a window of Java 3D content in a typical Java program, for example, you can simply create a frame and add a 3D canvas to it. After registering for mouse and keyboard input, you're ready to rock and roll. With OpenGL, however, the process is much more complicated; you must first determine what screen capabilities are available, select an appropriate one, create your window, separately register for mouse input and sound output, and, finally, render the content to the screen.

Java 3D versus Other Scene Graph APIs

Although Java 3D is a scene graph API, it's not the player in the game. A variety of popular scene graph APIs exist, including SGI's OpenInventor and Performer APIs, and to some extent VRML. Although VRML inspired the design of Java 3D considerably, it's usually not thought of as a programming API. Consequently, it's more accurate to compare SGI's OpenInventor and Performer to the Java 3D API.

SGI's OpenInventor was one of the first scene graph APIs to surface in the graphics programming industry. It was intended to be a simple approach to 3D graphics, and offered built-in user interface and file interaction capabilities. In the mid 1990s the OpenInventor file format was selected as the basis for the first VRML file format (the now obsolete VRML 1.0), which in turn heavily influenced the Java 3D scene graph structure.

OpenInventor suffered from flaws in the way its scene graph was interpreted that made it difficult to optimize the effect of changing the scene graph. Changes to the scene graph required that the whole scene graph be traversed to determine the state at each node. Contrast this approach to Java 3D, where the scene graph is structured so that the state of a node depends only on the nodes above it in the tree, allowing much more performance optimization. In other words, Java 3D uses optimized scene graph management and traversal techniques to gain a significant performance boost over OpenInventor.

OpenGL Performer is another scene graph API developed by SGI. Performer is also quite similar to Java 3D, although a few key differences are worth noting. Specifically, Performer utilizes a scene graph that's similar to that of Java 3D; both offer essentially the same type of scene graph optimization techniques to increase overall performance. Performer, however, is only available on SGI IRIX and Linux platforms using C and C++ bindings, whereas Java 3D is available on any system that can support Sun's Java 2 platform.

Performer is built on top of OpenGL, and it provides excellent interfaces for integrating custom OpenGL rendering with the scene graph rendering provided by Performer. Performer makes use of a variety of features available only in SGI's implementation of OpenGL. As a result, Performer is a great platform for building visual simulation applications on SGI systems. Unfortunately, Performer is only available on SGI systems and Linux systems, which is a significant disadvantage compared to Java 3D's cross platform compatibility.

Java 3D versus Modeling File Formats

On the other side of the divide are the 3D modeling file formats such as AutoCAD Drawing Interchange File (DXF), Lightwave Scene Format (LSF), VRML, Extensible 3D (X3D), and MPEG-4/BIFS. Unlike programming APIs that provide full-blown 3D graphics development facilities, 3D modeling file formats typically provide an encapsulated structure for the delivery of 3D content. To be fair, VRML, X3D, and MPEG4/BIFS are not merely file formats, as they embody a 3D scene description language as well as a file format in which this language is stored. Although most 3D file formats simply define 3D scenes, some, such as VRML, X3D, and MPEG-4/BIFS, also define runtime semantics. Neither VRML nor MPEG-4/BIFS, however, offers as robust a programming language as the combination of Java and Java 3D.

A primary difference between Java 3D and 3D modeling file formats lies in their execution models; 3D files are loaded into a program for display purposes, whereas Java 3D programs are executed directly by a Java runtime system. A VRML file, for example, is of no real value without a VRML browser (in the same way that an HTML file can't be viewed without an HTML browser). Stand-alone Java 3D applications, however, execute similar to any other software program, and Java 3D applets are executed within a Java-enabled Web browser (as you'll see later, Java 3D programs are often designed to run as dual-purpose stand-alone applications *and* Web-based applets).

Using the Java 3D loader mechanism, in fact, Java 3D programs can load and interact with content from a wide variety of 3D modeling file formats. The same cannot be said for 3D models; 3D file formats have no knowledge of Java 3D. You cannot, for example, load Java 3D classes into a VRML world, nor can you integrate Java 3D content directly with an MPEG4/BIFS scene.

Using loaders, however, Java 3D programs can work with a wide range of 3D file formats. Loaders currently exist for OpenFlight, 3D Studio (3DS), VRML, X3D, Wavefront OBJ, DXF, Caligari trueSpace COB, LSF, Lightwave Object Format (LOF), and many other formats. Developers can create their own loaders in cases where they need to access a file format for which a loader doesn't already exit, allowing Java 3D to accommodate new or proprietary 3D formats.

Java 3D does not have an external file format. Java 3D does, however, offer a file loader mechanism through which a variety of 3D file formats are supported. A utility binary file format is part of a utility package called Java 3D Fly Through. See java.sun.com/products/java-media/3D/ for more details.

Java 3D versus Other Java Media APIs

Although it took the software development industry by storm, the original version of Java was lackluster in terms of its multimedia capabilities. Even today the core Java libraries support only basic sound playback and relatively simple line and bitmap graphics, making it difficult, at best, to construct rich multimedia programs. With Java 1.1, however, Sun introduced a framework of multimedia APIs to bolster the Java core with serious multimedia capabilities.

The Java Media APIs are a collection of Java extensions that allow developers to create complex multimedia programs, including 3D. As a member of the Java Media family, Java 3D's siblings include:

- Java 2D, which offers advanced 2D graphics and imaging. Encompassing line art, text, and images, the Java 2D API supports enhanced lines, colors, image transforms, and composites.
- Java Advanced Imaging (JAI), which gives Java programs a wide range of image-processing capabilities, including image scaling, cropping, enhancing, distorting, and warping.
- Java Media Framework (JMF), which provides a unified architecture, messaging protocol, and programming interface for media playback, capture, and manipulation. JMF allows developers to synchronize and control audio, video, and other time-based media within their Java applications and applets.
- Java Shared Data Toolkit (JSDT), which offers interactive, network-based collaboration capabilities that developers can use to create communication programs such as multiuser whiteboards, chat systems, workflow applications, remote presentations, shared simulations, and networked games.
- Java Sound, which extends Java's otherwise limited audio capabilities to provide low-level audio features such as audio mixing, capture, MIDI (Musical Instrument Digital Interface) sequencing, and MIDI synthesis. Whereas Java itself supports only a limited form of AU format audio, Java Sound supports AIFF, AU, and WAV audio formats, as well as MIDI-based song file formats (TYPE 0 MIDI, TYPE 1 MIDI, and RMF).
- Java Speech, which gives developers the ability to add support for speech recognition and speech synthesis to their Java programs. Java Speech supports command and control recognizers, dictation systems, and speech synthesizers.
- Java Telephony, which integrates telephones with computers. By allowing Java programs to control telephony, Java Telephony can be used to create a wide range of applications including fax systems, voice mail, auto-dial programs, call logging and tracking, routing, automated attendants, and call center management.

Designed as an interoperable suite of multimedia packages, the Java Media APIs allow developers to integrate audio, video, animation, 2D and 3D graphics, speech, and telephony. Just as Java 3D can be integrated with core Java technologies (such as networking, i/o, database access, and graphic user interface [GUI] facilities), it can also be integrated with other members of the Java Media family.

As a result, media-rich applets and applications can be constructed by combining Java Media APIs with core Java classes.

Learn more about Sun's Java Media family, including Java 3D, online at java.sun.com/products/java-media/.

Java Media Packages, Development Cycles, and Versions

Although Java Media APIs are interoperable, it's important to realize that they're developed and delivered independent of one another. Some Java Media APIs are organized as a subpackage of the main Java Media Framework (JMF) `javax.media` package. Java 3D classes, for example, are found in the `javax.media.j3d` package, while Java Advanced Imaging (JAI) classes are found in the `javax.media.jai` package.

Other Java Media APIs, however, are organized into different packages. Java 2D, for instance, is bundled under the original `java.awt` Abstract Windowing Toolkit package (meaning that Java 2D classes are now considered part of the Java core, as they're delivered under the top-level Java package instead of as a Javax "extension" package). Java Sound classes, meanwhile, are found in the javax.speech package. Although some Java Media APIs are actually part of the Java core (such as Java 2D), most, like Java 3D, are simply extensions to the core.

Because Java Media APIs are developed and deployed separately, they do not share the same development cycle or version number. For example, as this was bing written, the current Java Media Framework release was 2.1.1, while the current Java 3D release was 1.2.1.

Hitting Pay Dirt: Exploring Key Java 3D Features

Java 3D is a Java programming interface to a comprehensive library of 3D classes. Later we'll examine the relationship between Java and Java 3D in more detail. Now, however, it's high time that we hit paydirt after digging through the previous introduction to Java 3D. In the sections that follow we'll explore key Java 3D features, including those features that make Java 3D particularly well suited as a platform for the example applications that we looked at earlier.

Scene Graph Programming Model

Java 3D is based on a high-level scene graph programming model. Scene graphs are treelike data structures used to store, organize, and render 3D scene information (objects, appearances, which tell how to draw the objects, lights, which illuminate the objects, and so forth). Java 3D scene graphs are made up of objects called *nodes*, as illustrated in Figure 1–14.

In Java 3D, the term *virtual universe* is used to describe a 3D space populated with 3D objects. The virtual universe can be viewed using a display device, such as a window on the screen. For each Java 3D scene object, transform, or behavior, the programmer creates a new object, calls methods on the object, and adds it to a parent object.

When complete, the scene graph is attached to a virtual universe, which makes the scene graph appear on the screen. Changes are made to the scene graph by calling methods on the objects. As changes are made to the scene graph, Java 3D automatically updates the display to reflect the changes.

Virtual universes can be extremely large, allowing Java 3D to model huge graphical databases, such as entire cities. Virtual universes represent the largest possible unit of aggregation in Java 3D, and as such can be thought of as graphical databases (see Figure 1–14).

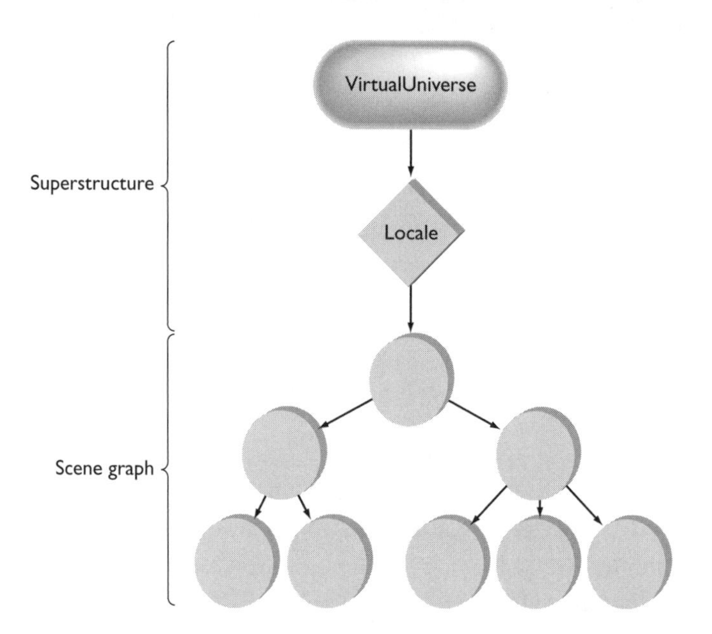

FIGURE 1–14 Nodes that make up a Java 3D scene graph are rooted to a Locale object, which in turn is rooted to VirtualUniverse object.

Rendering Control

The Java 3D renderer is responsible for traversing a Java 3D scene graph and displaying its visible geometry in an on-screen window (e.g., an applet canvas or application frame). In addition to drawing visible geometry, the Java 3D renderer is also responsible for processing user input and performing behaviors, which make automatic changes to the scene graph, such as animations. To handle these various tasks, the Java 3D renderer runs in a loop that has the following conceptual structure:

```
while(true) {
  Process user input
  If (request to exit == TRUE) break
  Perform Behaviors
  If (scene graph has changed) {
     Traverse scene graph and render visible
       Objects
  }
}
Cleanup and exit
```

Java 3D gives the developer extensive controls over the rendering process, including control over exactly what items are rendered to screen. In graphics parlance, an API's *rendering mode* specifies such control.

The Java 3D API supports two basic rendering modes, *retained mode* and *immediate mode*. These modes correspond to the level of control that the developer has over the rendering process, as well as the amount of liberty that Java 3D has to optimize. Although most Java 3D developers prefer the convenience and performance enhancements that come with retained mode, some require the fine-grained control offered by immediate mode rendering. Following is an overview of each:

- **Retained Mode** is the commonly used rendering mode. It strikes a balance between the amount of rendering control given to the developer and the amount of optimization control given to Java 3D. In retained mode, the developer constructs a scene graph and specifies the parts of the scene graph that may change in the rendering process. Java 3D then builds an internal version of the scene graph that is optimized for rendering. As the program makes changes to the scene graph, Java 3D updates its internal version and redraws the scene to make sure that the display reflects the current state of the scene graph.
- **Immediate Mode** gives the developer complete control over every aspect of rendering, which in turn gives Java 3D very little opportunity for optimization. For every frame drawn to the screen, the developer provides the raw rendering data (points, lines, or triangles) to a Java 3D draw method. Because Java 3D doesn't retain any of this information between frames, the developer is responsible for managing the rendering data between calls to

the draw method. This mode also gives developers the freedom to store and manage scene data in any way they see fit. Immediate mode can be used alone, or it may be combined with retained mode, where the immediate mode rendering happens after the retained mode completes each frame.

Java 3D Rendering Model

Java 3D uses a single programming interface, regardless of the underlying low-level API. Programs written to the Java 3D API can depend on the same features and semantics. As a high-level, scene-graph based API, however, Java 3D shields the developer from platform-specific details such as hardware acceleration. In a few cases, features of the low-level API are exposed in the Java 3D API, allowing features particular to that API to be used by Java 3D programs.

Scalable Performance

Java 3D was designed with the rapidly progressing state of CPU and graphics performance in mind. In particular, Java 3D is designed to scale as the balance between CPU and graphics power changes. In recent years, the power of graphics hardware has been growing even faster than CPU power. This makes it more and more difficult to write graphics code where the CPU can keep the graphics hardware busy. Java 3D was built with this problem in mind, structuring the scene graph to allow as much of the work as possible to be offloaded to the graphics hardware. As a result, developers don't have to rewrite or recompile their Java 3D programs to keep up with advances in hardware; Java 3D applets and applications scale automatically.

Java 3D was designed for scalability in many ways. As a layered API, Java 3D sits atop low-level graphics APIs (such as OpenGL and Direct3D), allowing it to benefit from hardware acceleration. The Java 3D scene graph structure was also designed for scalability, and can include a number of high-level optimization features including view culling, occlusion culling, execution culling, behavior pruning, parallel graph traversal, and parallel rendering.

Because it is based on Java, Java 3D inherently supports multithreading. *Threads*, also known as *lightweight processes* or *execution contexts*, allow a program to be divided into a number of smaller tasks that can be executed independent of one another. When run on multiprocessor systems, the threads can be executed concurrently on different processors. The result is a performance increase, as program execution is spread across CPUs.

Although multiprocessor systems are considered high-end today (primarily reserved for high-capacity servers and scientific workstations), consumer-level computers will eventually benefit from multiple CPUs as well. Using multithreading, a single Java 3D program can scale in performance across a wide variety of computer systems.

Java 3D is optimized for both the single CPU and multiprocessor configurations. When run on a single CPU, Java 3D partitions its work to maximize performance and interactivity. On multiprocessor systems, Java 3D changes its partitioning to take advantage of the extra processors. The speedup is especially dramatic on systems with multiple displays, where Java 3D can partition the rendering to make each processor render to a particular display.

Behaviors

Java 3D supports objects called *behaviors* that allow program logic to be imbedded into a scene graph. This allows objects in the virtual world to make automatic changes to the scene graph.

A spinning wheel, for example, could have an animation behavior associated with it. The input that drives the animation might be the passage of time. For example, the wheel could rotate once a second. A simulation or a user interface could also drive the behavior.

A behavior can be made active only when the viewer is near it. This allows a virtual world to have many more behaviors than could be active at once. Only the behaviors that affect what the viewer is experiencing can be made active.

Geometry Compression

Java 3D allows developers to compress scene geometry. Java 3D supports binary compression of specific object geometry through the API itself. Java 3D's geometry compression capabilities allow an object's geometry, or form, to be represented in an order of magnitude in less space than many popular 3D file formats.

With very little loss in object quality, Java 3D's binary compression format is typically used to reduce the bandwidth required to transmit geometric data over a network.

Sound

Java 3D uses a member of the Java Media family known as the Java Sound API to produce both 2D and 3D audio output capabilities for Java 3D programs. Although Java 3D uses the Java Sound API to support general sound and MIDI, the Java 3D API also supports fully spatialized audio.

Generally speaking, audio can be used in interactive and immersive 3D environments as simple *ambient sounds* that seem to have no particular source, or they may be very sophisticated forms of *spatialized sound*.

Ambient sounds are sometimes called *background sounds* because they aren't tied to a particular location or element of a 3D scene; instead, they seem to be coming from all directions. No matter where you are in a scene, ambient sounds have the same volume and direction. Blowing wind, for instance, is a good example of ambient sound because you can't really pinpoint where it comes from. Likewise, background music tracks (such as those used in video games) are typically played as ambient sound because there is no need for them to be emitted from a specific location.

Spatialized sounds, on the other hand, are tied to a specific location, or *emitter*, in a 3D scene and, as such, are more like the sounds we typically hear in the real world. The sound of a chirping bird, for example, is tied to the bird itself. As you move closer to the bird, the chirping becomes louder; as you move away, it lessens. If you walk around the bird, the chirping will differ, depending on your position relative to the bird. If you stand with the bird to your right, for example, your right ear will hear more of the chirping than your left ear. If you reposition yourself so that the bird is on your left-hand side, your left ear will then hear more of the chirping than your right ear will.

Convenience and Utility Classes

The core Java 3D API defines objects only in terms of strips of polygons, or triangles arranged in various forms. Although a bare 3D object skeleton can be formed using the core API classes, for example, it's up to the programmer to add the required behavior. In many cases, developers construct Java 3D programs by implementing code and structures common to other Java 3D programs. Realizing this, Sun provides a large number of convenience and utility classes designed to save Java 3D developers time, effort, and code.

Sun's Java 3D convenience classes are found in the `com.sun.j3d` package. Here you'll find convenience classes for a range of purposes, from basic scene graph construction, to mouse and keyboard navigation behaviors, to standardized audio device handling. In addition, a number of loaders are also included with the convenience classes, allowing Java 3D developers to take advantage of content stored in a variety of popular 3D file formats.

Versatile View Model

Java 3D uses a unique view model that separates the virtual world (the 3D space in which 3D objects reside) from the physical world that the user resides in. This model makes it easy to support traditional viewing mechanisms, like a window on the screen, but with simple configuration changes the same code can operate seamlessly across a wide range of viewing devices. A single Java 3D applet or application, for example, will work just as well when viewed on a standard desktop monitor as it will when viewed through a pair of stereoscopic virtual reality goggles, in a multiscreen immersive "cave," or on the wall of a stereo projection system.

The Java 3D view model makes a clean distinction between the virtual world and that of the user's physical world. In terms of the Java 3D API, the *ViewPlatform* object represents the viewpoint in the virtual world while the *View* object and its associated components represent the viewpoint in the physical world. Java 3D provides a bridge between the virtual and physical environment by constructing a one-to-one mapping from one space to another, allowing activity in one space to effect the other.

Traditional graphics APIs use camera-based view models, where the viewpoint is determined by emulating a camera placed in a virtual world. The programmer can then reposition a virtual camera in 3D space in an attempt to simulate a human being residing in a virtual world. Although camera-based viewing is appropriate in cases where the end user's display device is known (such as a standard computer monitor), it's not flexible enough to handle a wide range of display devices.

The Java 3D view model, on the other hand, was specifically designed to accommodate a variety of end user configurations. The Java 3D view model can handle head tracking devices seamlessly, without any effort on the programmer's part. In addition, the Java 3D view model can automatically generate stereo views (meaning various types of VR goggles and stereo viewing devices are supported without extra coding by the programmer).

The Java 3D view model degenerates smoothly to a traditional camera-based model in cases where the display is a single (non-stereo), standard computer monitor and no head tracking devices are detected.

Java 3D and the Java Platform

Although you don't need to be an expert in Java to customize existing Java 3D programs, you should, at the very least, be comfortable with the basics of Java programming.

If you are not already experienced with Java, you should first familiarize yourself with the language and Sun's Java development tools before continuing with this chapter and those that follow. As luck would have it, Sun provides a wealth of Java programming resources free of charge at the official Java home page (java.sun.com/) for just such purposes.

On the Java home page you'll find a link called "Docs and Training." The "Docs and Training" link will take you to a huge amount of documentation targeted at developers (which you can jump directly to at java.sun.com/infodocs/), including the Java tutorial (available directly at java.sun.com/docs/ books/tutorial/). You can learn how to program in Java by working through the Java tutorial online, or you can download the entire thing to your personal computer for off-line reading.

The Java tutorial's "Your First Cup of Java" lesson should be your first stop, as it starts at the very beginning. Not only does "Your First Cup of Java" guide you through the process of creating, compiling, and executing applets and applications, it also includes step-by-step installation instructions for the Java 2 Platform Software Development Toolkit (SDK). Following "Your First Cup of Java" you should complete all of the other lessons in the "Trails Covering the Basics" portion of the Java tutorial. Upon completing all of the basic Java programming lessons provided by the Java tutorial, you will have the fundamental experience necessary to learn Java 3D. In particular, you should know:

- The basic Java jargon, including class, class library, object, instance, method, field, bytecode, package, thread, exception, Java Archive (JAR), Java Virtual Machine (JVM), Just-in-Time (JIT) compiler, Java Plug-in, and so forth
- The basic code structure of a Java applet and application
- The basic functionality of the core Java classes, and the packages they are organized into
- How to compile and run premade Java applets and applications
- How to stitch an applet into a Web page using the <APPLET> tag
- How to use the Plug-in converter to make your applet run using the Java Plug-in
- How to write a simple Java applet and application from scratch
- How to import and use premade Java classes, especially those in the core libraries
- How to create custom classes and bundle them into custom packages

In addition to the "Docs and Training" area, through which the Java tutorial is available, you'll also find Sun's "Java Platform Documentation" site particularly useful when learning how to program in Java. Located online at java.sun.com/docs/, the "Java Platform Documentation" site provides links to a number of related online resources, including an overview of the Java platform, Frequently Asked Questions (FAQs), technical papers, design guidelines, the Java language specification, coding conventions, and even an overview of the Java standardization process.

Java 2 JDK, JRE, and the Java Plug-In

Java 3D is built on the Java 2 platform, so Java 3D must be run on Java 1.2 or later. The Java 2 platform consists of two levels of implementation, the JRE and the SDK. The JRE, or Java Runtime Environment, consists of the components that are needed to run Java 2 applications and applets. The SDK, or Software Developers Kit, consists of the JRE plus the Java compiler and other tools that developers need to make new applications and applets. End users need the JRE, while developers need the SDK. The native version of Java present in Netscape or Internet Explorer is Java 1.1, so Java 2 applets need to have a plug-in that adds support for Java 2 to the browser (see Figure 1–15). The plug-in is installed as a part of the JRE. The HTML files that use the applet have to be converted from using the simple APPLET tag to using special tags that direct the applet to the plug-in. The Java plug-in HTML converter tool makes this conversion simple. It is available from the plug-in page, java.sun.com/products/plugin/.

The first Java 2 release was Java 1.2. As of this writing, the current version of Java 2 is 1.3. The 1.3 release has significant performance advantages over 1.2 and should be used if possible.

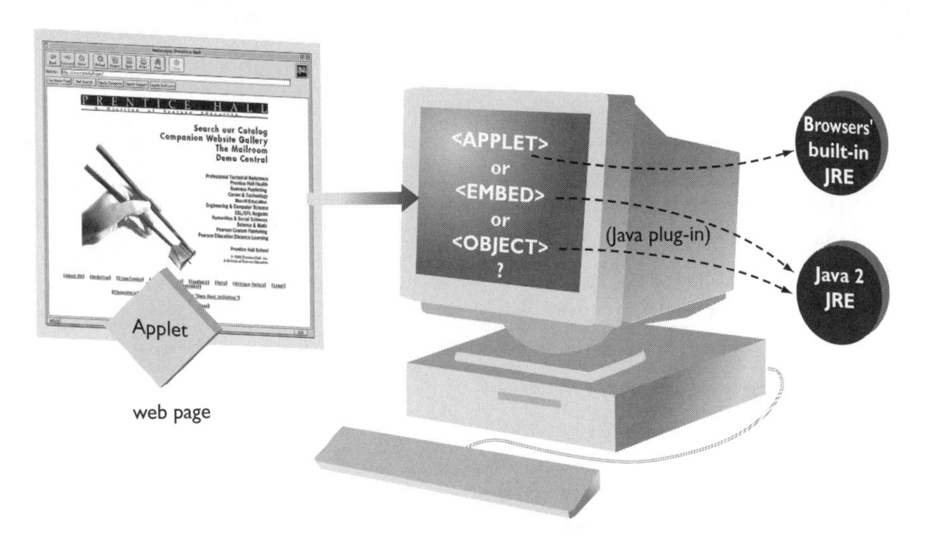

FIGURE 1-15 Because Java 3D programs can only execute on a Java 2 JRE, Java 3D applets can't run in today's Web browsers without the help of Sun's Java Plug-in. The Java Plug-in redirects appropriately configured applets away from the browser's internal JRE and onto a more capable Java 2 runtime.

Java 2 Platform

Sun Microsystems unveiled Java 2 in December of 1998. Prior to its official release, Java 2 was known as Java 1.2, following the previous Java 1.1 (Java 1.1 followed Java 1.0, which was released in 1995). Before releasing 1.2, Sun decided to recast Java 1.2 as the "Java 2 Platform." Primarily a marketing move to create a "Java 2" brand, the name change emphasized Sun's conviction that the latest version of Java was finally a platform upon which industrial-strength applications could be built.

Unfortunately, many technical publications were caught off guard by the name change from Java 1.2 to the Java 2 platform. As a result, a number of "Java 1.2" books, trade journals, programming magazines, and other publications (including much of Sun's own online Java documentation) were already rolling out the door by the time "Java 2" was officially announced. Sun's most current Java SDK is still labeled as SDK 1.3 because it's considered version 1.3 of the Java 2 development platform.

Because of the amount of Java 1.2 material now on the market, many developers tend to use the terms Java 1.2 and Java 2 interchangeably. To learn more about the relationship between Java 2 and Java 1.2, you can read Sun's position paper at java.sun.com/products/jdk/1.2/java2.html. To learn more about Java in general you can visit the official Java home page at java.sun.com/.

Java and Java 3D

Java 3D is an extension to Java. Java 3D can be thought of as a programming layer that resides on top of Java, as previously illustrated by Figure 1–13. Optional packages such as Java 3D add additional classes that aren't considered essential to every Java program. The ability to create a window is considered a core feature available to every Java program, for example, although drawing 3D content in that window is not as critical; consequently, the Java core includes a number of windowing classes but no 3D classes. Java 3D classes, on the other hand, provide very specific 3D graphics and sound capabilities not offered by the core Java class libraries. In this respect you can think of Java 3D classes as building blocks used in the construction of interactive 3D content.

As an optional package, Java 3D must be installed separately from Java 2. This process is simple; the details depend on whether you are installing to the JRE or the JDK. Windows users will need to select between the OpenGL and DirectX versions of Java 3D. See the upcomming "Java 3D DirectX versus Java 3D OpenGL" section.

End users who will be running Java 3D programs but not writing new programs should install the Java 2 JRE and the Java 3D Runtime. Installing the JRE is an automatic process if the HTML file for the applet has been converted using the plug-in converter. When the browser encounters the HTML file and the plug-in has not yet been installed, an automatic installation system is started to download and install the plug-in. As this was being written, Java 3D could not be installed using this mechanism, but it should work soon. In the meantime, users can go to the Java 3D download page (java.sun.com/products/java-media/3D/

download.html), select the version of Java 3D to download, and run the resulting executable. The installation tool will find the JRE and install Java 3D.

If you want to develop new Java 3D programs, you will need the Java 2 JDK and the Java 3D SDK. Install the JDK from java.sun.com/products/. Then install the Java 3D SDK from java.sun.com/products/java-media/3D/.

Java 3D Packages

The core Java 3D API classes are in the `javax.media.j3d` package. Java 3D also includes a collection of vector and matrix classes that are used to represent "vector math" data. These classes are packaged in the `javax.vecmath` package. The `javax.media.j3d` and `javax.vecmath` packages are an implementation of the Java 3D specificication. A set of useful utility classes is included in the `com.sun.j3d` package tree. The utilities provide loaders, geometric primitives, and other capabilities. The `com.sun.j3d` packages provide additional functionality not defined in the Java 3D specification. In practice, all three packages are available to all Java 3D programs, and the set of packages is considered the Java 3D API.

Java 3D Documentation

Be sure to install the Java 3D documentation to your SDK. The download link for the documentation is on the download page for the implementation (be sure to get the *implementation* documentation, not the *API* documentation, which does not include utilities). The javadocs for the Java 3D classes are an invaluable reference. This book does not include the basic class reference provided by the javadoc. Instead, this book will highlight the methods and concepts that are most important when learning Java 3D, leaving the detailed listing of the classes to the javadoc.

Java 3D Versions

As this was being written, Java 3D 1.2.1 was the current release and Java 3D 1.3 was being specified. Java 3D 1.2 was the second major release of Java 3D. The initial implementation of Java 3D was designated Java 3D 1.1, and the final release of that implementation was 1.1.3. In the release number, 1.1 refers to the version of the API, while the final number indicates subsequent releases that fix bugs and improve performance, so 1.1.3 was the third release of the version of the 1.1 API. Java 3D 1.2 represented a new implementation of the architecture, based on the lessons learned in the 1.1 implementation. The 1.2.1 release further improves the quality and performance of 1.2.

Platform Support

Java 3D is available on most of the platforms that support Java 2. Java 3D consists of class libraries and small native libraries that communicate with the low-level graphics APIs. Sun delivers versions of Java 3D for SPARC Solaris and Windows platforms. The other Java 2 licensees release their Java 3D ports as their resources and demands allow. The support level for Java 3D on a variety of platforms as of June 2001 is listed in Table 1–1.

TABLE 1–1 Java 3D Support Level

Platform	Java 3D Release	Low-Level API	Notes
SPARC Solaris	1.2.1	OpenGL	Delivered by Sun
Windows 98 Windows Me	1.2.1	OpenGL DirectX	Delivered by Sun
Windows 2000	1.2.1	OpenGL	Delivered by Sun
Linux	1.2.1	OpenGL	Delivered by Blackdown
HP-UX	1.2.1	OpenGL	Delivered by HP
AIX	1.2.1	OpenGL	Delivered by IBM
IRIX	1.1.3, 1.2.1 planned Q3 2001	OpenGL	Delivered by SGI

Sun continues to discuss making Java 3D available on other system vendor's platforms.

Platform Variations

Java 3D shares the basic Java "write once, run anywhere" philosophy. Like the rest of Java, there are subtle variations between Java 3D on different platforms. For the most part, the differences are due to inconsistencies and bugs in the OpenGL and DirectX drivers on the various platforms. Like any program that makes use of 3D hardware, Java 3D generally requires getting the latest drivers for your hardware to be sure of the best performance and stability. Outside of differences in the graphics drivers, Java 3D generally has the same behavior on different platforms since the large majority of Java 3D is written in Java, with only a small segment dependent on the underlying platform.

Java 3D DirectX versus Java 3D OpenGL

Java 3D is supported on both DirectX and OpenGL on Windows 98 and Windows Me. DirectX is supported on a wider range of hardware, and the DirectX drivers are frequently faster than the OpenGL drivers. On the other hand, some specific features that OpenGL supports are not supported on DirectX. These features will be noted in Chapter 4, "Appearances." For most users, DirectX should provide better performance and should be the default version of Java 3D installed.

Java 3D Resources

Many resources exist for Java 3D besides the material produced by Sun. Be sure to check out the collateral information and links available on the Java 3D home page. The collateral page includes a tutorial that covers many of the basic Java 3D concepts, performance guides, course notes, articles, and other useful reference material. The links page refers to several useful sites, including the Java 3D Community Site, which has a FAQ, utilities, and other reference material. Other sites on the links page include sites with file loaders, utilities, translations of the tutorial, and other useful information.

Summary

Java 3D is a Java interface for interactive 3D graphics. It is an optional extension to the Java 2 platform, providing platform-independent, high-performance applications and applets. Java 3D is being used to develop applications in the entertainment, eCommerce, data visualization, and collaborative engineering areas.

Java 3D provides advantages over other computer graphics APIs. Java 3D provides scene graph programming model which simplifies programming compared to low-level APIs like OpenGL and DirectX. Java 3D shares advantages of other scene graph APIs like OpenInventor and OpenGL Performer, while providing good performance and platform independence. Java 3D works with file formats like Open Flight and X3D, providing a platform for file loaders with the ability to control the file content using Java code.

The key features of Java 3D make it a compelling platform for creating 3D content for the Web. Java 3D's scene graph programming model, retained and immediate mode rendering, scalable performance, support for behaviors, geometry compression and sound, utilities, and a powerful view model support a huge range of application capabilities.

Java 3D is an optional package, installed on top of Java 2. Java 3D is supported on most of the platforms which support Java 2. A wide variety of resources are available on Java 3D.

Summary of URLs Found in This Chapter

Boston's Museum of Science **http://www.mos.org/**

Virtual FishTank™ **http://www.VirtualFishTank.com/**

Full Sail Real World Education **http://www.fullsail.com/**

Roboforge **http://www.roboforge.com/**

Xtivia **http://www.xtivia.com/**

VisAD **http://www.ssec.wisc.edu/~billh/visad.html**

SPLViz **http://www.slicer.org/**

INT **http://www.int.com/**

SDRC I-DEAS Viewer **http://www.sdrc.com/ideas/ideas-viewer/features.html**

Webscope **http://www.webscopeinc.com/**

Java 3D Home Page **http://java.sun.com/products/java-media/3D/**

Java home page **http://java.sun.com/**

Java "Docs and Training" **http://java.sun.com/infodocs/**

Java tutorial **http://java.sun.com/docs/books/tutorial/**

Java Platform Documentation **http://java.sun.com/docs/**

Sun Microsystems **http://www/sun.com/**

Java plug-in **http://java.sun.com/products/plugin/**

Java 1.2vs. Java 2 **http://java.sun.com/products/jdk/1.2/java2.html**

Java 3D download **http://java.sun.com/products/java-media/3D/download.html**

Java 2 SDK **http://java.sun.com/products/**

Java 3D 1.2 API **http://java.sun.com/products/java-media/3D/1_2_api/**

Javadoc **http://java.sun.com/products/jdk/javadoc/**

Java Media APIs **http://java.sun.com/products/java-media/**

CHAPTER 2 Scene Graph Basics

TOPICS IN THIS CHAPTER

- ▼ EXPLORING HELLOUNIVERSE, A SIMPLE JAVA 3D PROGRAM
- ▼ SCENE GRAPH COMPONENTS
- ▼ WORKING WITH THE SCENE GRAPH
- ▼ USING GROUPS TO STRUCTURE YOUR WORLD
- ▼ RECIPE FOR A JAVA 3D PROGRAM

After taking a bird's eye view of Java 3D in the previous chapter, it's time to dive into the basics of programming with the API. Because Java 3D employs a scene graph programming model, your application will create a description of a scene, then Java 3D will manage the on-screen display of the scene. In this chapter we'll show you how to do exactly that. Here you'll explore the basic class structure used for Java 3D programming, how to make changes to the scene graph while it is being displayed, and how to build up the scene graph using grouping objects.

Firing Up HelloUniverse

Throughout this chapter we'll explore elements of a basic Java 3D program by examining Sun's example HelloUniverse application. HelloUniverse is provided along with the Java 3D SDK. Once you've installed the Java 3D SDK you should spend a few minutes looking at the various example programs that it comes with. In particular, you should run HelloUniverse by changing your directory to the HelloUniverse directory found in the SDK's example programs directory, and issue the following command at the command line:

```
> java HelloUniverse
```

If Java 3D is properly installed, and you're in the correct directory, this will fire up the HelloUniverse program. Once running, HelloUniverse will display the spinning colored cube frozen in time as shown in Figure 2–1.

FIGURE 2–1 HelloUniverse displays a spinning color cube, which we see here frozen in time.

The complete source code for HelloUniverse is found in Listing 2–1 at the end of this chapter. You can flip through this printed version of the program as we explore its features, or open the HelloUniverse.java file provided with the Java 3D SDK.

Stepping into a Virtual Universe

Java 3D programs use a *scene graph* data structure to describe and organize the graphics that will be drawn on the user's display. In Java 3D terminology the scene graph is more commonly called the *virtual universe* or the *virtual world*. These interchangeable terms describe an imaginary space where you create and view your scene. The virtual universe contains all of the graphical aspects of your scene: the objects to be displayed and the lights and other elements of the environment, along with structure that organizes the data.

Java 3D renders scene graphs to the screen based on the viewpoint of an observer in that virtual universe. For example, in HelloUniverse, the virtual universe consists of the spinning cube and a viewer looking at the cube. The images on the screen are what the viewer would see. This simple model, a virtual world being observed by a virtual viewer, allows Java 3D to handle a large variety of applications, from a simple case, like the spinning cube of HelloUniverse, to huge simulations in which the world is drawn on several screens at once (i.e., immersive environments).

In the sections that follow we'll explore a number of elements common to most Java 3D virtual universes.

Scene Graphs

The *scene graph* is a treelike data structure used to store, organize, and render 3D scene information such as objects, materials, lights, and other aspects of a scene. The scene graph is made from *nodes*, which represent objects to be displayed, aspects of the environment of the virtual world, or groups of nodes. A Java 3D programmer can construct node hierarchies by adding child nodes to grouping nodes.

For example, a scene might contain a house group, with the children of the house being the rooms of the house, and the children of each room being the furniture in the room. Nodes can be made from smaller pieces, called *node components*. Several nodes in a scene graph can share a node component.

Figure 2–2 illustrates a scene graph for our theoretical house scene. The house group contains two room groups, each of which has a bed node. The beds are made from node components that specify their shape and color. The beds share the shape for the beds, but have different colors.

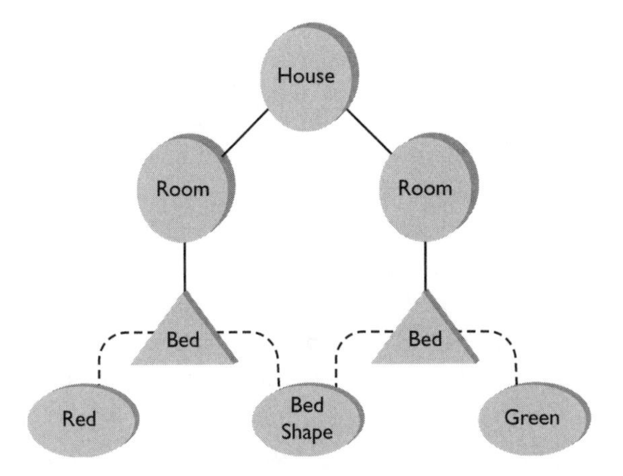

FIGURE 2–2 Scene graphs are treelike data structures used to store, organize, and render 3D scene information such as objects, materials, lights, and other aspects of a scene. This figure illustrates a simple Java 3D scene graph of a house.

Figure 2–2 is an example of a scene graph diagram. A scene graph diagram is a visual representation that acts as a "map" for the scene graph. By looking at the scene graph diagram you can get a good feel for how the scene graph is actually structured in code. The shapes appearing in the diagram represent Java 3D objects, while lines represent connections between the objects. A complete legend for scene graph "map" diagrams such as this is shown in Figure 2–3.

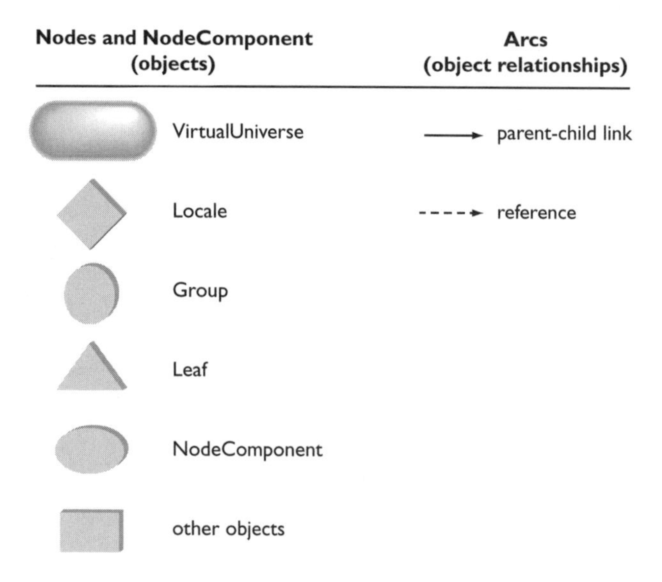

FIGURE 2–3 Symbols commonly used to graphically represent Java 3D scene graphs.

A *subgraph* is a piece of the scene graph. It can be a single node or a large tree. The *root node* of a subgraph is the top-level group. For example, in the subgraph above, the root node is the house group.

SceneGraphObjects

The base class for objects in the scene graph is **`SceneGraphObject`**. **`Node`** and **`NodeComponent`** are subclasses of **`SceneGraphObject`**. **`Nodes`** can be further divided into **`Group`** nodes, which have children and **`Leaf`** nodes that do not, as seen in the class diagram in Figure 2–4

Methods on **`SceneGraphObjects`** build the structure and modify the properties of your world. **`SceneGraphObjects`** are connected via references. For example, in the house described previously, the left bed is red as specified by an **`Appearance`** node component. Changing the **`Appearance`** changes the color of the bed.

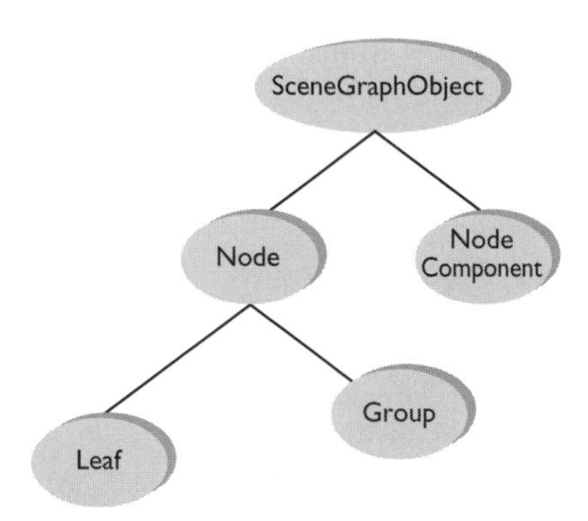

FIGURE 2–4 Java 3D class diagram of SceneGraphObject. (Note: This is not a scene graph diagram, it is a class diagram.)

Node Types Nodes are the basic elements of the scene graph. Nodes can be divided into the following basic categories:

- Shape nodes, which represent 3D objects in your world
- Environment nodes, which represent characteristics of areas of your world, such as the light shining in an area
- Group nodes, which organize the scene graph
- The **`ViewPlatform`**, which is a place where a viewer can look at your world

A node can only appear in one group in a scene graph; nodes can't be shared between groups. A special group, called a **`SharedGroup`** allows a subgraph to appear multiple times in the scene graph.

The Java 3D scene graph is a *directed acyclic graph* (DAG). Connections between nodes in a scene graph are *directed,* which means they are connected using parent-child relationships. Java 3D scene graphs are *acyclic,* which means that the parent-child relationship can't form loops; for example, the child of a group can't contain the parent of the group.

NodeComponents **`NodeComponents`** are pieces of nodes that hold properties or data. **`NodeComponents`** can be shared between nodes and may be referred to many times in a scene graph. **`NodeComponents`** are shared for two main reasons: shared memory and shared functionality. In the example of the house, the bed shape is shared between the beds in the two rooms, sharing the memory used for the bed. An example of shared functionality would be a room where a sofa and chair share an appearance, perhaps making them appear to be upholstered in the same fabric (see Figure 2–5).

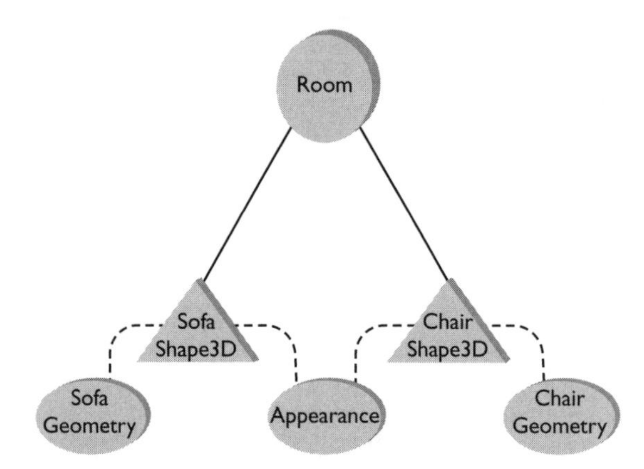

FIGURE 2–5 Scene graph objects can be shared to save memory and share functionality within the scene. Here we see a variation on Figure 2–2, in which the bed is shared.

The sofa and chair have different shapes, but the same appearance. This shares the functionality of the appearance: a program could change the color for both the sofa and chair by changing the shared appearance.

Shape Nodes Shape nodes are the graphical objects in your virtual world. A shape consists of two pieces: the geometry, which specifies the 3D coordinates and other geometric data for the shape, and the appearance, which specifies the color and other properties of the shape.

Java 3D supports several kinds of shape nodes. The basic type of shape is a **`Shape3D`**. It consists of **`Geometry`** and **`Appearance`** node components. There are several classes of **`Geometry`** node components:

- **`GeometryArray`** is used to draw primitives like points, lines, and polygons that are defined using vertices.
- **`Text3D`** is used to draw text as 3D "block" characters.
- **`Raster`** is used to draw images on the screen.
- **`CompressedGeometry`** is a way to draw **`GeometryArray`** primitives using a compressed format that is faster to send over a network.

Classes related to **`Shape3D`** which add functionality are as follows:

- **OrientedShape3D** nodes automatically face toward the user. They are used for drawing objects such as text labels that need to face the viewer to be seen properly.
- **Morph** nodes allow several **GeometryArray** primitives to be combined to allow a smooth transition from one shape to another. For example, a **Morph** could be used to represent a hand that can be opened and closed.

Utility classes which function as shapes are as follows:

- **Primitives** are high level shapes like **Cone**, **Cylinder**, and **Sphere**.
- **Text2D** is used to draw a text label on a flat polygon, like a sign.

Shape nodes will be covered in Chapter 3, "Creating and Loading Geometry," and Chapter 4, "Appearances."

Group Nodes

Group nodes are containers that hold sets of nodes. The **Group** class does basic grouping. Subclasses of **Group** add different properties. The **Group** class (javax.media.j3d.Group) is a subclass of **Node** and is able to contain children. The primary role of a **Group** object is to act as the parent of other nodes, specifically other **Group** nodes and Leaf nodes. Subclasses of **Group** are considered *grouping nodes* (see Figure 2–6).

Group is the base class for a number of classes that position, orient, and control scene graph objects in the virtual universe. Following is an overview of the **Group** subclasses:

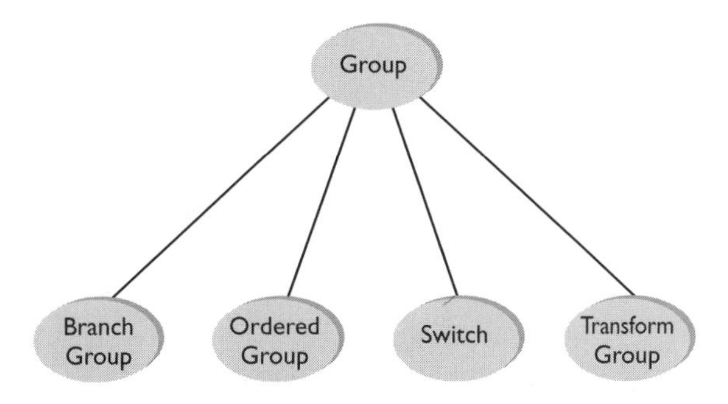

FIGURE 2–6 Group class diagram.

The subclasses of **Group** are:

- **BranchGroup** holds subgraphs that can be added and removed while the scene is being displayed.

- **OrderedGroup** specifies that its children be rendered in the order they appear in the group.
- **Switch** allows the display of each of its children to be turned on and off.
- **TransformGroup** changes the transformation of its children, giving its children a different position, orientation, or size.

SharedGroup Another subclass of **Group** is **SharedGroup**, which allows a subgraph of your scene to appear in more than one group. A **SharedGroup** is an independent subgraph, not the child of another **Group**. Instead, another node, called a **Link**, is used to connect the **SharedGroup** to other groups. Figure 2–7 illustrates this concept.

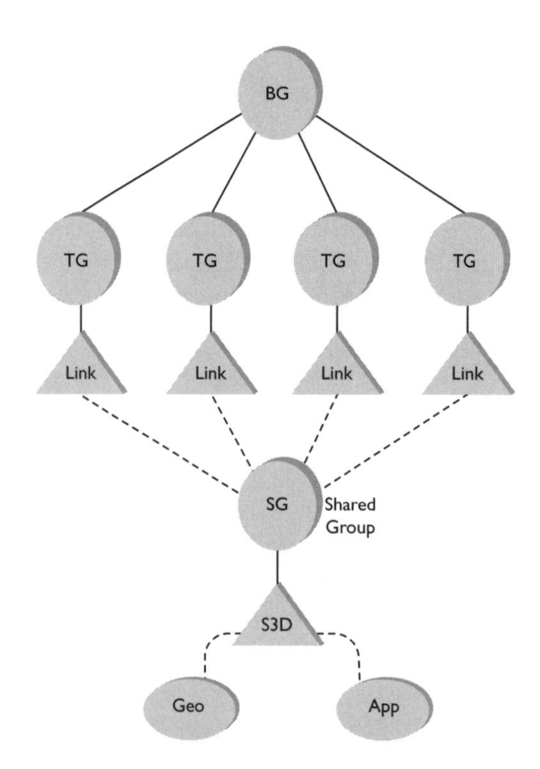

FIGURE 2–7 The **SharedGroup** node provides the ability to share a subgraph among different portions of a scene graph tree.

The top-level **BranchGroup** holds a car. The **SharedGroup** holds the definition for a wheel for the car. The **TransformGroups** position each wheel and the **Links** connect the **SharedGroup** with the **TransformGroups**.

Groups will be covered in more detail in the "Groups" section later in this chapter.

Environment Nodes

Environment nodes affect the environment in an area of the virtual universe. They are not directly visible, but instead they change the space in which the shape nodes are viewed. You'll learn how to use environment nodes in Chapter 5, "Environment Nodes." The kinds of environment nodes are:

- **`Light`** nodes light the scene. These include directional, positional, and spot lights.
- **`Background`** nodes define the background for the current scene. The background can be a solid background color, an image that fills the window, or geometry that is drawn in the back of the scene.
- **`Fog`** nodes simulate atmospheric effects like fog or smoke. They can be used to increase the realism of a scene by fading the appearance of objects that are farther from the viewer.
- **`Behavior`** nodes make changes to the scene graph based on events such as time passing, moving the viewer, or using the mouse. There are many predefined behaviors. For example, a **`Billboard`** behavior updates a **`TransformGroup`** to keep the group's children facing towards the viewer.
- **`Clip`** nodes keep objects that are far away from the viewer from being drawn.
- **`ModelClip`** nodes can be used to cut away sections of a model. For example, a program could use **`ModelClip`** nodes to slice away the housing for a car's transmission, revealing the gears inside.
- **`AlternateAppearance`** nodes are used to selectively override the **`Appearance`** component of **`Shape`** nodes. For example, a program could highlight the shapes being pointed to by the mouse by using an **`AlternateAppearance`**.
- **`Sound`** nodes define sound sources.
- **`Soundscape`** nodes set up the aspects of the listener's "aural environment" such as reverberation.

The ViewPlatform

The scene graph is drawn on the screen from the viewpoint of a virtual observer. The viewer observes the virtual universe using a node called the **`ViewPlatform`**. This is the place where the scene is being viewed. The **`ViewPlatform`** can be moved around like any other node, allowing the observer to move through the scene. For example, if the virtual world is a house, the **`ViewPlatform`** could be moved from the point of view of a person walking through the house.

Shape nodes can move along with the **`ViewPlatform`**. For example, in a space simulation, the viewer might be inside a space ship. The **`ViewPlatform`** could then be located with a control panel in front of it inside the space ship. As the space ship moves around, the **ViewPlatform** moves with it, with the control panel drawn in front of the viewer.

The VirtualUniverse and Locale

VirtualUniverse and **Locale** form the root of the scene graph. Connecting a scene graph to a **Locale** makes it available for display, an active state known as making the scene graph *live* (a scene graph that is connected to a **Locale** is said to be live). The scene graph is connected to the **Locale** using a **BranchGroup**. The subgraph held by a **BranchGroup** is called a "branch graph." A utility class called **SimpleUniverse** usually manages the **VirtualUniverse** and **Locale**.

SimpleUniverse manages several objects that control the drawing of your scene:

- The **VirtualUniverse** and **Locale** hold the virtual world you want displayed
- The **ViewPlatform** is where the viewer is located in your world

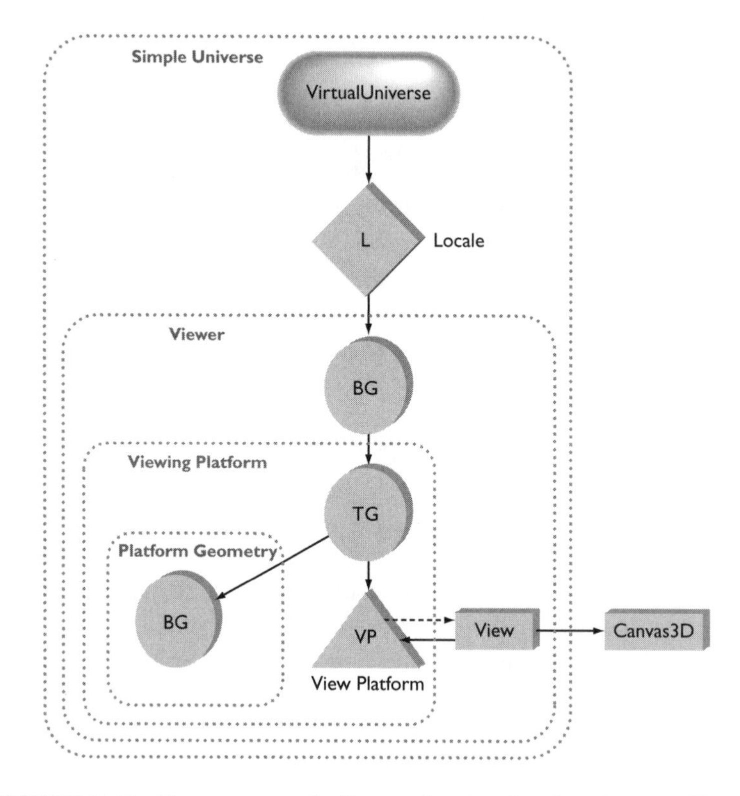

FIGURE 2–8 The scene graph diagram for the SimpleUniverse utility class.

- The **View** tells how to turn what the viewer sees into a 2D picture
- The **Canvas3D** tells where to draw the 2D picture on your computer screen

Figure 2–8 illustrates a scene graph diagram for SimpleUniverse.

Use **SimpleUniverse** to attach the branch graph for your world to the **Locale**. This is called the "content" branch of the scene graph. **SimpleUniverse** manages the "view" branch graph. You can move your viewer through your world by changing the **TransformGroup** that holds the **ViewPlatform**.

Exploring the HelloUniverse Scene Graph

The scene graph for HelloUniverse is shown in Figure 2–9. Here we see that the "content branch" for **HelloUniverse** consists of a **TransformGroup** that holds a **ColorCube** shape node, and **Behavior** that changes the transformation on the **TransformGroup** to make the cube rotate.

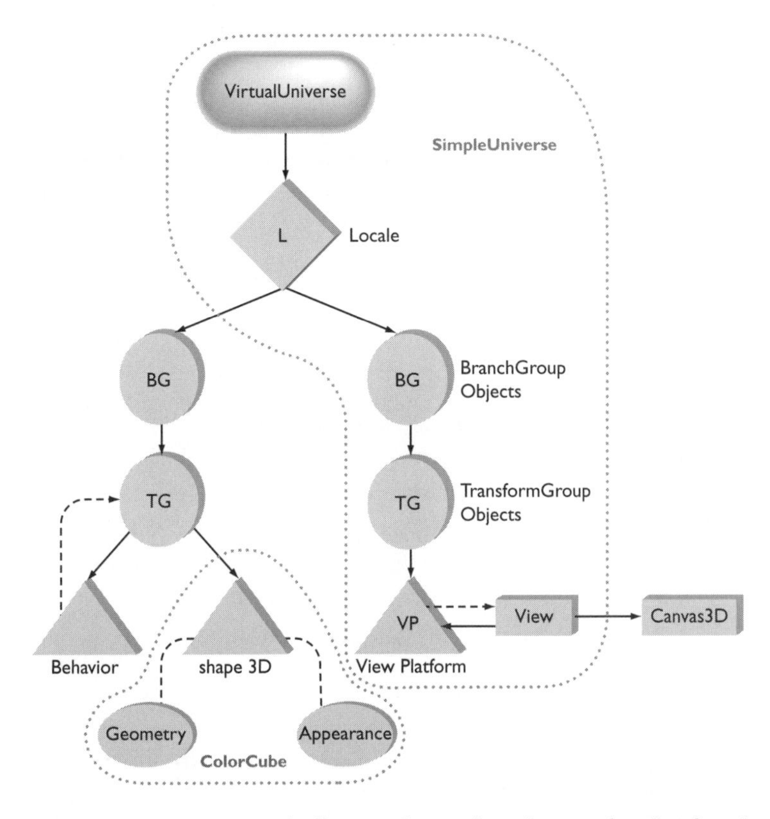

FIGURE 2–9 A scene graph diagram for HelloUniverse. The SimpleUniverse portion of the scene graph has been simplified.

HelloUniverse uses the **SimpleUniverse** utility to set up the basic scene graph and the view branch graph. This is done in the `init()` method:

```
init () {
   GraphicsConfiguration config =
        SimpleUniverse.getPreferredConfiguration();
   Canvas3D c = new Canvas3D(config);

      // Create a simple scene and attach to the virtual
      // universe
      BranchGroup scene = createSceneGraph();

      SimpleUniverse u = new SimpleUniverse(c);

      // This will move the ViewPlatform back a bit so the
      // objects in the scene can be viewed.
      u.getViewingPlatform().setNominalViewingPlatform();

      u.addBranchGraph(scene);
}
```

The first couple of lines create a **Canvas3D**, which is the component where the graphics get drawn. It is created using a **GraphicsConfiguration**, which ensures that Java 3D will be able to use the graphics hardware in your computer to draw to the canvas efficiently.

Next, the `createSceneGraph()` method is called to create the content branch graph. We'll look at this method in more detail later.

The call:

```
u.getViewingPlatform().setNominalViewingPlatform();
```

moves the **ViewPlatform** so that the viewer can see the area around the origin (0,0,0). Finally, the content branch graph is attached to the **SimpleUniverse** using `addBranchGraph()`. This makes the branch graph "live" or available for viewing and so the cube starts to be drawn on the **Canvas3D**.

Working with the Scene Graph

So far, we have looked at the basic elements of the scene graph. Shapes are the objects in your world, environment nodes affect areas of your world, group nodes organize and control other nodes, and everything gets viewed from the **ViewPlatform**. In this section, we'll look at how the scene graph gets interpreted, how to make changes to the scene graph once it is being displayed, and other ways you can use the scene graph.

Scene Graph Interpretation

The scene graph is a description of your world that Java 3D uses to render to the **Canvas3D**. Java 3D doesn't render the scene directly from the scene graph; instead, it builds an internal representation of the scene graph. This conversion allows Java 3D to optimize the scene graph for rendering, minimizing the overhead of working with the underlying graphics API. It is important to understand how Java 3D interprets your scene graph when building the rendering representation so that the final image is correct. Consider the scene graph illustrated in Figure 2–10.

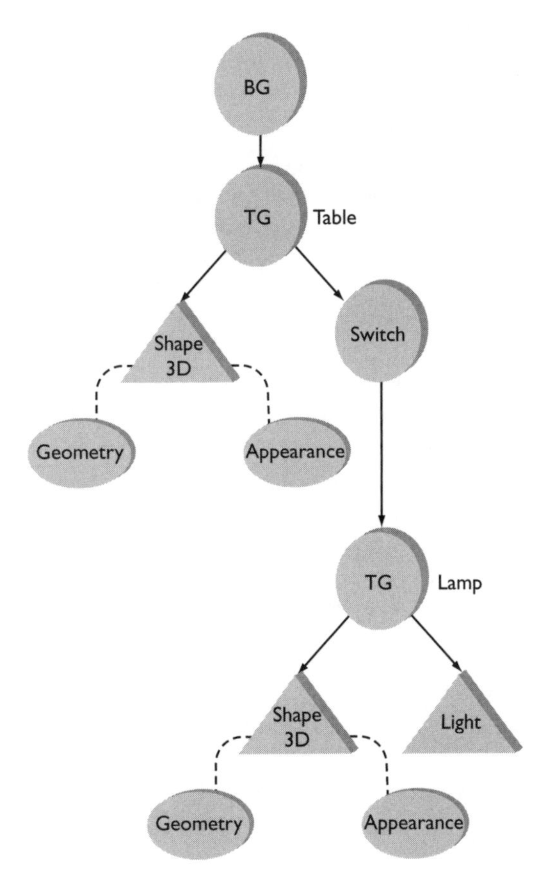

FIGURE 2–10 Scene graph of a table with a lamp.

This is a scene graph for a table with a lamp on it. The **BranchGroup** holds the subgraph, allowing it to be added to a virtual world. The top level **Transform-**

Group controls the positioning of the table and lamp. The children of the **TransformGroup** are the **Shape3D** for the table and a **Switch** for the lamp. The **Switch** controls whether the subgraph under the switch is active. If the **Switch** selects the lamp **TransformGroup** child, then the lamp's **Shape3D** and **Light** are part of the scene graph (the lamp has a separate **Shape3D** and **Light** since a **Light** is an environment node, affecting shape nodes without a visible appearance of its own). If the lamp isn't selected, then the lamp isn't included in the scene graph, as neither the shape or the light is active. The lamp **Transform-Group** controls the positioning of the lamp on the table.

This scene graph shows how Java 3D interprets the hierarchy in the scene graph. The group nodes affect their descendents: the top **TransformGroup** moves both the table and the lamp; the **Switch** controls the lamp's shape and **Light**. The effect of group nodes chain from the root to leaves of the tree: both the table **TransformGroup** and the lamp **TransformGroup** affect the lamp. The state for the leaf nodes, the **Shape3Ds**, and the **Light** comes from the ancestors of the leaf nodes. The effect of environment nodes, such as the **Light** comes from the node's properties, not the hierarchy. In other words, the light illuminates the table because the table is near the light, even though the table and light are not on the same branch of the scene graph.

When building the optimized version of the scene graph, Java 3D preserves the relationships specified by the group and environment nodes, but otherwise it is free to reorganize your data. It may group all the shapes with common properties together or do other optimizations. This means that you can't infer any ordering for the rendering from the scene graph. The shapes are drawn in whatever order Java 3D decides (unless a specific ordering is specified by an **OrderedGroup**). The *depth buffer*, a part of the graphics hardware, makes sure that closer shapes obscure shapes that are farther away.

Making Changes to the Scene Graph

When you attach your scene to the **Locale**, it starts being displayed in the **Canvas3D** associated with the **View** that is attached to the **Locale**. (As you make changes to the scene graph, Java 3D updates its internal representation and draws the new picture). For example, in **HelloUniverse**, the transformation for the cube is being changed, making the cube rotate. Drawing the new picture is called *rendering* the scene. Each picture is called a *frame*.

To make the updates to the internal representation more efficient, Java 3D makes a "contract" with your program that spells out what changes you will be making to the scene graph when it is live. This contract is specified using a mechanism called *capability bits*. For each change that you can make to the scene graph, there is a corresponding capability bit, an integer constant that is part of the class definition for the scene graph object. To make the change available when the scene graph is live, you set the capability bit using the method:

```
void setCapability(int bit);
```

By default, no capabilities are set so that you can't make any changes to live scene graph objects. You must explicitly set capability bits that correspond to the changes you want to make, telling Java 3D not to optimize these portions of the scene graph. Capability bits can be inquired and reset using the methods:

```
boolean getCapability(int bit)
void clearCapability(int bit)
```

Capability Bits Example: TransformGroup

Let's looks at a concrete example. In **HelloUniverse** the cube is rotating because the **TransformGroup** holding the cube is changing the transform for the cube. **TransformGroup** inherits the `clearCapability()`, `getCapability()`, and `setCapability()` methods from **SceneGraphObject**. The transformation for the cube is changed by calling the method

```
void setTransform(Transform3D t);
```

on the **TransformGroup**. This copies the transform from the **Transform3D** into the **TransformGroup**. This method can be called anytime when the **TransformGroup** is not live, but by default this method can't be called when the **TransformGroup** is live without generating an exception. The **TransformGroup** class also defines a field used for setting the capability bits for these methods:

```
static int ALLOW_TRANSFORM_WRITE;
```

To make the `setTransform()` method available when the scene graph is live, call `setCapability()` with the corresponding field. In **HelloUniverse**, this is done when the **TransformGroup** for the cube is created as follows:

```
// Create the transform group. Enable the
// TRANSFORM_WRITE capability so that our
// behavior code can modify it at runtime.
TransformGroup objTrans = new TransformGroup();
objTrans.setCapability(TransformGroup.ALLOW_TRANSFORM_WRITE);
// a call to objTrans.setTransform() is now legal!
```

Capability Bits Details

Capability bits can only be changed when a scene graph is not live. That is, you can only change the contract between you and Java 3D when the contract is not active. If you try to change the capability bits on a live scene graph you'll get a **RestrictedAccessException**. If you need to change your capability bits, it is legal to detach your branch graph, adjust that capability bits, and reattach the branch graph, but it will be more efficient if you set up your capability bits correctly from the beginning.

It is also legal for you to turn on all of the capability bits all the time. However, this may disable optimizations that Java 3D could make to your scene graph. How much performance difference will this make? It is hard to say. In a very few cases, it could make a large difference (perhaps slowing performance down by a factor of 3 to 4 times), but most of the time the difference is fairly small (somewhere in the range of 0 to 10%).

Your best bet is to set the capability bits you think you'll need but don't worry about keeping their usage to an absolute minimum. A handy way to work with this is to subclass the node type and set the capability bits in the constructor. For example, if you are going to use **TransformGroup** nodes for the joints on a robot arm where you know you'll want to be changing the transforms while the scene graph is live, you can make a subclass of **TransformGroup** called **JointTG**, which sets the ALLOW_TRANSFORM_READ and ALLOW_TRANSFORM_WRITE cap bits in its constructor.

More Optimizations: compile()

You can further optimize a **BranchGroup** or a **SharedGroup** by calling the method:

```
void compile()
```

This tells Java 3D to finalize the capability bit contract and spend extra time trying to make the compiled group as optimized as possible. After compiling, no further changes to the capbility bits can be made. Compiling is typically the last operation before making a **BranchGroup** live.

Other Scene Graph Operations

Rendering the scene is the primary operation of Java 3D, but other operations are supported as well. Picking is used to determine the shapes that are in a specific area of your virtual world. Collision detection is used to determine when the movement of shapes leads to a collision and where the shapes intersect with one another.

Picking is primarily used to select shapes using the mouse. The **PickCanvas** utility class is used to turn the mouse location into an area of space, or *pick shape*, that projects from the viewer through the mouse location into the virtual world. **PickCanvas** extends the more general **PickTool** class. A **PickTool** can be used to select shapes without the mouse; for example, all the shapes that are near a specific location. All **Shapes** are pickable by default. To disable picking for a **Shape** or the children of a **Group**, use the **Node** method:

```
void setPickable(boolean pickable);
```

Picking can use different levels of detail, from the general area of the shape down to the exact geometry of the shape. Picking will be discussed in more detail in Chapter 6, "Tools: Transformation, Viewing, and Picking."

Collision detection is a more advanced operation. When moving a shape results in the shape intersecting with another shape, Java 3D can generate an event that can be processed by a collision **Behavior**. Collision detection can be combined with the code that moves the **ViewPlatform** to keep the viewer from moving though other shapes, such as walls. Picking can also be used for collision prevention, using a pick shape to query whether moving the viewer would result in a collision.

Groups

Earlier in this chapter we talked briefly about the basic classes of groups. In this section you'll learn more about working with groups. Groups form the structure of the scene graph. They organize the data, control what pieces of the scene are rendered, and change the position, orientation, and size of objects in your scene. In this section you'll learn the basics of working with **Group** nodes, the subclasses of **Group**, and the added capabilities of each subclass.

Group is the base class for nodes that have children. The base class defines the methods that are used when working with child nodes:

```
void addChild(Node child);
void insertChild(Node child, int index);
void removeChild(int index);
void setChild(Node child, int index);
java.util.Enumeration getAllChildren();
Node getChild(int index);
int numChildren();
```

These methods have the same semantics (meaning) as the `java.util.Vector` class. Adding a child appends it to the end of the list. Insertion and removal change the length of the list; `setChild()` replaces a child without changing the length of the list.

There are `ALLOW_CHILDREN_READ` and `ALLOW_CHILDREN_WRITE` capability bits that correspond to the methods that get and set children. There is also an `ALLOW_CHILDREN_EXTEND` bit that must be set if the additional child will add to the number of children in a **Group**.

The children of a **Group** are in an ordered list, so that each child can be referenced using an index. However, there is no guarantee that the children will be rendered in index order (except for **OrderedGroup**, discussed below). In general, you can't assume *any* ordering for the rendering of your scene graph unless you explicitly define it. This is because Java 3D builds an optimized version of your scene graph for rendering which doesn't preserve the order of children unless explicitly instructed to do so.

The **Group** class is not abstract. **Groups** are useful for holding sets of nodes. The subclasses of **Group** add different functionality or operations on their children.

Group Subclasses

Each subclass of **Group** adds capabilities to the basic **Group** functionality.

BranchGroup

BranchGroups are the root nodes for branch graphs, subgraphs that can be added or removed from a live scene graph. Adding a branch graph to a live scene graph makes it "live" or available for display. **BranchGroups** are the only node that can be attached to a **Locale** or **SimpleUniverse** using the method:

```
void addBranchGraph(BranchGroup branchGroup);
```

Remove the **BranchGroup** from a **Locale** or **SimpleUniverse** using the method:

```
void removeBranchGraph(BranchGroup BranchGroup);
```

A **BranchGroup** can be added to a live **Group** using any of the methods that add children, such as `addChild()`. It can be removed from a group by calling any of the methods that remove children, such as `removeChild()`. A **BranchGroup** can also be removed from a live scene graph by calling:

```
void detatch();
on the BranchGroup.
```

When a **BranchGroup** is made live, **Java 3D** makes an internal representation of the subgraph, optimized for rendering. This process takes time and memory. This work is lost when the **BranchGroup** is detached, so it is wise to keep **Branch-Groups** attached to the scene graph whenever possible. **Groups** support a special method to keep **BranchGroups** live:

```
void moveTo(BranchGroup branchGroup);
```

This method moves a **BranchGroup** to the **Group** without detaching the **BranchGroup**. This is more efficient than detaching the **BranchGroup** and adding it to the group since the **BranchGroup** will not have to be made live after the operation.

A **BranchGroup** can be further optimized by calling:

```
void compile();
```

This optimizes the branch graph and finalizes the capability bits of the scene graph objects in the branch graph.

OrderedGroup

An **OrderedGroup** ensures that its children are rendered according to their index order. Children of an **OrderedGroup** are rendered from the lowest index to the highest. In general, **Java 3D** will not render children of a group in any particular order. Only the children of an **OrderedGroup** (and its subclasses) are rendered in index order. **DecalGroup** is a subclass of **OrderedGroup** that is used to define an **OrderedGroup** where the children of the group are coplanar, such as when a decal is applied to a surface.

OrderedGroups are not commonly used. Most of the time, shapes are drawn using *depth buffering*, which is a process that decides which shapes are visible based on their distance to the viewer; close objects obscure distant objects. The depth buffering process does not depend on the order of the shapes being drawn, which is why Java 3D doesn't ordinarily use ordering for the rendering. **OrderedGroup** is a way to force an ordering. It is used when the specific order of rendering is important. For example, a program might have a user interface where buttons are drawn on top of a panel. If the buttons and the panel are coplanar, the buttons must be drawn after the panel to be sure that they are visible. An **OrderedGroup** could specify that the panel is drawn first, followed by the buttons.

SharedGroup

A **SharedGroup** is used to share a subgraph between different groups in a scene graph. The **SharedGroup** has no parent. Instead, another node type, called a

Link, is used to refer to a **SharedGroup**. **Links** are then the children of other groups (refer back to Figure 2–7). Figure 2–7 shows a **SharedGroup** that might be used for the wheels on a car. The **SharedGroup** holds the shape for the wheel. The **TransformGroups** set up the transforms for each instance of the wheel and the **Links** connect the **SharedGroup** with the **TransformGroups**.

The **SharedGroup** is added to a group using a **Link**; for example, if wheelSG is the **SharedGroup** for the wheel and rightFrontTG is the **TransformGroup** to position the right front wheel, the wheel could be added to the **Transform-Group** by calling:

```
rightWheelTG.addChild(new Link(wheelSG));
```

This creates a new **Link** that refers to the wheelSG and adds it to the **TransformGroup**.

The scene graph for the **SharedGroup** can be much more complex than a single shape. A **SharedGroup** could hold an entire assembly. For example, the **SharedGroup** for the wheel could contain an axle, a brake assembly, the tire, etc.

Certain node types can't appear in a shared subgraph. The legal node types for a SharedGroup are: Group nodes (except another SharedGroup, since SharedGroups can't have parents), Light, Link, Morph, Shape3D, OrientedShape3D, and Sound. Putting other node types into a SharedGroup will generate an exception.

Like a **BranchGroup**, a **SharedGroup** may be compiled by calling the method:

```
void compile();
```

This has the same effect as for **BranchGroup**. The subgraph is optimized and the capability bits are frozen.

Switch

A Switch selects which of its children are active. The selection is set and inquired using the methods:

```
void setWhichChild(int whichChild)
int getWhichChild();
```

The switch value can be the index of the child in the **Switch** or one of the constants:

```
CHILD_NONE
CHILD_ALL
CHILD_MASK
```

If the selection value is `CHILD_NONE`, none of the children are drawn. If the value is `CHILD_ALL`, all of the children are drawn. If the selection value is `CHILD_MASK`, then the children are selected using a `java.util.BitSet` to specify the children, as follows:

```
void setChildMask(java.util.BitSet childMask);
java.util.BitSet getChildMask();
```

The bits of the **`BitSet`** correspond to the children of the **`Switch`**. Bit 0 corresponds to child 0, etc. For example, for a **`Switch`** called `switch`, we would turn on the rendering of child 3 and turn off the rendering of child 2 using **`BitSet`** `childMask` as follows:

```
childMask.set(3);
childMask.clear(2);
switch.setChildMask(childMask);
```

To activate or deactivate a subgraph it can be more efficient to use a **`Switch`** than to attach and detach a **`BranchGroup`** since the **`Switch`** remains live even when its children are not active.

TransformGroup

`TransformGroup` changes the size, position, or orientation of its children. The **`TransformGroup`** may have other **`TransformGroups`** as children, allowing hierarchies of objects to be constructed.

The transform for a **`TransformGroup`** is set using a **`Transform3D`** object. You'll learn how to work with **`Transform3D`** objects in Chapter 6, "Tools: Transformation, Viewing, and Picking." For now, think of the **`Transform3D`** as a "black box" which specifies how to move, size, and orient the children of the **`TransformGroup`**.

The **`TransformGroup`** has an internal **`Transform3D`** that holds the transform it uses. Your program doesn't have access to that **`Transform3D`**. Instead, the **`TransformGroup`** methods allow you to copy your **`Transform3D`** into and out of the **`TransformGroup`**:

```
void setTransform(Transform3D newTransform);
void getTransform(Transform3D inqTransform);
```

If you change the **`Transform3D`** after you call `setTransform()`, it won't affect the **`TransformGroup`** unless you call `setTransform()` again.

A **TransformGroup** starts out with an identity **Transform3D**. This means that the **TransformGroup** starts out acting like a simple **Group** with the children of the **TransformGroup** having the same transformation as the **TransformGroup**.

The Java 3D scene graph exists in a coordinate space called virtual world or VWorld coordinates. The children of a **TransformGroup** are affected by the **TransformGroup**'s transform, so they are in a different coordinate system called "local coordinates." Each **TransformGroup** produces a new local coordinate system for its children.

The transformation from the local coordinate system to VWorld coordinates for any node can be inquired by calling:

```
void getLocalToVWorld(Transform3D trans)
```

on the node. This can be useful when you need the "real" location of an object.

Groups in HelloUniverse

HelloUniverse makes use of a few groups in the content branch graph. The scene graph diagram for the content branch is shown in Figure 2–11.

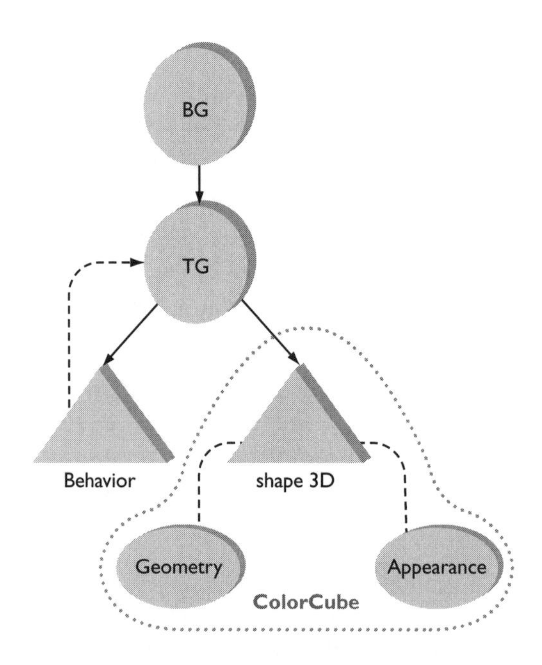

FIGURE 2–11 The HelloUniverse content branch.

The content branch group is created in the createSceneGraph() method. This begins by creating the **BranchGraph**:

```
public BranchGroup createSceneGraph() {
   // Create the root of the banch graph
   BranchGroup objRoot = new BranchGroup();
```

Next, we set up the **TransformGroup** and add it to the **BranchGroup**:

```
// Create the TransformGroup node. Enable the
// TRANSFORM_WRITE capability so that our behavior
// node can modify it at runtime. Add it to the
// root of the subgraph
TransformGroup objTrans = new TransformGroup()
objTrans.setCapability(
            TransformGroup.ALLOW_TRANSFORM_WRITE);
objRoot.addChild(objTrans);
```

Next, we create the color cube and add it to the **TransformGroup**:

```
// Create a simple Shape3D node; add it to the scene
// graph
objTrans.addChild(new ColorCube(0.4));
```

Next, we set up the rotation interpolator which will spin the cube and add it to the **TransformGroup**:

```
// Create a new Behavior object that will perform the
// desired operation on the specified transform and add
// it to the scene graph
Transform3D yAxis = new Transform3D();
// The Alpha turns produces repeating 0->1 values over
// time
Alpha rotationAlpha = new Alpha(-1, 4000);
  // The interpolator turns the 0->1 values into
 // rotations
  RotationInterpolator rotator =
        new RotationInterpolator(rotationAlpha, objTrans,
              yAxis, 0.0f,(float) Math.PI*2.0f);
// The bounds tell where the interpolator is active.
// in this case, as long as the viewer is within 100
// meters of 0,0,0.
  BoundingSphere bounds =
        new BoundingSphere(
                    new Point3d(0.0, 0.0, 0.0), 100.0);
  rotator.setSchedulingBounds(bounds);
```

```
  // adding the interpolator to the group makes it active
  objTrans.addChild(rotator);
```

Finally, the **BranchGroup** is compiled; this optimizes the scene graph and finalizes the contract specified by the capability bits:

```
// Have Java 3D perform optimizations on this scene
// graph.
objRoot.compile();
```

Recipe for a Java 3D Program

We have looked at how pieces of **HelloUniverse** are structured, now we'll look at how **HelloUniverse** implements the basic steps that Java 3D programs include:

1. Create a **Canvas3D** to display the scene
2. Create a **SimpleUniverse** to manage the basic scene graph; attach the **Canvas3D** to the **SimpleUniverse**
3. Create a content branch to describe the scene to be rendered and connect it to the **SimpleUniverse**

We've already looked at most of these steps in the earlier discussion. The complete source code to HelloUniverse is in Listing 2–1. Let's look at the other details. **HelloUniverse** is an applet, but it uses a utility class, **MainFrame**, to allow it to run as an application using the main() method:

```
public static void main(String[] args) {
    new MainFrame(new HelloUniverse(), 256, 256);
}
```

The **MainFrame** simply creates a stand-alone frame for the applet when it is run as an application.

The other part of **HelloUniverse** is the basic code that puts the **Canvas3D** into the applet panel:

```
public HelloUniverse() {
  // set up the layout for the applet
  setLayout(new BorderLayout());
  // Get a configuration that will make a good Canvas3D
  // for Java 3D
  GraphicsConfiguration config =
          SimpleUniverse.getPreferredConfiguration();
```

```
    // Create the Canvas3D using the configuration
    Canvas3D c = new Canvas3D(config);
    // Add it to the applet container.
    add("Center", c);

    // Create a simple scene and attach it to the virtual //universe
    BranchGroup scene = createSceneGraph();
    SimpleUniverse u = new SimpleUniverse(c);

    // This will move the ViewPlatform back a bit so the
    // objects in the scene can be viewed.
    u.getViewingPlatform().setNominalViewingTransform();

    u.addBranchGraph(scene);
}
```

We've already looked at much of this. First, a layout is set for the applet (applets are subclasses of **Panel**, so `setLayout()` sets the layout for the applet panel). The **Canvas3D** is created using a **GraphicsConfiguration** to ensure that it is rendered efficiently by the graphics hardware. Then it is added to the applet panel. The **SimpleUniverse** is created and the scene **BranchGroup** is added to the universe.

Listing 2–1 HelloUniverse.java

```
/*
 *      @(#)HelloUniverse.java 1.52 01/01/11 07:33:44
 *
 * Copyright (c) 1996-2001 Sun Microsystems, Inc. All Rights Reserved.
 *
 * Sun grants you ("Licensee") a non-exclusive, royalty free, license to use,
 * modify and redistribute this software in source and binary code form,
 * provided that i) this copyright notice and license appear on all copies of
 * the software; and ii) Licensee does not utilize the software in a manner
 * which is disparaging to Sun.
 *
 * This software is provided "AS IS," without a warranty of any kind. ALL
 * EXPRESS OR IMPLIED CONDITIONS, REPRESENTATIONS AND WARRANTIES, INCLUDING ANY
 * IMPLIED WARRANTY OF MERCHANTABILITY, FITNESS FOR A PARTICULAR PURPOSE OR
 * NON-INFRINGEMENT, ARE HEREBY EXCLUDED. SUN AND ITS LICENSORS SHALL NOT BE
 * LIABLE FOR ANY DAMAGES SUFFERED BY LICENSEE AS A RESULT OF USING, MODIFYING
 * OR DISTRIBUTING THE SOFTWARE OR ITS DERIVATIVES. IN NO EVENT WILL SUN OR ITS
 * LICENSORS BE LIABLE FOR ANY LOST REVENUE, PROFIT OR DATA, OR FOR DIRECT,
```

```
 * INDIRECT, SPECIAL, CONSEQUENTIAL, INCIDENTAL OR PUNITIVE DAMAGES, HOWEVER
 * CAUSED AND REGARDLESS OF THE THEORY OF LIABILITY, ARISING OUT OF THE USE OF
 * OR INABILITY TO USE SOFTWARE, EVEN IF SUN HAS BEEN ADVISED OF THE
 * POSSIBILITY OF SUCH DAMAGES.
 *
 * This software is not designed or intended for use in on-line control of
 * aircraft, air traffic, aircraft navigation or aircraft communications; or in
 * the design, construction, operation or maintenance of any nuclear
 * facility. Licensee represents and warrants that it will not use or
 * redistribute the Software for such purposes.
 */

import java.applet.Applet;
import java.awt.BorderLayout;
import java.awt.event.*;
import java.awt.GraphicsConfiguration;
import com.sun.j3d.utils.applet.MainFrame;
import com.sun.j3d.utils.geometry.ColorCube;
import com.sun.j3d.utils.universe.*;
import javax.media.j3d.*;
import javax.vecmath.*;

public class HelloUniverse extends Applet {

  private SimpleUniverse u = null;

  public BranchGroup createSceneGraph() {
      // Create the root of the branch graph
      BranchGroup objRoot = new BranchGroup();

      // Create the TransformGroup node and initialize it to the
      // identity. Enable the TRANSFORM_WRITE capability so that
      // our behavior code can modify it at run time. Add it to
      // the root of the subgraph.
      TransformGroup objTrans = new TransformGroup();
      objTrans.setCapability(TransformGroup.ALLOW_TRANSFORM_WRITE);
      objRoot.addChild(objTrans);

      // Create a simple Shape3D node; add it to the scene graph.
      objTrans.addChild(new ColorCube(0.4));

      // Create a new Behavior object that will perform the
      // desired operation on the specified transform and add
      // it into the scene graph.
      Transform3D yAxis = new Transform3D();
      Alpha rotationAlpha = new Alpha(-1, 4000);

      RotationInterpolator rotator =
```

```
        new RotationInterpolator(rotationAlpha, objTrans, yAxis,
               0.0f, (float) Math.PI*2.0f);
      BoundingSphere bounds =
        new BoundingSphere(new Point3d(0.0,0.0,0.0), 100.0);
      rotator.setSchedulingBounds(bounds);
      objRoot.addChild(rotator);

      // Have Java 3D perform optimizations on this scene graph.
      objRoot.compile();

      return objRoot;
  }

  public HelloUniverse() {
  }

  public void init() {
    setLayout(new BorderLayout());
      GraphicsConfiguration config =
      SimpleUniverse.getPreferredConfiguration();

    Canvas3D c = new Canvas3D(config);
    add("Center", c);

    // Create a simple scene and attach it to the virtual universe
    BranchGroup scene = createSceneGraph();
    u = new SimpleUniverse(c);

      // This will move the ViewPlatform back a bit so the
      // objects in the scene can be viewed.
      u.getViewingPlatform().setNominalViewingTransform();

    u.addBranchGraph(scene);
  }

  public void destroy() {
   u.removeAllLocales();
  }

  //
  // The following allows HelloUniverse to be run as an application
  // as well as an applet
  //
  public static void main(String[] args) {
      new MainFrame(new HelloUniverse(), 256, 256);
  }
}
```

Summary

Java 3D uses a scene graph-programming model in which your program makes a description of the virtual world and Java 3D renders the world from the viewpoint of a virtual viewer. The scene graph is a treelike data structure made from **`Nodes`**. **`Nodes`** can share pieces of nodes called **`NodeComponents`**. The basic node types are shape nodes, which describe objects in the virtual world; environment nodes, which describe properties of the virtual environment; group nodes, which organize and structure the scene graph; and the **`ViewPlatform`**, which holds the virtual viewer. The scene graph must be made "live" or attached to a **`VirtualUniverse`** to be visible on the screen. A live scene graph can only be modified within the contract specified by the capability bits, which tell Java 3D which methods you intend to call while the scene graph is live. **`Group`** nodes collect sets of nodes together. Subclasses of **`Group`** add other capabilities, such as changing the transformation for the children of the **`Group`**, selectively displaying the children of the **`Group`**, or allowing the group to be added and removed from a live scene graph.

CHAPTER

3 Creating and Loading Geometry

TOPICS IN THIS CHAPTER

- ▼ FIRING UP THE JAVA 3D EXPLORER
- ▼ WORKING WITH JAVA 3D'S GEOMETRY CLASSES AND METHODS
- ▼ SPECIFYING SHAPE GEOMETRY USING COORDINATES, NORMALS, AND COLORS
- ▼ CREATING GEOMETRY STRIPS AND INDEXED GEOMETRY
- ▼ TAPING INTO GEOMETRY UTILITIES
- ▼ CREATING 2D AND 3D TEXT
- ▼ EXPLORING HIGHER-LEVEL PRIMITIVES
- ▼ USING LOADERS TO IMPORT DATA FROM A FILE

Shapes are the objects in your virtual world. Shapes consist of two pieces, the *geometry,* which specifies the shape of the object, and the *appearance,* which specifies how the object gets rendered. In this chapter, we'll focus on the geometric aspects of shapes. As you'll soon see, geometry can be added to a virtual world in several different ways. It can be explicitly created, building up the object from individual vertices, created from higher-level classes such as spheres or 3D text, or loaded from files that hold previously created geometry. We'll begin our exploration by firing up the Java 3D Explorer program created especially for this book.

Most of the examples and illustrations in this chapter come from the Java 3D Explorer, which is freely available to Java 3D API Jump-Start readers online at web3dbooks.com/java3d/jumpstart/. You can more closely examine the topics discussed in this chapter by running the Java 3D Explorer and experimenting with the application as we walk through different kinds of Java 3D geometry in the sections that follow.

Shape3D Nodes

The basic node for shape data is **Shape3D**. All of the shape nodes discussed in this chapter will use **Shape3D** nodes (or one of its variants) to hold the shapes. The exact usage depends on the way the shape is created. If you make the geometry yourself, you'll work with the **Shape3D** nodes directly. If you create the geometry using utility classes or a file loader, the **Shape3D** nodes will be imbedded in the scene graph that holds your shapes.

A **Shape3D** is simply a container for **Geometry** and **Appearance** node components. The basic usage of **Shape3D** holds a **Geometry** and an **Appearance**, as follows:

```
Shape3D();
Shape3D(Geometry geo);
Shape3D(Geometry geo, Appearance app);
void setGeometry(Geometry geo);
void setAppearance(Appearance app);
Geometry getGeometry();
Appearance getAppearance();
```

The constructors take the initial geometry and appearance, and the mutator methods let you update the geometry and appearance. The `set()` methods can be called on a live scene graph if the corresponding capability bits are set (see Chapter 2, "Scene Graph Basics"). For example, set the `ALLOW_GEOMETRY_WRITE` bit to enable changing the geometry when the scene graph is live.

More than one **Geometry** can be associated with a **Shape3D**. This allows a single **Shape3D** to manage lots of pieces of geometry, which can be an efficient way to construct your scene graph. The geometry components are managed with the following methods:

```
void addGeometry(Geometry geo);
void insertGeometry(Geomtery geo, int index);
void removeGeometry(int index);
void setGeometry(Geometry geo, int index);
java.util.Enumeration getAllGeometries();
Geometry getGeometry(int index);
int numGeometries();
```

The geometry objects form a list. The single geometry methods affect the geometry at index 0 of the list.

The subclasses of **Shape3D** add additional functionality. An **OrientedShape3D** automatically faces towards the viewer. We'll look at an example of this kind of shape when we look at text labels later. A **Morph** allows several **GeometryArrays** to be combined to allow a smooth transition from one shape to another. **Morph** nodes are beyond the scope of this book.

In the following sections you'll learn about the different kinds of geometry that you can use with **Shape3D** nodes.

Geometry

There are a few basic kinds of **Geometry**. Most **Geometry** subclasses deal with points, lines, and polygons. These primitives are defined using **GeometryArray** node components. Other kinds of **Geometry** are used for special purposes. **Text3D** is a special geometry for drawing text as polygons that form "block" letters. Other advanced kinds of geometry are **Raster,** a special geometry for drawing images, and **CompressedGeometry,** a special geometry for efficiently transmitting a block of **GeometryArray** primitives over a network. In the next section we'll look at the many kinds of **GeometryArrays**, followed by **Text3D**.

GeometryArrays

The basic kinds of geometry (points, lines, and polygons) are created using **GeometryArray** node components. For these primitives, your program specifies the data for each location of the object, called a *vertex*. Because you must specify each vertex explicitly, this method is not usually used for very complex geometry; instead, complex geometry is usually created using utility classes or loaded from a file produced by another program that creates the data. But there are lots of cases where you may work with low-level geometry classes. For example, you may want to create a simple figure or graph, add support for a new file format, or modify existing geometry. Even if you only use the higher-level primitives, it is helpful to understand the basics of vertex-based geometry to understand the options to the higher-level primitives.

The basic types of geometry are points, lines, and polygons. Polygons can be either triangles or quadrilaterals (convex four-sided polygons). More complex polygons are handled using utility classes, which we'll discuss later along with the geometry utilities.

Each kind of geometry is constructed from a list of vertices, hence, the name for the base class **GeometryArray**. The subclasses of **GeometryArray** interpret the data in different ways to form different kinds of geometry. Figure 3–1 shows a class diagram for the subclasses of **GeometryArray**.

In a **PointArray,** each vertex is drawn as a point. In a **LineArray,** each pair of vertices forms a line segment. In a **TriangleArray,** each set of three vertices

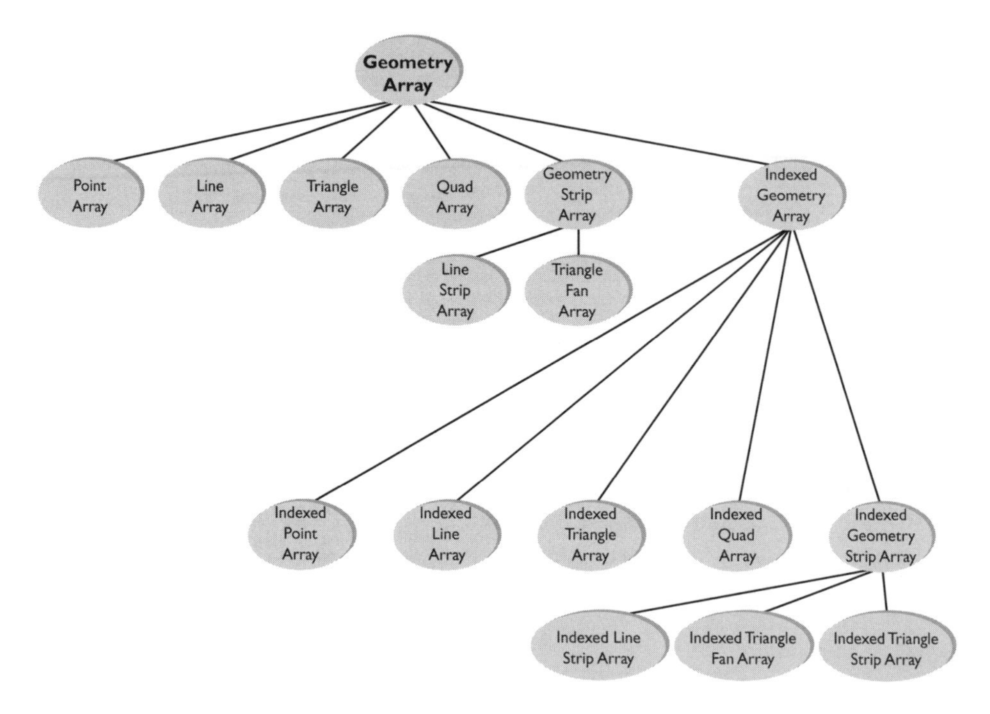

FIGURE 3–1 Class diagram for GeometryArray subclasses.

forms a triangle, and in a **QuadArray,** each set of four vertices forms a quad. Lines and triangles can also be combined into connected primitives. In a **LineStripArray,** groups of vertices form connected line segments, where the end of one line segment is the beginning of the next. In a **TriangleStripArray,** the second and third vertices of one triangle are used as the first and second vertices of the next triangle. In a **TriangleFanArray,** the first point of the first triangle is reused along with the third point of the previous triangle. Figure 3–2 shows examples of each.

Another way to construct geometry using a list of vertices is to share the list between several subprimitives and use an index into the array to specify each vertex. For example, in an **IndexPointArray**, each point is specified as an index into the list of points. Each of the main geometry classes has a corresponding indexed form: **IndexLineArray**, **IndexTriangleArray**, **IndexQuadArray**, **IndexLineStripArray**, **IndexTriangleStripArray**, and **IndexTriangleFanArray**.

In the following sections we'll look at how these primitives are defined. First, we'll look at the kinds of data that are associated with vertices and at the classes that are used to represent the data. Then we'll look at the classes that represent

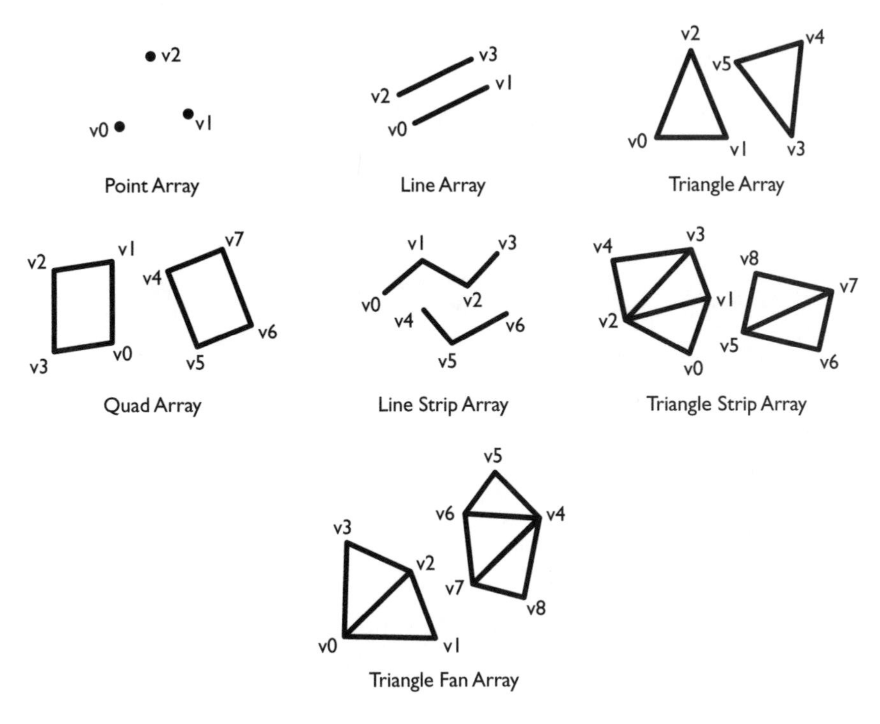

FIGURE 3–2 Basic geometry types.

the different kinds of geometry. Finally, we'll look at utility classes that make it easier to create geometry.

Vertex Data

Points, lines, and polygons are built from vertices. Each vertex has data associated with it. At a minimum, each vertex has a coordinate, which specifies the location of the vertex in 3D space. The other kinds of vertex data are optional. They are normals, colors, and texture coordinates.

Normals indicate the orientation of the geometry at the vertex. Normals are usually used for polygon primitives to indicate the orientation of the surface, although normals can be associated with points and lines as well. Normals are used for *lighting*, which is the process of coloring the geometry based on its orientation relative to lights in the scene. If the surface faces towards the light, it is lit more brightly, if it faces away from the light, it is lit less brightly or not at all.

Color can be specified with the vertices of geometry. Normally, color is specified as part of the appearance, but the color can also be specified for each vertex of the geometry. This is most often done when the color represents a property being visualized. For example, a scientific analysis might use the vertex color to indicate the temperature at the vertex, with red vertices indicating hot areas of the surface and blue vertices indicating cool areas of the surface.

Texture coordinates are used when an image or *texture* is attached to a surface. For example, an image of woodgrain might be used to make a surface appear to be made of wood. The texture coordinates specify the place on the texture that should correspond to the vertex.

Lighting, coloring, and texturing are discussed in Chapter 4, "Appearances."

Basic Data Classes: javax.vecmath

Java 3D uses the `javax.vecmath` package classes to help specify vertex data. This package contains classes for basic vector math. These classes are the basic data types for Java 3D geometry as well as many of the attributes and other interactions that Java 3D supports.

Each kind of data has several variations to support different kinds of data and precision, leading to a large number of classes. The complexity of the variations is managed using naming conventions and base classes. The class name indicates the data type, dimension, and precision. For example, a **`Point3f`** is an instance of the "Point" data type, with a dimension of three and a precision of "f," indicating float data.

The data type indicates the form kind of data held by the class. The types used for vertex data are shown in Table 3–1.

TABLE 3–1 Data classes

Data Type	Class Prefix
Coordinate	Point
Normal	Vector
Color	Color
Texture Coordinate	TexCoord

The dimension is the number of components. For example, a **`Point3f`** coordinate has X, Y, and Z components and a dimension of three. The number of components depends on the usage. Coordinates usually have three components. Normals always have three components. Colors can have three or four components. Texture coordinates can have two or three components. We'll discuss how many components to use in Chapter 4, "Appearances."

The precision letter indicates the data type used for each component, as shown in Table 3–2.

TABLE 3–2 Precision type abbreviation

Data Precision	Type Letter
Byte	b
Integer	i
Float	f
Double	d

So a **Vector3f** has three float components. A **Color4b** has four byte components and a **TexCoord2f** has two float components. **Point** classes can use either float or double data; **Color** classes can use byte or float data, and **Vector** and **TexCoord** classes use only float types (the `javax.vecmath` package defines **Vector** classes with double values, but the Java 3D **Geometry** classes take only the float variations).

Classes that have the same dimension and precision share a common base class called a **Tuple**. For example, **Point3f** and **Color3f** both extend the **Tuple3f** base class. The base class specifies the basic methods for working with the data. The data can also be set in the constructor:

```
Point3f point = new Point3f(1.0f, 1.0f, 1.0f);
```

Or via a `set()` method:

```
Point3f point = new Point3f();
point.set(1.0f, 1.0f, 1.0f);
```

The set() method can also be used to copy a **Tuple**:

```
Point3f point1 = new Point3f(1.0f, 1.0f, 1.0f);
Point3f point2 = new Point3f();
point2.set(point1);
```

Also, the components of the data are exposed as fields so that the data can be set explicitly:

```
Point3f point = new Point3f();
point.x = 1.0;
point.y = 1.0;
point.z = 1.0;
```

The subclasses of **Tuple** add specific functionality. For example, **Point3f** supports the `distance()` method, which calculates the distance between two **Point3f** objects. **Vector3f** has the `length()` method, which returns the length of the vector, and the `normalize()` method, which makes the vector have a length of 1.0, making it a *unit vector*.

See Sun's Java 3D javadocs for details on specific classes and methods that may be useful in this context.

Geometry Classes and Methods

The base class for point, line, and polygon primitives is **GeometryArray**. **PointArray**, **LineArray**, **TriangleArray**, and **QuadArray** are subclasses of **GeometryArray**, and differ only in the way the list of vertices is interpreted. The constructor for a **GeometryArray** sets the number of vertices and the data associated with each vertex. The specific constructors are:

```
PointArray(int vertexCount, int vertexFormat)
LineArray(int vertexCount, int vertexFormat);
TriangleArray(int vertexCount, int vertexFormat);
```

Each takes the number of vertices for the primitive and the format for the vertices. The format indicates the data associated with each vertex. The format is specified using an integer that is a combination of static integer fields that are OR'd together. The data type fields are:

```
COORDINATES
NORMALS
COLOR_3
COLOR_4
TEXTURE_COORDINATE_2
TEXTURE_COORDINATE_3
```

The color and texture coordinate fields have variations for the different numbers of components the color and texture coordinate can have. For example, creating a **TriangleArray** with the vertex format:

```
GeometryArray.COORDINATES|
GeometryArray.NORMAL|
GeometryArray.TEXTURE_COORDINATE_2
```

tells Java 3D that you will be specifying coordinates, normals, and two component texture coordinates for the **TriangleArray**.

Geometry Array Methods

GeometryArray defines methods to set each kind of vertex data. Each method has several variations that allow the data to be set using different forms of data. Other variations allow different sections of the array of vertices to be set—from individual vertices to a range of vertices within the array to the entire array. Rather than list all the variations, we'll look at how each variation is represented (consult the javadocs for **GeometryArray** for a complete listing of the methods).

The data for vertex coordinates can be set using **Point3f** objects, or arrays of floats. The **Point3f** methods can take either a single **Point3f** or an array as follows:

```
void setCoordinate(int index, Point3f coord);
void setCoordinates(int index, Point3f[] coords);
void setCoordinates(int index, Point3f[] coords, int start,
                    int length);
```

The first method sets the coordinate data for the vertex at `index`. The second sets the data for the vertices from `index` through `(index + coords.length - 1)`. The third sets the data for vertices from `index` through `(index + length - 1)` copying a range of coordinates out of `coords`, starting at `start` and ending at `(start + length - 1)`. These methods can take either **Point3f** or **Point3d** objects to specify the coordinates.

The coordinate data can also be set using arrays of floats. Each set of three floats in the array specifies the coordinates for one vertex:

```
void setCoordinate(int index, float[] coords);
void setCoordinates(int index, float[] coords);
void setCoordinates(int index, float[] coords, int start,
                                                int length);
```

The first method sets the data for the vertex at `index` using `coords[0]`, `coords[1]`, and `coords[2]` for X, Y, and Z, respectively. The second copies groups of three floats from `coords` starting at `index`. The number of vertices set is `coords.length / 3`. The third copies groups of floats from `coords` starting with `coords[start*3]`. The number of vertices set is `length`, with `length * 3` floats being copied from `coords`. The data for setting coordinates using this kind of method can be either an array of floats or an array of doubles.

The methods for setting normals, colors, and texture coordinates are all variations on this theme. Normals are set using three floats in either **Vector** objects or arrays. Colors are set using either three or four values that can be bytes or floats in either **Color** objects or arrays. Texture coordinates are set using either two or three float values in either **TexCoord** objects or arrays. The methods that set texture coordinate methods have an additional parameter, the texture coordinate set. For example, the **TexCoord2f** methods are:

```
void setTextureCoordinate(int texCoordSet, int index,
                          TexCoord2f coord);
void setTextureCoordinates(int texCoordSet, int index,
                           TexCoord2f[] coords);
void setTextureCoordinates(int texCoordSet, int index,
                           TexCoord2f[] coords, int start,
                           int length);
```

This parameter is usually 0, unless your program is using the advanced "multitexture" feature. This will be discussed further in Chapter 4, "Appearances."

Specifying color values using bytes has a problem. Computer graphics usually work with byte values for colors as unsigned values. That is, the range for each component is [0, 255] with 0 being no intensity and 255 being maximum intensity. The problem is that Java does not have an unsigned byte data type, so the values for bytes are [-128, 127]. Java 3D recognizes this and, for color, treats bytes as if the range were [0, 255]; that is, as if the values were unsigned. This means that byte color values in the range [0, 127] are represented by the signed values [0, 127]. Color byte values in the [128, 255] range are represented by the signed values [-128, -1].

Internally, Java 3D converts data to arrays of floats. You should use `vecmath` objects or data types other than float if that makes it easier to write your program, but under the covers Java 3D will copy your data into floats.

Let's look at how this works in a couple of examples. Here is a **PointArray** with three points:

```
PointArray pa = new PointArray(3, PointArray.COORDINATES);
Point3f[] pts = new Point3f[3];
pts[0] = new Point3f(0.0f, 0.0f, 0.0f);
pts[1] = new Point3f(1.0f, 0.0f, 0.0f);
pts[2] = new Point3f(0.0f, 1.0f, 0.0f);
pa.setCoordinates(0, pts);
```

Note that the vertex format is specified using `PointArray.COORDINATES`. The `COORDINATES` field really is defined in **GeometryArray**, but **PointArray** is a subclass of **GeometryArray** so it is legal to use **PointArray** and make the code a bit clearer. Adding the **PointArray** to a **Shape3D** with `setGeometry()` and putting this into a scene graph results in the picture shown in Figure 3–3.

FIGURE 3–3 A PointArray with three points.

Next, let's draw a pair of lines with vertex colors.

```
LineArray la = new LineArray(4, LineArray.COORDINATES|
                                 LineArray.COLOR_3);
Point3f[] pts = new Point3f[4];
pts[0] = new Point3f(0.0f, 0.0f, 0.0f);
pts[1] = new Point3f(1.0f, 0.0f, 0.0f);
pts[2] = new Point3f(0.0f, 1.0f, 0.0f);
pts[3] = new Point3f(1.0f, 1.0f, 0.0f);
Color3f clrs = new Color3f[4];
clrs[0] = new Color3f(0.0f , 0.0f, 0.0f); // black
clrs[1] = new Color3f(1.0f , 1.0f, 1.0f); // white
clrs[2] = new Color3f(1.0f , 0.0f, 0.0f); // red
clrs[3] = new Color3f(0.0f , 1.0f, 0.0f); // green
la.setCoordinates(0, pts);
la.setColors(0, clrs);
```

Note that the number of vertices in the constructor is the total number of vertices in the array (not the number of lines). The line array produces the pair of lines shown in Figure 3–4.

FIGURE 3–4 Lines created using a LineArray with vertex colors.

Finally, let's draw a triangle with colors and normals:

```
  TriangleArray ta = new TriangleArray(3,
                 TriangleArray.COORDINATES|
                 TriangleArray.COLOR_3|
                 TriangleArray.NORMALS);
Point3f[] pts = new Point3f[3];
pts[0] = new Point3f(0.0f, 0.0f, 0.0f);
pts[1] = new Point3f(1.0f, 0.0f, 0.0f);
pts[2] = new Point3f(0.0f, 1.0f, 0.0f);
Color3f clrs = new Color3f[3];
clrs[0] = new Color3f(1.0f , 0.0f, 0.0f); // red
clrs[1] = new Color3f(0.0f , 1.0f, 0.0f); // green
clrs[2] = new Color3f(0.0f , 0.0f, 1.0f); // blue
Vector3f[] norms = new Vector3f[3];
Vector3f triNormal = new Vector3f(0.0f, 0.0f, 1.0f);
norms[0] = triNormal;
norms[1] = triNormal;
norms[1] = triNormal;
ta.setCoordinates(0, pts);
ta.setColors(0, clrs);
ta.setNormals(0, norms);
```

Note that the triangle has the same normal at each vertex. While each kind of data specified by the vertex format must be specified for each vertex (in this case coordinate, color, normal), it is legal to use the same value for different vertices.

Polygon Vertex Details

There are two more important details you should be aware of when creating polygons: the order of the vertices is important for defining the orientation of the polygon; and vertices of a quad must form a convex, planar polygon.

Polygons are defined with front and back sides. The orientation is used to determine which way the polygon is facing for lighting operations. The orientation can also be used to remove, or *cull*, polygons from the scene that are facing away from the viewer (see the sections on lighting and culling in Chapter 4, "Appearances").

The front side of a polygon is defined to be the orientation where the vertices of the polygon form a counter-clockwise loop. Figure 3–5 shows a front-facing and back-facing triangle:

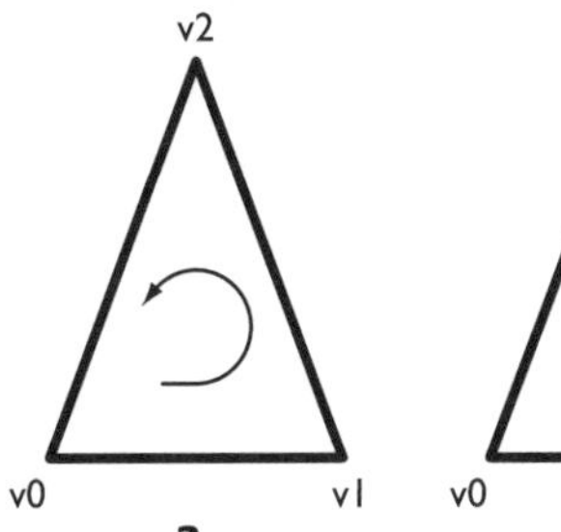

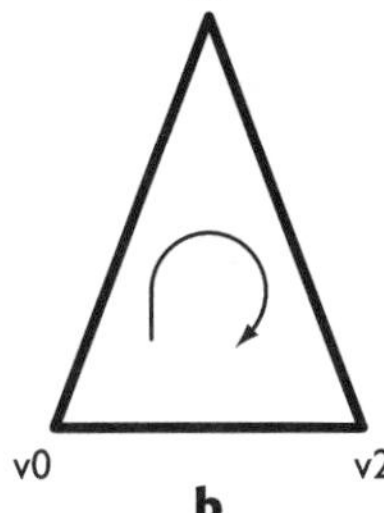

FIGURE 3–5 (a) Front- and (b) back-facing triangles.

The triangle on the left is front facing; its vertices form a counter-clockwise loop. The triangle on the right is back facing; its vertices form a clockwise loop.

When defining polygonal geometry, make sure that your polygons are oriented in the direction you intend. If the polygon has normals, it should be oriented so that the normals come out of the front side of the polygon. If polygons are joined together in a surface, the orientations of adjacent polygons should be the same.

The other detail is that the points of a quadrilateral must form a convex, planar polygon. The quad must be convex or some graphics hardware may render the quad incorrectly. The quad must be planar because a convex quad can turn non-convex if the quad is not planar. For example, consider this case of the geometry shown in Figure 3–6.

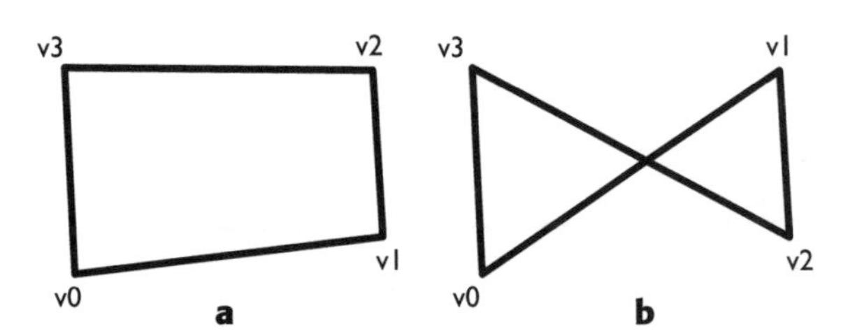

FIGURE 3-6 Rectangle (a) and bow tie (b) geometry.

These are two views of the same quad. The vertices of the quad are defined so that the top-right corner of the left quad is closer to you than the other vertices. The view on the left shows the quad rotated so that the top edge comes towards you. Notice how the quad now resembles a bow tie. You can avoid this problem by using triangles instead of quads for non-planar data.

BY_REFERENCE and INTERLEAVED Arrays

By default, Java 3D copies your data into the GeometryArray object. If your program needs to access the data it can use the get() methods. However, it may be better for your application to *share* the data array with Java 3D. The field `BY_REFERENCE` specifies that Java 3D should share the array with your program. Using this mechanism, the methods with the Ref suffix are used, for example, instead of calling `setCoordinates()` you call `setCoordinatesRef()`. Using the `BY_REFERENCE` scan saves memory, but it can also have slightly slower performance because Java 3D may not be able to use the fastest rendering methods for your data.

Internally, Java 3D does more than just convert your data into floats. It also combines the different data for the vertices into a single array of floats with the data for each vertex grouped together. This format is called an interleaved array. If you can organize your data into this format you can optimize the way Java 3D works with your data. Using the `BY_REFERENCE` and `INTERLEAVED` flags, you can share the data for your vertices in the fastest format for rendering possible with `BY_REFERENCE` data.

The interleaved format stores the data for each vertex in a specific order: texture coordinates, color, normal, coordinate, where each component is included and sized-based on the vertex format. For example, a vertex list with `COORDINATES|NORMALS`, is stored with six floats per vertex. The first three floats are the normal; the next three floats are the coordinate.

You can specify your vertex data using interleaved arrays with the method:

```
void setInterleavedVertices(float[] vertexData);
```

If you share your data with Java 3D using `BY_REFERENCE` and later need to change the data, you have to call the `updateData()` method to inform Java 3D of changes to the data. See the javadoc for complete details.

Geometry Strips

Geometry strip primitives share vertices between the pieces of the shape. Strip primitives are subclasses of the abstract class **GeometryStripArray**, which adds a parameter, the strip vertex count array, to the constructor for GeometryArray. The types of **GeometryStripArray** are **LineStripArray, TriangleStripArray**, and **TriangleFanArray:**

```
LineStripArray(int vertexFormat, int vertexCount,
                              int[] stripVertexCounts);
TriangleStripArray(int vertexFormat, int vertexCount,
                              int[] stripVertexCounts);
TriangleFanArray(int vertexFormat, int vertexCount,
                              int[] stripVertexCounts);
```

The `stripVertexCounts` array specifies the number of strips and the length of each strip. The number of strips is the length of the `stripVertexCounts` array and the numbers of vertices in each strip are the elements of the array. The sum of the strip lengths is equal to the number of vertices.

For example, here is a line strip with five vertices making two lines, one with three vertices and one with two vertices:

```
int[] stripLength = new int[2];
stripLength[0] = 3;
stripLength[1] = 2;
LineStripArray lsa = new LineStripArray(5, LineArray.COORDINATES,
stripLength);
Point3f[] pts = new Point3f[5];
pts[0] = new Point3f(0.0f, 0.0f, 0.0f);
pts[1] = new Point3f(1.0f, 0.0f, 0.0f);
pts[2] = new Point3f(0.0f, 1.0f, 0.0f);
pts[3] = new Point3f(1.0f, 1.0f, 0.0f);
pts[4] = new Point3f(0.0, 0.0f, 0.0f);
lsa.setCoordinates(0, pts);
```

Indexed Geometry

Indexed geometry is another way to define Java 3D geometry. With indexed geometry the vertices in the geometry array are shared between the pieces of the primitive, as illustrated by Figure 3–7. For example, a cube consists of six faces with four points each, for a total of 24 points.

The cube has eight unique coordinates, but representing the cube as a **QuadArray** would require 24 vertices. Each face of the cube shares its vertices with the adjacent faces. Using indexed geometry a cube can be defined using an array of eight vertices and 24 indices into the array:

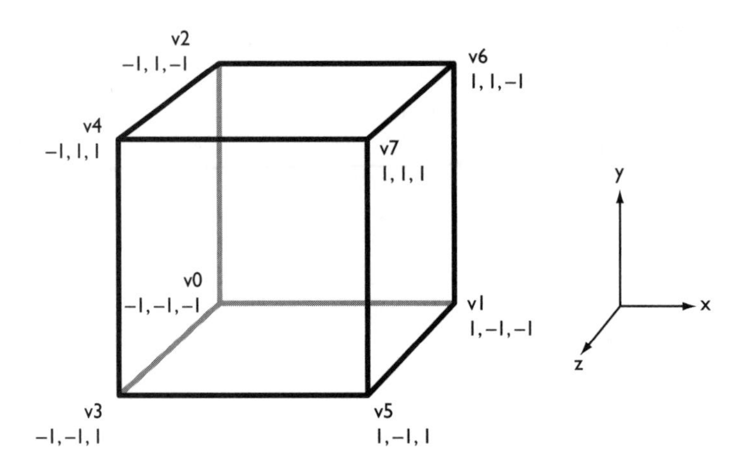

FIGURE 3–7 A cube.

```
Point3f[] pts = new Point3f[8];
pts[0] = new Point3f(-1.0f, -1.0f, -1.0f);
pts[1] = new Point3f(1.0f, -1.0f, -1.0f);
pts[2] = new Point3f(-1.0f, 1.0f, -1.0f);
pts[3] = new Point3f(-1.0f, -1.0f, 1.0f);
pts[4] = new Point3f(-1.0f, 1.0f, 1.0f);
pts[5] = new Point3f(1.0f, -1.0f, 1.0f);
pts[6] = new Point3f(1.0f, 1.0f, -1.0f);
pts[7] = new Point3f(1.0f, 1.0f, 1.0f);
int[] indices = {
      0, 3, 4, 2, // left face   x = -1
      0, 1, 5, 3, // bottom face y = -1
      0, 2, 6, 1, // back face   z = -1
      7, 5, 1, 6, // right face  x =  1
      7, 6, 2, 4, // top face    y =  1
      7, 4, 3, 5  // front face  z =  1
      }
IndexedQuadArray iqa = new IndexedQuadArray(8,
            GeometryInfo.COORDINATES);
iqa.setCoordinates(0, pts);
iqa.setCoordinateIndices(0, indices);
```

So the front face is made from the points:

```
pts[7] = [1, 1, 1]
pts[4] = [-1, 1, 1]
pts[3] = [-1, -1, 1]
pts[5] = [1, -1, 1]
```

It defines the square with z = 1, as seen in Figure 3–8.

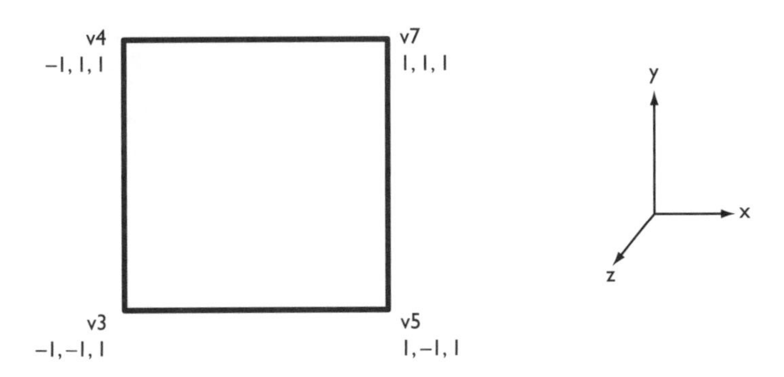

FIGURE 3–8 The z=-1 face of the cube.

The coordinates, colors, normals, and texture coordinates each have separate index lists, so each kind of data can share the vertex data in different ways. The methods to set the indices are defined in the base class **`IndexedGeometryArray`** using the usual variety of different options. For example, the coordinate indices can be set using the methods:

```
void setCoordinateIndex(int index, int coordinateIndex);
void setCoordinateIndices(int index, int coordinateIndices[]);
```

There are similar methods to set the color, normal, and texture coordinate indices. The number of indices per face must be the same for each data type and, just as in the non-indexed case, the vertex list for each kind of data must have the same number of elements.

Using indexed geometry can make it simpler to define complex geometry. Internally, Java 3D generally converts indexed geometry into a non-indexed format for rendering since most graphics hardware does not support indexed rendering.

Some hardware does support indexed rendering if the index lists for each kind of data have the same value. Java 3D may support this kind of indexed rendering in the future, so if you want your data to be rendered using indexed rendering, use the same indices for each kind of data in the vertex format.

Geometry Utilities

So far we have been looking at some simple examples of geometry. You may, however, want to render more complex geometry that doesn't match the **`GeometryArray`** classes directly. For example, you might have polygons that have more than four vertices, or which have holes in them. Or you may have a surface that you want to render with lighting, but the data does not include vertex normals. Or you may have a mesh of polygons that you want to render more quickly. Java 3D provides geometry utilities that solve these problems.

To use the geometry utilities, define your geometry using the **GeometryInfo** class instead of a **GeometryArray** class. Then pass your geometry to a tool class for processing. The tool classes are the **Triangulator**, which breaks up complex polygons into triangles, the **NormalGenerator**, which calculates vertex normals for a set of polygons, and the **Stripifier**, which turns a mesh of triangles into triangle strips to improve performance. After processing, you can extract a **GeometryArray** from the **GeometryInfo** and use that in your scene graph.

GeometryInfo

The constructor to the **GeometryInfo** specifies the kind of polygons you will be defining:

```
GeometryInfo(int primType)
```

Where the primitive type is one of:

```
POLYGON_ARRAY
QUAD_ARRAY
TRIANGLE_ARRAY
TRIANGLE_FAN_ARRAY
TRIANGLE_STRIP_ARRAY
```

The quad and triangle arrays are defined the same way as the corresponding **GeometryArray** classes, except that instead of specifying the number of vertices, the vertex format, and other data in the constructor, this data is set implicitly based on the methods you call to define the geometry.

The number of vertices is set by the number of vertices you call—`setCoordinates()`, `setColors()`, and so forth—except there is less flexibility. The methods only let you set the entire array, not a range of the array. For example, instead of the **GeometryArray** method that lets you set a range of coordinates starting at an index:

```
void setCoordinates(int index, Point3f[] coords);
```

the **GeometryInfo** method always replaces the entire array:

```
void setCoordinates(Point3f[] coords);
```

The vertex format comes from the set of vertex data arrays you define. If you set coordinates and normals, the format is COORDINATES | NORMALS. Since colors and texture coordinates can have different numbers of components, the methods indicate the number of components. For example, the color methods include:

```
void setColors(Color3f[] colors);
void setColors3(float[] colors);
void setColors(Color4f[] color);
void setColor4(float[] color);
```

The first two methods specify three component colors; the second two methods specify four component colors.

To use indexed representation in the **GeometryInfo**, simply set the indices using the methods:

```
void setColorIndices(int[] indices);
void setCoordinateIndices(int[] indices);
void setNormalIndices(int[] indices);
void setTextureCoordinateIndices(int[] indices);
```

Calling these methods implicitly specifies that the data be indexed.

As with the **GeometryArray** classes, the length of each vertex data array must be the same and the length of each index array must the same.

Strip lengths are set using the method:

```
void setStripCounts(int [] stripCounts);
```

This is the same as the strip counts array in the **GeometryStripArray** constructor.

The POLYGON_ARRAY value is used to specify complex polygons, which have more than four vertices or contain holes. Each polygon is made from one or more *contours*, each of which defines a boundary of the polygon. The first contour specifies the outer border of the polygon; each subsequent contour specifies a hole in the interior of the polygon. The outer contour has counter-clockwise ordering (see the previous Polygon Details section), while the holes have clockwise ordering. Figure 3–9 shows a triangle with a hole in it.

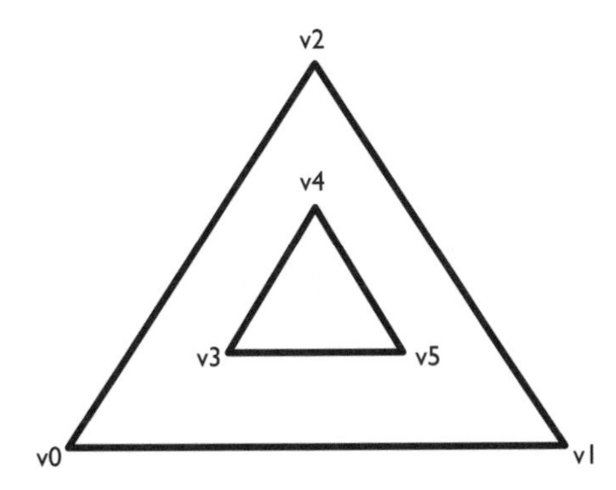

FIGURE 3–9 A triangle with a hole.

For a complex polygon the strip counts array specifies the number of vertices in each contour (that is, each strip is a contour). The **GeometryInfo** can hold several polygons; the number of contours in each polygon is specified by the method:

```
void setContourCounts(int[] contourCounts);
```

The length of the `contourCounts` array specifies the number of polygons. The integers in the `contourCounts` array specify the number of contours in each polygon. The total of the integers in the `contourCounts` array is the same as the number of contours, which is the length of the `stripCounts` array passed to `setStripCounts()`. For example, for the triangle with a hole, the strip counts array is [3, 3], indicating two contours with three points each, and the contour counts array is [2], indicating one polygon with two contours.

After defining the geometry, pass the **GeometryInfo** to the tool classes for processing and then extract the resulting data using:

```
GeometryArray getGeometryArray();
```

Note that the tools may completely reorganize your data as part of their processing, so it is generally not possible to correlate your input data with the output **GeometryArray**.

Triangulator

The **Triangulator** breaks complex polygons into triangles. Use a **GeometryInfo** with POLYGON_ARRAY to define the polygons and then pass the **GeometryInfo** to a **Triangulator** to generate the triangles. For example, here is the triangle with a hole that we just defined:

```
int[] stripCounts = new int[2];
stripCounts[0] = 3;
stripCounts[1] = 3;
int contourCounts = new int[1];
contourCounts[0] = 2;
Point3f[] pts = new Point3f[6];
pts[0] = new Point3f(-1.0f, -1.0f, 0.0f);
pts[1] = new Point3f(1.0f, -1.0f, 0.0f);
pts[2] = new Point3f(1.0f, 1.0f, 0.0f);
pts[3] = new Point3f(-0.6f, -0.8f, 0.0f);
pts[4] = new Point3f(0.8f, 0.6f, 0.0f);
pts[5] = new Point3f(0.8f, -0.8f, 0.0f);
GeometryInfo gi = new GeometryInfo(GeometryInfo.POLYGON_ARRAY);
gi.setCoordinates(pnt);
gi.setStripCounts(stripCounts);
gi.setContourCounts(contourCounts);

Triangulator tr = new Triangulator();
```

```
tr.triangulate(gi);
GeometryArray triWithHole = gi.getGeometryArray();
```

The **Triangulator** produces a **GeometryArray** with triangles in the shape of the polygon. Figure 3–10 shows the resulting polygon rendered as a filled polygon and using lines:

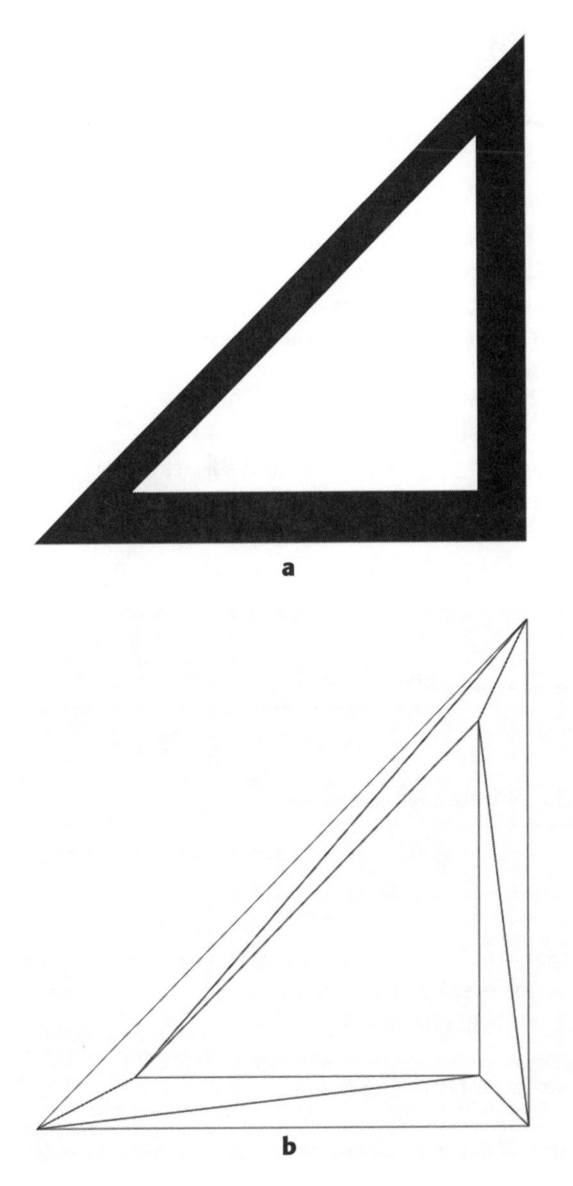

FIGURE 3–10 Triangle with hole, filled (a) and wireframe (b).

NormalGenerator

The **NormalGenerator** tool adds vertex normals to a set of polygons specified by a **GeometryInfo** containing a set of connected polygons that form a surface. The **NormalGenerator** analyzes the surface and decides where the surfaces meet smoothly and where the surfaces meet in a crease. It then calculates the normals for the surface. The smooth joints share normals between the adjacent polygons; the creased joints get separate normals as seen in Figure 3–11.

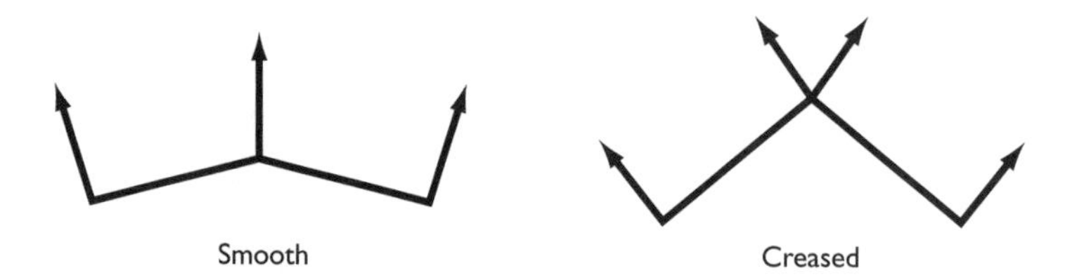

FIGURE 3–11 NormalGenerator adds vertex normals to GeometryInfo polygons. Surface normals are calculated based on a surface analysis by NormalGenerator that determines which areas share joints (resulting in smooth joints) and which create a crease (resulting in separate normals).

Here we see the surface as viewed edge-on. The faces on the left form a smooth surface, so the normal is shared between the two faces. The faces on the right form a creased surface, so that each face has a separate normal. The **NormalGenerator** decides whether the joints are creased or not based on the crease angle. If the joint angle is less than the crease angle, the joint is smooth. If the joint angle is greater than the crease angle, the joint is creased (see Figure 3–12).

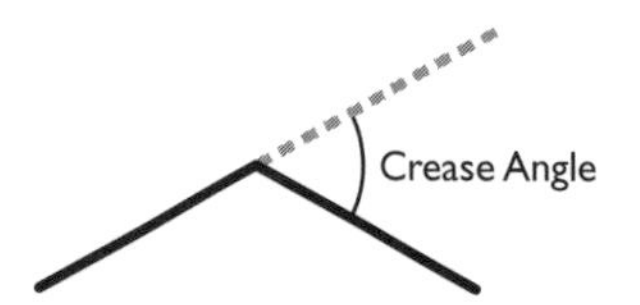

FIGURE 3–12 This joint is creased because Normal-Generator determined that the joint angle is greater than the crease angle for this surface.

The methods on the NormalGenerator are:

```
void setCreaseAngle(float radians);
void generateNormals(GeometryInfo gi);
```

The first method is used to set the crease angle. The second is used to generate the normals. The angle is set using radians. To use degrees instead, use the `java.lang.Math` class to convert degrees to radians using the method:

```
double toRadians(double degrees);
```

For example, we can add vertex normals to the cube we defined as follows:

```
GeometryInfo gi = new GeometryInfo(GeometryInfo.QUAD_ARRAY);
Point3f[] pts = new Point3f[8]
pts[0] = new Point3f(-1.0f, -1.0f, -1.0f);
pts[1] = new Point3f(1.0f, -1.0f, -1.0f);
pts[2] = new Point3f(-1.0f, 1.0f, -1.0f);
pts[3] = new Point3f(-1.0f, -1.0f, 1.0f);
pts[4] = new Point3f(-1.0f, 1.0f, 1.0f);
pts[5] = new Point3f(1.0f, -1.0f, 1.0f);
pts[6] = new Point3f(1.0f, 1.0f, -1.0f);
pts[7] = new Point3f(1.0f, 1.0f, 1.0f);
int[] indices = {
      0, 3, 4, 2, // left face   x = -1
      0, 1, 5, 3, // bottom face y = -1
      0, 2, 6, 1, // back face   z = -1
      7, 5, 1, 6, // right face  x =  1
      7, 6, 3, 4, // top face    y =  1
      7, 4, 3, 5  // front face  z =  1
      }
gi.setCoordinates(pts);
gi.setCoordinateIndices(indices);
NormalGenerator ng = new NormalGenerator();
ng.setCreaseAngle((float) Math.toRadians(45));
ng.generateNormals(gi);
GeometryArray cube = gi.getGeometryArray();
```

This code uses a crease angle of 45 degrees. Since the cube faces form 90-degree edges, this code generates creases between the faces. If we change the crease angle to 100 degrees, the normal generator forms smooth creases between the faces. Figure 3–13 shows the cube with creased and smooth edges.

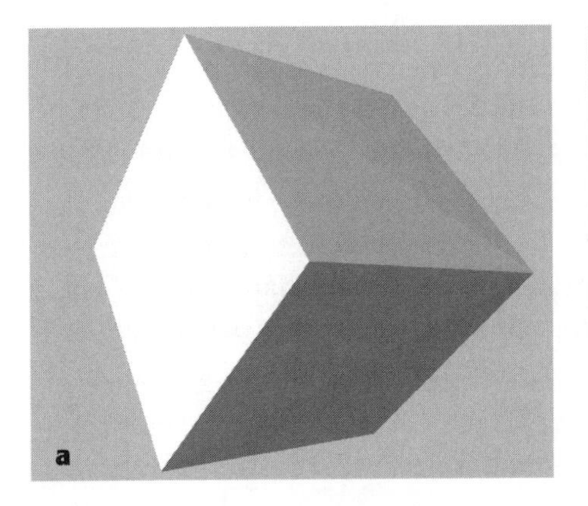

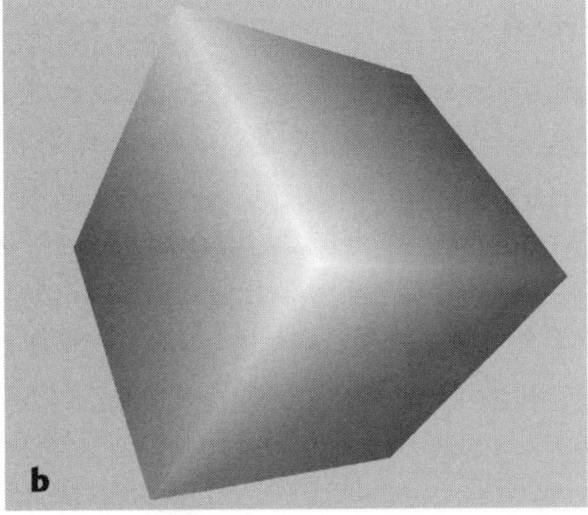

FIGURE 3–13 A cube has 90-degree angles at the edges. Calculating normals with a crease angle of (a) 45 degrees makes "creased" edges and (b) 100 degrees makes "smooth edges."

Stripifier

The **Stripifier** can be used to optimize the rendering of large surfaces by looking for places where adjacent triangles can be combined into triangle strips. Long triangle strips render faster than isolated triangles, so the **Stripifier** tries to make the strips as long as possible. The action of the **Stripifier** is just like the **Triangulator** and **NormalGenerator**. A **GeometryInfo** is passed to the **Stripifer**, which modifies the contents of the **GeometryInfo**:

```
GeometryInfo gi; // initialized above
Stripifier st = new Stripifier();
st.stripify(gi)
GeometryArray ga = gi.getGeometryArray();
```

The **Stripifier** can improve performance, but you should know a couple of details. First, if you are going to generate normals and stripify a surface, you should generate the normals first, since creases will create places where the **Stripifier** has to break the strips. Second, there are cases where the data cannot be made more optimized by the **Stripifier**, so you should compare the performance with and without the **Stripifier**. You can also get statistics on the tool's performance by calling

```
StripifierStats getStripifierStats();
```

Consult the Java 3D javadoc files to learn more about StripifierStats.

Text3D

Text3D is another kind of **Geometry**. A **Text3D** is a string represented as 3D "block" letters made from polygons that can be lit and shaded. See Figure 3–14.

Text3D is a 3D extension of the basic Java text model that uses a **String** and a **Font** to specify how the text is drawn. The **String** tells what characters are to be rendered, but not shapes of the individual characters. The shapes come from the **Font**. A **Text3D** object is created using a **String** and a **Font3D** object.

A **Font3D** object is a 3D version of a Java font. A constructor for **Font3D** specifies the **Font** that defines the shape of each character and the **FontExtrusion**, which tells how the 3D font should be generated from the 2D font:

```
Font3D(java.awt.Font font, FontExtrustion extrudePath);
Font3D(java.awt.Font font, double tolerance,
                           FontExtrustion extrudePath);
```

FIGURE 3–14 Text3D geometry is a string represented as 3D block letters. Here we see the string "Text3D" represented as Text3D geometry.

The font is an AWT font. The details of the font aren't important (see the javadoc `java.awt.Font` for details), but the size of the font will determine the size of the Text3D characters. For example, the **Font**:

```
import java.awt.Font;
Font font = new Font(null, Font.PLAIN, 2);
```

creates a **Font** in the default font, a plain style with a size that will make the **Text3D** characters 2 meters tall.

The **Font3D** creates a 3D version of this font. The outlines of the characters define the X and Y shape of the characters. The **FontExtrusion** projects the outline in the Z direction, making block letters. The default **FontExtrusion** makes characters that are 0.2 meters deep. For example, the **Text3D** shown in Figure 3–14 used the **Font3D**:

```
Font3D f3d = new Font3D(new Font(null, Font.PLAIN, 2),
      new FontExtrusion());
```

The **FontExtrusion** can be used to make different 3D versions of the **Font** (see the javadoc for **FontExtrusion**). For most uses, the default **FontExtrusion** is fine. Specifying `null` for the FontExtrusion makes characters that have no depth. This is useful if you are going to use an **OrientedShape3D** to keep the **Text3D** facing towards the user, since it eliminates the polygons that the user won't see. We'll look at an example of this next.

The `tolerance` parameter tells how finely to approximate the outline of the characters. The smaller the tolerance, the more polygons will be used for the 3D version of the characters. The default tolerance usually looks pretty good.

The **Text3D** is created using the **Font3D** and a **String**:

```
Text3D(Font3D font3d, java.langString string);
Text3D(Font3D font3d, java.langString string,
      Point3f position);
Text3D(Font3D font3d, java.langString string, Point3f position,
      int alignment, int path);
```

Options to **Text3D** set the text position, alignment, and path. The position is the location of the **Text3D**. The alignment tells how the string should be placed in reference to the position; choices are to place the string so that the first, center, or last part of the string is placed at the text position. The path controls whether the characters are drawn to the right, left, up, or down. By default, the **Text3D** will be positioned at 0, 0, 0 with the beginning of the string aligned at the text position and the characters drawn from left to right.

Here is an example of **Text3D** that makes a label that rotates around a 0, 0, 0 and always points towards the eye:

```
// null FontExtrusion == flat characters:
Font3D f3d = new Font3D(font, null);
Text3D t3d = new Text3D(f3d, "Hello");

// default appearance, white, non-lit:
Appearance app = new Appearance();
Point3f pnt = new Point3f(0.0f, 0.0f, 0.0f); // rotation point
OrientedShape3D os3d = new OrientedShape3D(app, t3d, pnt);
```

The **OrientedShape3D** can also be used to rotate the geometry around a fixed axis instead of a fixed point.

Consult the Java 3D javadoc files for more details about `OrientedShape3D`.

Higher-Level Primitives

Geometry node components are one way to create shapes. Java 3D supports several other mechanisms for defining shapes. These higher-level primitives let you define the parameters of the geometry and Java 3D fills in the details. The higher-level primitives are defined in the `com.sun.j3d.utils.geometry` package. This package includes the **ColorCube** and **Text2D** classes, and a set of shape classes that share a base class called **Primitive**. Subclasses of **Primitive** are **Box**, **Sphere**, **Cone**, and **Cylinder**.

ColorCube

ColorCube is a simple test class. It makes a cube one meter on a side with a different color on each face (see the **HelloUniverse** example in Chapter 2, "Scene Graph Basics"). **ColorCube** is useful as at test shape since it has a very simple constructor:

```
ColorCube();
```

ColorCube extends **Shape3D** so that you can change its appearance using the **Shape3D** method:

```
void setAppearance(Appearance app);
```

Text2D

Text2D is another way to draw text. A **Text2D** is a rectangle with a texture map (image) of the string attached to it. The constructor for a **Text2D** is similar to the constructor for **Text3D:**

```
Text2D(java.lang.String text, Color3f color,
    java.lang.String fontName, int fontSize, int fontStyle);
```

The text parameter specifies the string to go on the polygon. The color specifies the color of the string. The remaining parameters specify the font. See the javadoc for `java.awt.Font` for more details on the `fontName` and `fontStyle`. As with **Font3D**, using `null` and `Font.PLAIN` produces a reasonable default. The `fontSize` specifies the size of the font in pixels. The `fontSize` affects two aspects of the **Text2D**. First, a larger `fontSize` will produce a text with a smoother appearance; second, the size of text in the **Text2D** will be approximately equal to the `fontSize / 256` meters.

Text2D is handy for doing simple text labels. It can be faster than **Text3D** since it uses one texture-mapped quad instead of many non-textured polygons (it can also be slower if your hardware doesn't support texture mapping, although most hardware does these days). Some graphics cards have trouble with long strings rendered as **Text2D** if the resulting texture is too wide for the hardware. If your **Text2D** comes out as a white box, try using a shorter string or use a **Text3D** instead.

Text2D extends **Shape3D** and initializes both the geometry and appearance. It is possible to modify a **Text2D** once it has been created, but it is simpler to just make a new one.

Utility Shape Primitives

Java 3D supports several basic shapes through utility classes: **Box**, **Sphere**, **Cone**, and **Cylinder**. These classes give you the ability to create versions of these shapes with specific dimensions and properties. These are subclasses of the **Primitive** base class in the `com.sun.j3d.utils.geometry` package.

The properties of the **Primitive** are set in the constructor. For example, a **Cone** is created with a specific radius and height (see Figure 3–15).

FIGURE 3–15 Primitive cones are constructed based on radius and height values that you specify.

The cone is created centered around the origin (0, 0, 0). This cone has a radius of 1.0 and a height of 2.0:

```
Cone cone = new Cone(1.0f, 2.0f);
```

A **Primitive** is like a **Shape3D** node with an internal **Geometry** component. The **Primitive** can have an **Appearance** associated with it, but the **Primitive** manages the **Geometry**. **Primitive** is actually a subclass of **Group**, and the shape may be made of several **Shape3D** nodes, each of which holds a piece of the shape. For example, a **Cone** contains two **Shape3D** nodes, one for the base and one for the body (sides) (see Figure 3–16).

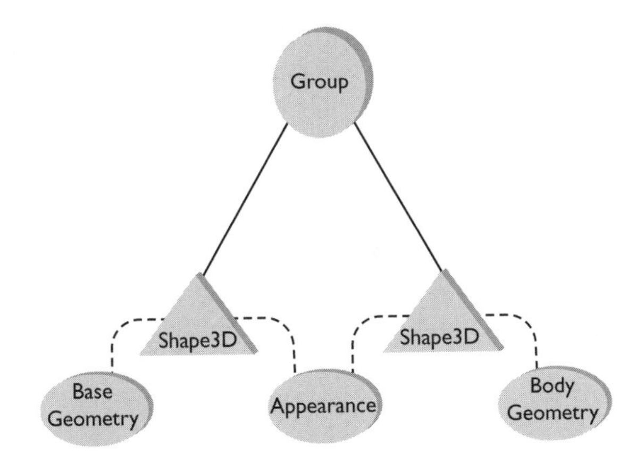

FIGURE 3–16 Scene graph diagram for a primitive cone.

The appearance for the **Shape3D** node(s) can be specified with the constructor or set via the method:

```
void setAppearance(Appearance app);
```

Several options can be specified in the constructor for a **Primitive**. For example, a Cone may be created using several different constructors:

```
Cone()
Cone(float radius, float height);
Cone(float radius, float height, Appearance ap);
Cone(float radius, float height, int flags, Appearance ap);
Cone(float radius, float height, int flags, int xdiv,
      int ydiv, Appearance ap);
```

In addition to the dimensions and the appearance, the other options that can be set are the flags and the resolution. The flags specify properties of the shape, such as whether the geometry should be created with normals. The resolution specifies how many polygons should be used to represent the shape. If a parameter is not in the constructor, its default is used.

The flags parameter controls the options for the shape via integer fields. The values for the fields are:

```
ENABLE_APPEARANCE_MODIFY
ENABLE_GEOMETRY_PICKING
GENERATE_NORMALS
GENERATE_NORMALS_INWARD
GENERATE_TEXTURE_COORDS
GEOMETRY_NO_SHARED
```

The ENABLE_APPEARANCE_MODIFY flag specifies that the **Shape3D** nodes for the shape have the ALLOW_APPEARANCE_READ and ALLOW_APPEARANCE_WRITE capability bits set to allow the appearance to be read and written while the scene graph is live. The ENABLE_GEOMETRY_PICKING flag specifies that the geometry generated for the shape have the ALLOW_INTERSECT bit set so that the geometry can be picked. The GENERATE_NORMALS flag specifies that the geometry should be created with normals for lighting. The GENERATE_NORMALS_INWARD specifies that the normals should be oriented towards the inside of the surface; this is used when the viewer will view the inside of the surface instead of the outside. The GENERATE_TEXTURE_COORDINATES flag indicates that texture coordinates should be generated for the vertices of the shape. The GEOMETRY_NO_SHARED flag indicates that the geometry for the **Primitive** should not be shared with other **Primitives**.

The resolution parameter(s) specify the number of polygons to generate for the shape. The parameters specify the number of subdivisions of each aspect of the shape. For example, for a **Cone,** the number of subdivisions around the outside edge of the circle and the number of subdivisions along the side of the cone can be specified. Using a lower number of divisions results in a shape with fewer polygons and lower visual quality. Figure 3–17 shows a sphere rendered with 10 subdivisions compared to a sphere with 45 subdivisions (the shading has been set up to show the subdivisions more clearly).

It is easy to generate a surface with more polygons than necessary, which can make your scene render slowly. For example, the subdivisions parameter for a sphere are applied in the x and y directions, so that the number of polygons with 10 subdivisions is about 10x10 = 100, and the number of polygons with 45 subdivisions is about 45x45 = 2025, so 45 subdivisions uses about 20 times the number of polygons as 10 subdivisions.

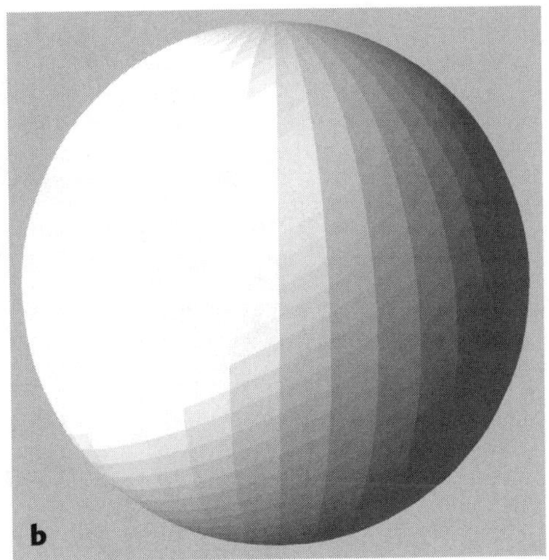

FIGURE 3–17 This sphere has been rendered with (a) 10 subdivisions and (b) 45 subdivisions. Note that the shading for this figure has been set up specifically to show the subdivisions more clearly.

For example, this code creates a **Sphere** of radius 1.0 that can be texture-mapped and lit using the appearance appTex that sets up the texture:

```
Sphere sphere = new Sphere(1.0, Sphere.GENERATE_NORMALS|
                         Sphere.GENERATE_TEXTURE_COORDINATES
                         appTex);
```

This creates the sphere with normals for lighting and texture coordinates for texture mapping. Figure 3–18 shows the resulting sphere with the texture of the earth's surface applied.

If the **Primitive** is made from several **Shape3D** nodes, the class will define fields that can be used to look up each shape from the group. For example, a cone has BODY and BASE fields. Retrieve the **Shape3D** for the base by calling:

```
Shape3D baseShape = cone.getChild(Cone.BASE);
```

Primitives are created so that the center of the shape is at the origin (0, 0, 0). The dimensions, shapes, and subdivisions for the different shape types are summarized in Table 3–3 (see the Java 3D javadocs for details on specific classes).

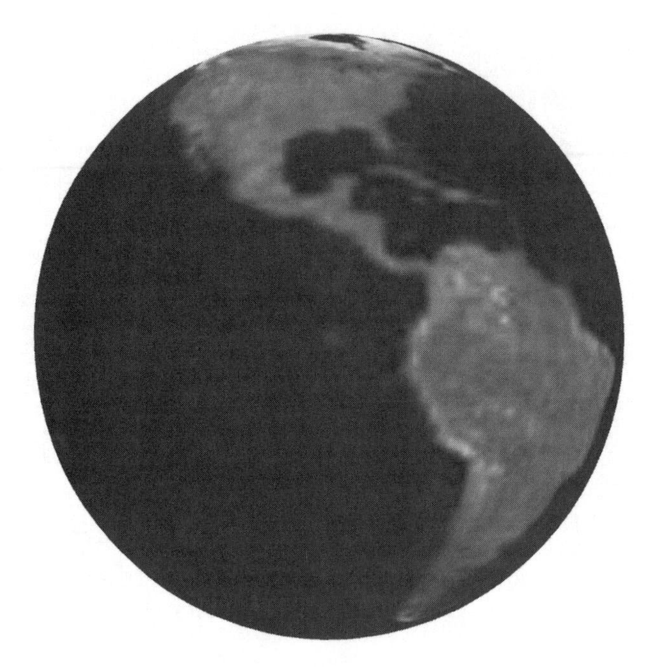

FIGURE 3–18 A texture is used to give the surface of this sphere an extremely detailed appearance that would be impractical using geometry alone.

TABLE 3–3 Primitive Summary

Class	Dimensions	Shapes	Resolution
Box	Xdim (width) Ydim (height) Zdim (depth)	BACK, FRONT TOP, BOTTOM, RIGHT, LEFT	None (not subdivided)
Cone	Radius (around Y Axis) Height (along Y Axis)	BODY BASE	Xdiv (around circle) Ydiv (along body)
Cylinder	Radius (around Y Axis) Height (along Y Axis)	BODY BASE	Xdiv (around circle) Ydiv (along body)
Sphere	Radius (around 0, 0, 0)	BODY	Ndiv (along X and Y)

Loading Geometry from Files

A very powerful way to bring shapes into your virtual world is importing data from a file. Loading data from a file lets you access data created in other applications, freeing you from the work of creating the shapes explicitly or using the utility classes. There are many applications available today which can be used to create amazing content. Exporting this content to a file and importing that file into Java 3D lets you bring that amazing content into your virtual world.

In this section, we'll explore the general interface that Java 3D uses for loading data from files. We'll use a file loader included with the Java 3D utilities that handles Wavefront .obj files. This is a commonly used file format; many objects are available in this format on the net. We'll explore the data that can be loaded from these files and then look at the other file loaders that are available for Java 3D.

The interface for importing data from files consists of two classes, **Loader** and **Scene**. A **Loader** takes a location and flags for the file, which indicate how it should be loaded, and produces a **Scene**. The **Scene** contains a scene graph for the content in the file along with methods that let you look up individual nodes in the scene, such as specific shapes.

The Loader

A **Loader** is a class for importing data from a file into Java 3D. Different loaders support different file formats. A single application can use multiple loaders, and can therefore integrate files created by a variety of authoring tools. This effectively makes Java 3D independent of the underlying graphics file formats that are used by the different authoring tools.

A **Loader** is a class that implements the `com.sun.j3d.loaders.Loader` interface. This interface defines the methods used to specify the file and options for loading. For example, the loader for .obj files is called **ObjectFile**, and it implements the **Loader** interface.

The **Loader** interface defines some options for file loading, but most options are specific to the particular file loader. For example, **ObjectFile** doesn't use any of the **Loader** options, but it does support a couple options via parameters to its constructor:

```
ObjectFile();
ObjectFile(int flags);
ObjectFile(int flags, float creaseAngle);
```

The flags parameter for **ObjectFile** specifies how the data is to be created. The flag values are:

```
RESIZE
REVERSE
STRIPIFY
TRIANGULATE
```

These are integer fields which can be OR'd together. RESIZE indicates that the geometry should be resized as it is loaded so that the object fits into the range (-1, -1, -1) to (1, 1, 1). This is useful when you want to browse through objects of different sizes using a constant setup. All the objects will be loaded into approximately the same size. REVERSE is used for data that was created with the polygons oriented the wrong way. If you load a file and the shading looks all wrong, try reloading with REVERSE and see if that corrects the problem. Use TRIANGULATE if the file contains complex polygons that must broken up by the **Triangulator** to be rendered property. STRIPIFY tells the loader to use the **Stripifier** utility to try to improve the rendering performance for the scene by combining adjacent triangles into strips.

The creaseAngle is used for file data that does not include normals. It specifies the sharpness of edges for normal generation. See the preceeding discussion of the **NormalGenerator**.

A **Loader** can be told to load a scene from a filename on your local system, from a URL, or from a **Reader** object:

```
Scene load(java.io.String filename)
Scene load(java.net.URL url);
Scene load(java.io.Reader reader);
```

The **Scene** is loaded and returned by these methods.

The Scene

The object returned by a loader is called a **Scene**. It stores several important pieces of information, the most significant being a **BranchGroup** containing the scene graph created by the loader. It also contains an array of all the lights in the scene, an array of viewpoints, and so on.

The most important data returned with the scene is a **BranchGroup** that holds the scene. This is called the scene group and it is returned by the method:

```
BranchGroup getSceneGroup();
```

This returns the root node for the scene. Figure 3–19 shows a model of a ship loaded from a .obj file.

The code that loads this model looks like this:

```
java.net.URL galleonURL; // initialized to point to the
                         // galleon .obj file
int flags = ObjectFile.RESIZE; // resize to fit
ObjectFile f = new ObjectFile(flags);
Scene s = null;
```

FIGURE 3–19 A loader was used to import this ship into our Java 3D program.

```
Try {
    s = f.load(galleonURL);
} catch (Exception e) {
    System.err.println("Can't load file, exception: " + e);
}
BranchGroup sceneGroup = s.getSceneGroup();
```

Other methods allow you to access nodes inside the scene graph for the **Scene**. The most useful of these let you look up objects in the scene that have names associated with them by the creating program:

```
java.util.Hashtable getNamedObjects();
```

For example, each **Shape3D** node loaded by the **ObjectFile** loader may have a name associated with it. We can print out these names by getting the named object, **Hashtable**, and printing out the keys:

```
Hashtable namedObjects = s.getNamedObjects();
Enumeration e = namedObjects.keys();
while (e.hasMoreElements()) {
    String name = (String) e.nextElement();
    System.out.println("name = " + name);
}
```

This prints out the names: "hull," "lamp," "keel," "aft," etc. In this file, each name corresponds to a **Shape3D** for a piece of the ship. The **ObjectFile** loader associates an **Appearance** with each shape. If we want to override the **Appearances** so that our program can modify the appearance of the shape, we can get the **Shape3D** from the hashtable:

```
Shape3D shape = (Shape3D) namedObjects.get(name);
shape.setAppearance(appearance);
```

Other file formats may make other parts of the scene available in the named object table.

Loading Other File Formats

Java 3D supports several other file formats. A loader for scene files from the Lightwave application is available as part of the Sun utilities. Loaders for other file formats are freely available from other developers. The Java 3D Community site, www.j3d.org/, has a wealth of useful information, including a list of the available Java 3D loaders at www.j3d.org/utilities/loaders.html. A few of the notable loaders are the NCSA Porfolio, which includes loaders for a number of commonly used file types; the Xj3D loader, which can load VRML97 and X3D files; the Full Sail OpenFLT loader, which can load OpenFLT data files produced by animation applications, and the Starfire Research 3Ds loader, which can load 3Ds files from 3D Studio Max. In addition, the utility Java 3D Fly Through provides a binary file format for Java 3D scene graphs.

The NCSA portfolio is a package of Java 3D utilities. It is available at www.ncsa.uiuc.edu/~srp/Java3D/porfolio/. In addition to other functionality, it includes loaders for several file formats. The porfolio includes another loader for OBJ files, loaders for DXF files from AutoCAD, VRML97 files, 3DS files from 3D Studio Max, and DEM digital elevation files; plus loaders for several other file formats.

The Xj3D loader is part of the X3D project, which is developing the next-generation Extensible 3D (X3D) Graphics specification. It expresses the geometry and behavior capabilities of the Virtual Reality Markup Language (VRML97) using the Extensible Markup Language (XML). Information on X3D is at www.web3d.org/x3d.html. Xj3D is an implementation of the X3D specification on top of Java 3D that supports loading both VRML97 and X3D files.

OpenFlight is a file format developed by MultiGen. OpenFlight is becoming a commonly used format for visual simulation. The Full Sail OpenFLT loader is available from Full Sail Real World Education (www.fullsail.com), an accredited school that offers training in computer animation, digital media, game design, and other areas. The OpenFLT loader loads scene files from MultiGen, Maya, and other content creation applications.*

See the color plates at the center of this book for a color example of an OpenFLT file created by Full Sail students.

3DS is a file format developed by Discreet for its popular 3D Studio Max application. This is another commonly used format for visual simulation. Starfire Research (www.starfireresearch.com) has made available a Java 3D loader for 3DS files. The loader allows 3DS models to be loaded into Java 3D with almost all of the 3DS model features supported. The loader is intended to load models and not scenes, so lights and animation in the 3DS file are ignored.

Java 3D Fly Through

Java 3D Fly Through is an extensible utility application that shows how to load and navigate through scenes loaded from many file formats. It is available from java.sun.com/products/java-media/3D/index.html. It can be used as a demonstration platform or as a basis for your application. It integrates the Sun and third-party loaders into a common framework. Once loaded the scene can be stored in a binary file format that can speed up file loading by an order of mangnitude. Users can navigate around the scene using "fly," "hover," or "drive" behaviors.

XJ3D is available online at www.web3D.org/TaskGroups/x3d/Xj3D/HowToInstall.html; the Full Sail OpenFLT loader can be found at www.fullsail.com/ and the 3Ds loader can be found at www.starfireresearch.com/services/java3d/inspector3ds.html.

*See Plate 11 in the color insert at the center of this book. Image courtesy of Full Sail Real World Education. Used by permission.

Summary

Geometry describes the shape of objects in a Java 3D scene. Java 3D supports two basic kinds of **`Geometry`** classes. Most **`Geometry`** subclasses deal with points, lines, and polygons. These primitives are defined using **`GeometryArray`** node components. Other kinds of **`Geometry`** are used for special purposes. **`Text3D`** is a special geometry for drawing text as polygons that form "block" letters. Utility classes let you create 2D text and geometric shapes like spheres, cones, and cylinders. Using the geometry utilities, you can create geometry from complex polygons, attach normals to a surface, or optimize the format of your triangles. Loaders allow geometry to be imported from other programs, such as Multigen or 3D Studio Max. Java 3D Fly Through can be used to integrate data from loaders and includes a binary file format.

Summary of URLs Found in This Chapter

Java 3D Explorer **web3dbooks.com/java3d/jumpstart/**

Java 3D Community site **www.j3d.org/**

Java 3D loaders site **www.j3d.org/utilities/loaders.html**

NCSA Java 3D portfolio **www.ncsa.uiuc.edu/~srp/Java3D/porfolio/**

Extensible 3D (X3D) **www.web3d.org/x3d.html**

XJ3D install docs **www.web3D.org/TaskGroups/x3d/Xj3D/HowToInstall.html**

Full Sail OpenFLT loader **www.fullsail.com/**

3DS loader **www.starfireresearch.com/services/java3d/inspector3ds.html**

Java 3D Fly Through **java.sun.com/products/java-media/3D/index.html**

CHAPTER 4 Appearances

TOPICS IN THIS CHAPTER

- ▼ SPECIFYING THE LOOK OF RENDERED OBJECTS USING APPEARANCES
- ▼ SETTING COLORING, RENDERING, AND MATERIAL ATTRIBUTES
- ▼ WRAPPING IMAGES AROUND SHAPES USING TEXTURE-MAPPING

Java 3D shape nodes reference a geometry component that tells Java 3D *what* to render, as well as an appearance component that tells Java 3D *how* to render the shape's geometry. In this chapter we'll examine the many ways that you can alter the look, or appearance, of Java 3D objects. We'll see how proper use of appearances can dramatically affect your scene in terms of the colors, rendering styles, and textures that the end user eventually sees. Before digging into these details, we'll begin with a closer look at Java 3D appearances in general.

Appearance Basics

An **`Appearance`** is a node component that holds the appearance information for a shape node. The **`Appearance`** class itself does not directly contain appearance information; instead, it maintains references to appearance components, which in turn hold pieces of the appearance information. For example, basic color attributes are held by the **`ColoringAttributes`** node component, as illustrated in

Figure 4–1. To set the coloring attributes, your program creates a **ColoringAttributes** object, sets the properties it needs, and then associates the **ColoringAttributes** with an **Appearance** by calling `setColoringAttributes()` on the **Appearance**.

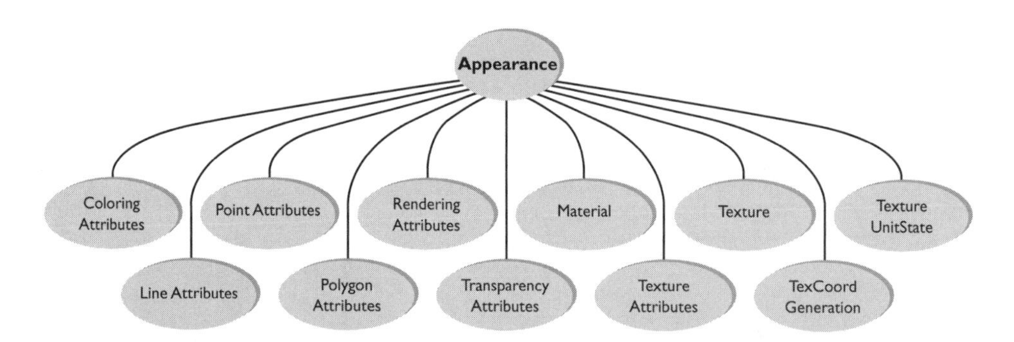

FIGURE 4–1 The **Appearance** node doesn't actually contain appearance information; it merely maintains *references* to appearance components that in turn contain appearance information, as this figure illustrates.

If the appearance does not have an appearance component associated with it, the **Appearance** takes on the default value for the component. For example, if an appearance does not have a **ColoringAttributes** associated with it, the appearance will use the default value for the **ColoringAttributes** component when determining the coloring attributes. The exception to the default attributes case is the **Material** appearance component. The **Material** component controls whether the shape is affected by lighting and specifies the colors used for lighting. By default, **Material** enables lighting. Lighting is *not* enabled if an **Appearance** does not have an associated **Material** component.

Appearance Attributes

Appearance objects can reference a number of node components known as *appearance components*. Appearance components encapsulate rendering properties related to a shape's color, transparency, texture, etc. The components of an **Appearance** are:

- **ColoringAttributes** define attributes which are used in color selection and shading.
- **LineAttributes** define attributes that apply to lines, such as line width and line pattern.
- **PointAttributes** define attributes that apply to point primitives, such as point size and antialiasing.

- **PolygonAttributes** define attributes that apply to polygon primitives, such as face culling and rasterization mode (i.e., POINT, LINE, or FILL).
- **RenderingAttributes** define attributes common to the rendering of all primitives, such as whether depth buffering should be used and whether the shape is enabled for rendering.
- **TransparencyAttributes** define attributes that affect the transparency of objects.
- **Material** defines attributes that apply to primitives when a light illuminates them.
- **TextureAttributes** define the general texture-mapping attributes such as the texture mode.
- **Texture** defines the texture image and filtering parameters used when texture mapping is enabled.
- **TexCoordGeneration** defines the attributes that control the automatic generation of texture coordinates.
- **TextureUnitState**. A program may specify that several textures be applied when texture mapping. To do so it defines several texture unit states on the **Appearance**. Each **TextureUnitState** contains a **TextureAttribute**, **Texture**, and **TexCoordGeneration**.

Each of these components defines a number of attributes that can be applied to shapes, encompassing a wide range of functionality. In this chapter we'll take a detailed look at a variety of attributes your program is likely to need. If your program needs an attribute that isn't discussed in this chapter, be sure to check the javadoc to see if Java 3D already supports the one you have in mind.

Color Classes

Color is an important part of many appearance components. Before we talk about the appearance components it is important to understand how color is actually represented and manipulated in Java 3D. Colors are represented using classes from the javax.vecmath package. These classes represent colors using three or four components. Three-component colors are represented using red, green, and blue (r, g, b) color values, while four-component colors use an additional value to specify the alpha (transparency) of a color (r, g, b, a). The term RGB is used to describe three-component colors, while four-color components are referred to as RGBA colors (red, green, blue, alpha).

The color components are represented using a floating-point value in the range of zero (0.0f) to one (1.0f), where (0.0f) specifies that no amount of light for a given color component should be used, and (1.0f) specifies that all (100%) of that color component should be used. Values between (0.0f) and (1.0f) are used to specify varying degrees of color-component intensity.

Colors can be specified in the constructor for the color object, or via mutator methods. The following code block initializes and copies several simple colors:

```
// Start by constructing a few basic colors:
Color3f black  = new Color3f(0.0f, 0.0f, 0.0f);
Color3f white  = new Color3f(1.0f, 1.0f, 1.0f);
Color3f red    = new Color3f(1.0f, 0.0f, 0.0f);
Color3f green  = new Color3f(0.0f, 1.0f, 0.0f);
Color3f blue   = new Color3f(0.0f, 0.0f, 1.0f);
Color3f cyan   = new Color3f(0.0f, 1.0f, 1.0f);
Color3f magenta= new Color3f(1.0f, 0.0f, 1.0f);
Color3f yellow = new Color3f(1.0f, 1.0f, 0.0f);

// Now create a color that we'll modify a few times:
Color3f myColor = new Color3f(black); // start as black

// Change by passing a new color object to the set() method:
myColor.set(white); // set to white
myColor.set(red);   // set to red
myColor.set(green); // set to green
myColor.set(blue);  // set to blue
myColor.set(yellow);  // set to yellow

// Change by passing raw (r,g,b) values to the set() method:
myColor.set(1.0f, 1.0f, 1.0f); // set to white
myColor.set(1.0f, 0.0f, 0.0f); // set to red
myColor.set(0.0f, 1.0f, 0.0f); // set to green
myColor.set(0.0f, 0.0f, 1.0f); // set to blue
myColor.set(1.0f, 1.0f, 0.0f); // set to yellow
```

Colors can be combined or mixed in the rendering process. For example, shining a white light on a red object could brighten the red areas and produce a white highlight if the surface is shiny. Additional lights add to the intensity of the red and white coloring, but keep in mind that the maximum intensity for color components is 1.0. If lighting leads to a color component having a value greater than 1.0, the value for that component will be clamped (restricted) to 1.0. Using too many bright lights will result in colors that saturate at their maximum values.

Appearance Methods

An appearance is a collection of attribute components that tells how a shape appears. The appearance for a shape can be changed at three different levels. The entire **Appearance** for the shape can be changed; an appearance component, such as a **ColoringAttributes**, can be changed; or a specific attribute of an appearance component, such as the current color in a **ColoringAttributes**, can be changed. Changing the **Appearance** or the appearance component is useful for switching between sets of attributes, while changing an individual attribute allows an **Appearance** to be edited.

The methods on the **Appearance** connect the appearance components with the **Appearance**. These are used to set up the initial appearance settings and to change the appearance settings when the scene graph is live. For example, an application could change the color for a shape using two **ColoringAttributes** components. At initialization, the application would set up the **Appearance** and two **ColoringAttributes** components. Consider, for example, the following snippet of code (`red` and `green` are **Color3f** objects taken from the previous example):

```
Appearance appearance = new Appearance();
appearance.setCapability(
    Appearance.ALLOW_COLORING_ATTRIBUTES_WRITE);
ColoringAttributes redColoring =
    new ColoringAttributes(red, ColoringAttributes.SHADE_FLAT);
ColoringAttributes greenColoring =
    new ColoringAttributes(green, ColoringAttributes.SHADE_FLAT);
appearance.setColoringAttributes(redColoring);
```

This creates a default appearance, indicates that the coloring attributes should be changeable when the scene is live, creates red and green **ColoringAttributes**, and sets the appearance to use the red **ColoringAttributes**. The program can switch to the green coloring by calling:

```
appearance.setColoringAttributes(greenColoring);
```

All of the methods on **Appearance** which set appearance components can be called on a live scene graph if the corresponding capability bit is set.

Switching between two **ColoringAttributes** is one way to change the color. Changing the color on a single **ColoringAttributes** can achieve the same effect. The initialization sets up the coloring attributes to be writeable:

```
Appearance appearance = new Appearance();
ColoringAttributes colrAttr =
    new ColoringAttributes(red, ColoringAttributes.SHADE_FLAT);
    colrAttr.setCapability(ColoringAttributes.ALLOW_COLOR_WRITE);
    appearance.setColoringAttributes(colrAttr);
```

When the scene graph is live, modifying the **ColoringAttributes** object changes the color of the shape:

```
coloringAttributes.setColor(green);
```

Most attribute methods can be called on a live scene graph if the corresponding capability bit is set. However, some methods on some classes, in particular **Texture** and **TexCoordGeneration**, do not have "write" capability bits, so they must be changed by replacing the attribute component instead of changing the component.

Each appearance component has several attributes associated with it. In this chapter we'll discuss most of the attributes and look at some code examples that change the attributes. Consult the javadoc for the attribute component classes for a complete listing of the methods that set and acquire the attributes.

Examining Appearance Attributes with Java 3D Explorer

Most of the figures found in this chapter come from the example program Java 3D Explorer, which is freely available at web3dbooks.com/java3d/jumpstart/. You can closely examine the various attributes discussed in the sections that follow by running the Java 3D Explorer application while you read about each attribute component. Look at the source for the Java 3D Explorer to see how the explorer changes the attributes as you interact with the user interface.

Java3DExplorer is available online at web3dbooks.com/java3d/jumpstart/.

ColoringAttributes

The **ColoringAttributes** component specifies the basic coloring properties for shapes. It sets the "unlit" color and the shading model for the shape. The color is used if lighting is *not* enabled; this happens if the appearance does not have a **Material** component, or if the **Material** disables lighting. The shading model tells whether the primitive should have a single color for each facet of the primitive or if the color should be smoothly interpolated between the colors specified at each vertex of the primitive.

A **ColoringAttributes** component is used to specify the color for unlit primitives, which are usually point or line primitives. Figure 4–2 shows a wire-frame sphere with a red color specified by a **ColoringAttributes** component.

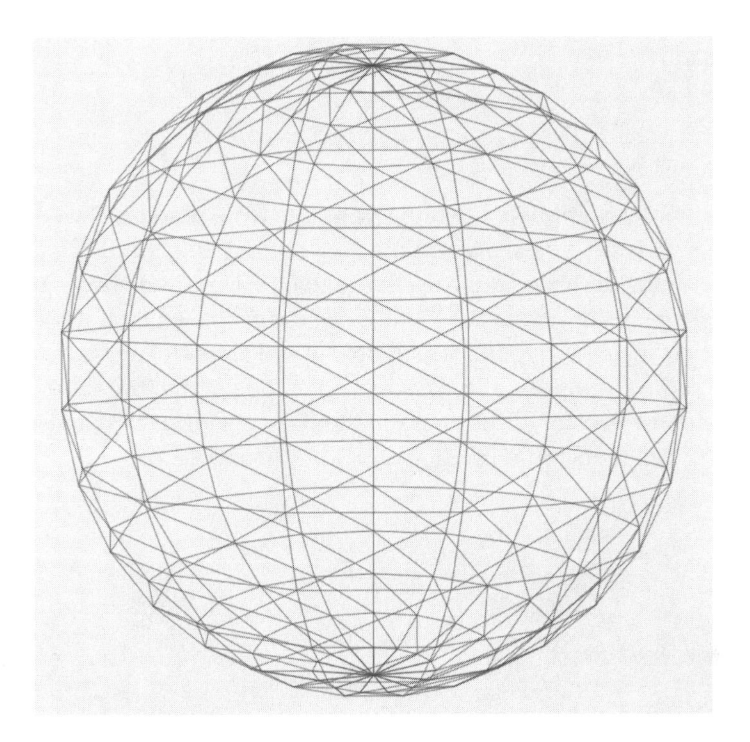

FIGURE 4–2 The red color for this wire-frame sphere was specified using a ColoringAttributes component.

ColoringAttributes are usually not used for filled polygon primitives because these types of primitives are normally lit (consequently their color comes from the **Material**). Color can also be specified using vertex colors specified in the geometry of a shape. When specified, vertex colors override coloring attributes.

The code that sets up the **ColoringAttributes** looks like this:

```
// First, create an Appearance object:
Appearance appearance = new Appearance();
// Next, create a ColoringAttributes object:
ColoringAttributes ca = new ColoringAttributes(1.0f, 0.0f, 0.0f,
                              ColoringAttributes.SHADE_FLAT);
```

```
// Set Appearance object to reference ColoringAttributes:
appearance.setColoringAttributes(ca); // set coloring attributes
```

The constructor specifies the color red (`1.0, 0.0, 0.0`) and the "flat" shading model. The values for the shading model are:

```
SHADE_GOURAUD
SHADE_FLAT
NICEST
FASTEST
```

The shading model is applied when the primitive to be rendered has different colors at each vertex. Typically, this is the result of lighting, but it can also be the result of specifying vertex colors with the geometry. Gouraud shading uses interpolation to shade pixels across the surface of a shape (based on the color of each vertex of the enclosing polygon), which produces a smooth appearance. Flat shading, by comparison, sets all pixels in a given polygon to the same color (based on one vertex color of the enclosing polygon). Figure 4–3 shows a cube with vertex colors rendered with `SHADE_GOURAUD` and `SHADE_FLAT`.

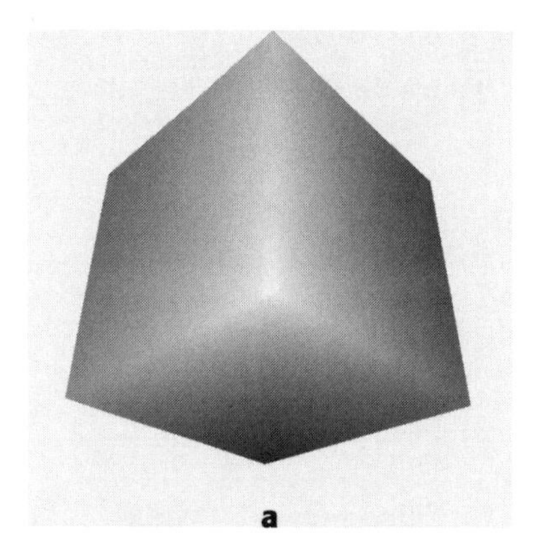

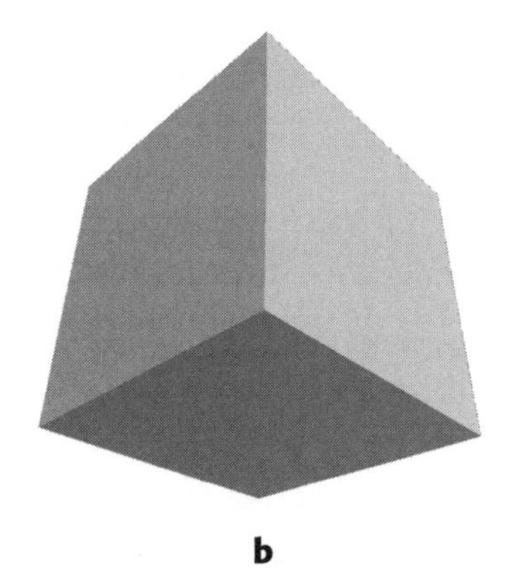

FIGURE 4–3 The vertex colors in this cube are rendered using (a) SHADE_GOURAUD and (b) SHADE_FLAT.

The color for the faces in the `SHADE_FLAT` color comes from the last vertex of the face.

The values `NICEST` and `FASTEST` are used for several attributes. These allow your program to express the tradeoff it desires (quality versus speed) and allow Java 3D to determine the appropriate value at runtime. For the shading method, in most Java 3D implementations `SHADE_FLAT` shading is no faster than SHADE_GOURAUD, so NICEST and FASTEST both specify SHADE_GOURAUD shading.

The defaults for **ColoringAttributes** are white color (1.0, 1.0, 1.0) and SHADE_GOURAUD shading.

With most Java 3D implementations, SHADE_FLAT shading is no faster than SHADE_GOURAUD. In such cases, NICEST and FASTEST both specify SHADE_GOURAUD shading.

PointAttributes

PointAttributes specify the attributes related to rendering points. You can specify the size and antialiasing state for points. Figure 4–4 shows a sphere rendered as antialiased points of size 5.0.

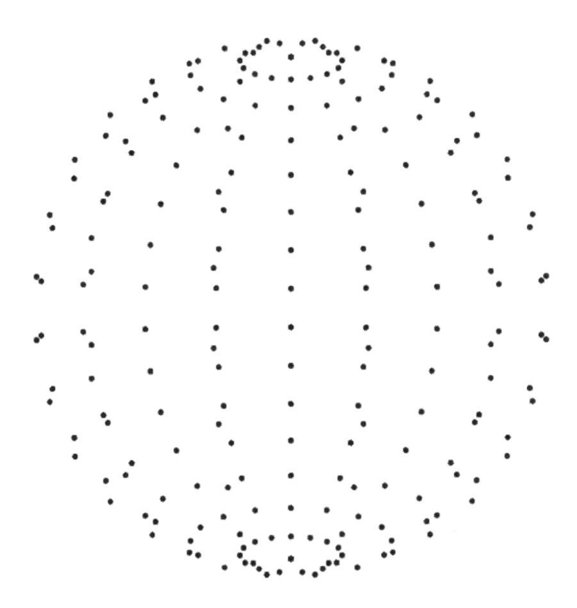

FIGURE 4–4 This sphere is rendered using antialiased points of size 5.0.

The point size sets the size in pixels for the points. Antialiasing controls whether the edges of the points are smooth. With antialiasing disabled, points are drawn as squares. With antialiasing enabled, points are drawn as smooth-edged circles. Figure 4–5 shows an enlarged view of aliased and antialiased size 5.0 points.

FIGURE 4–5 Detail of (a) aliased and (b) antialiased points.

By default, point primitives are one pixel in size and do not use antialiasing. Note that antialiased points are "transparent": the smooth edges of the point are drawn by blending the color of the pixels along edges of the point with the underlying image (see the note on transparent rendering that appears later in this chapter).

Point size is not supported by DirectX 7.0, but is supported in DirectX 8.0. Point antialiasing is not supported by DirectX.

LineAttributes

`LineAttributes` specify the attributes related to rendering lines. You can specify the width, pattern, and antialiasing state for lines. The line width specifies how many pixels wide the line is. The line pattern is the on/off pattern used to draw the line. Figure 4–6 shows lines of varying width and patterns.

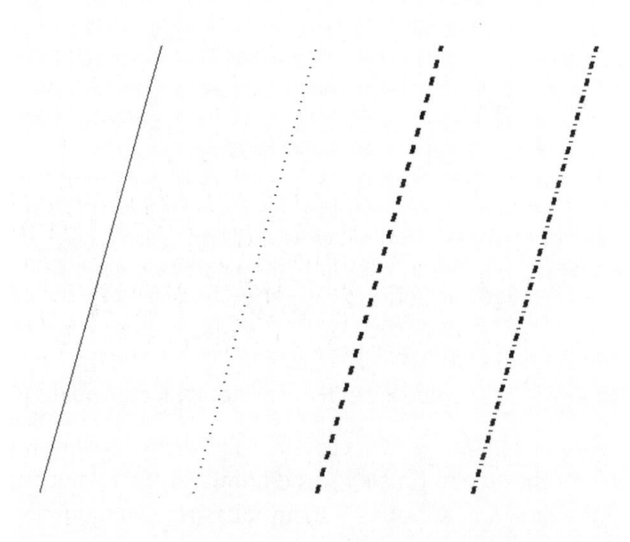

FIGURE 4–6 Lines created with a variety of width and pattern settings.

Plate 1
Nearlife's Virtual Fishtank™ Java 3D application allows exhibit visitors to create and release their very own digital fish into a tank that consists of jumbo computer monitors mounted to the museum walls.

Plate 2
Cosm is an online fantasy world developed in Java 3D.

a

b

Plate 3
In the Java 3D game Roboforge, players (a) create and train their own digital robots for online battle; (b) the robots battle in the Gigadrome.

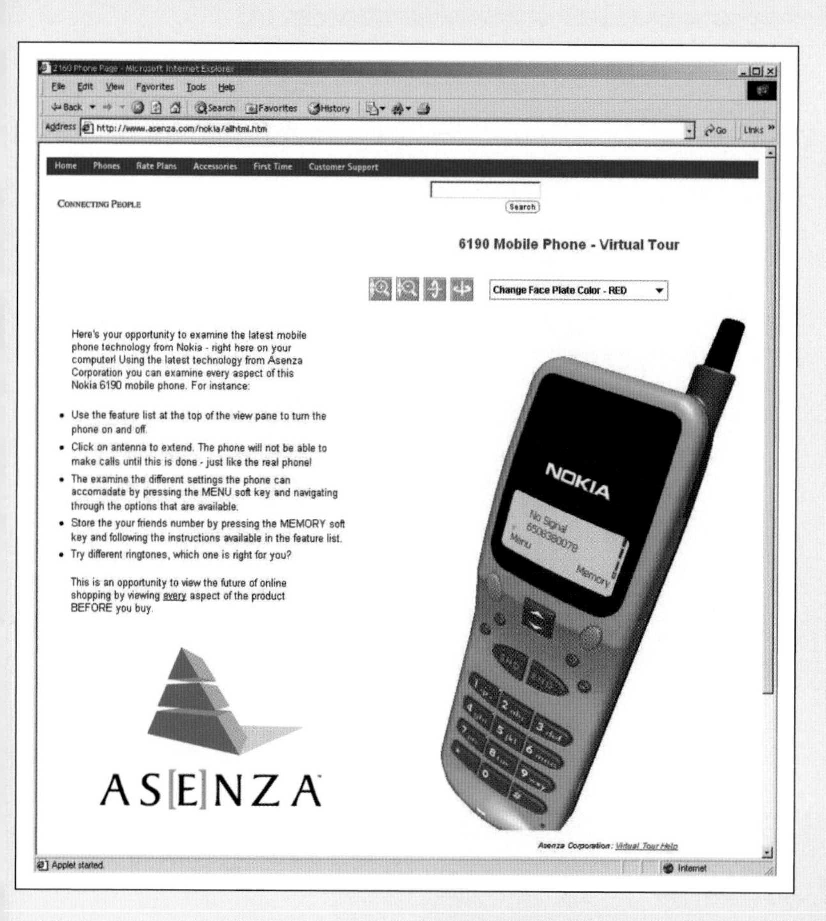

Plate 4
This Nokia mobile phone product visualization is only one of the Java 3D visualizations developed by Asenza Corp as part of its eProducts electronic commerce application.

Plate 5
With Java 3D, Xtivia is able to represent a store using a 3D interactive view rather than simple 2D images or animations.

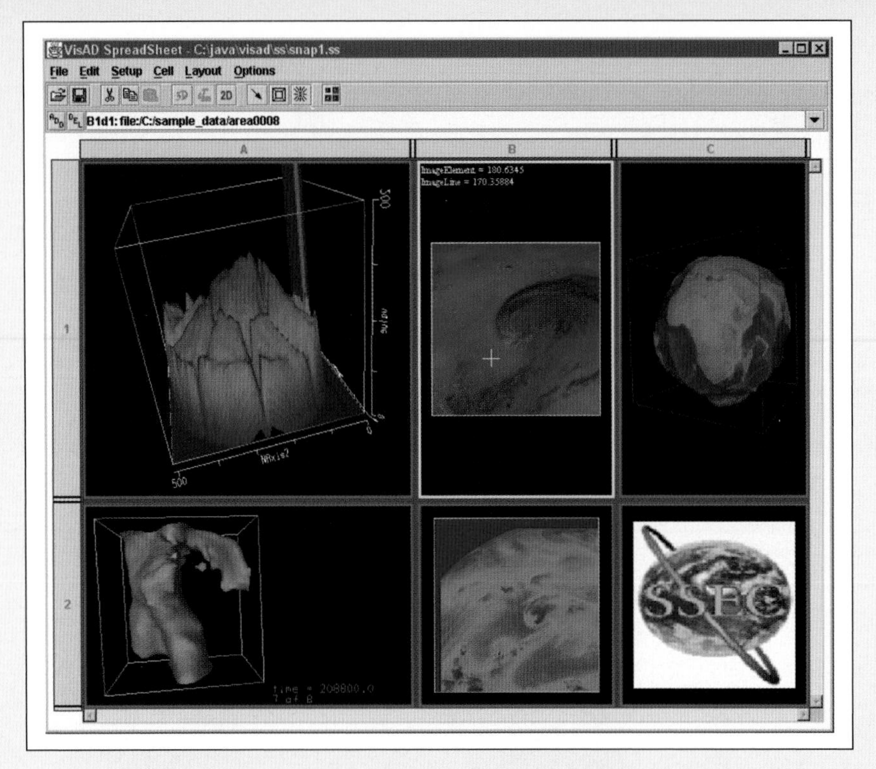

a

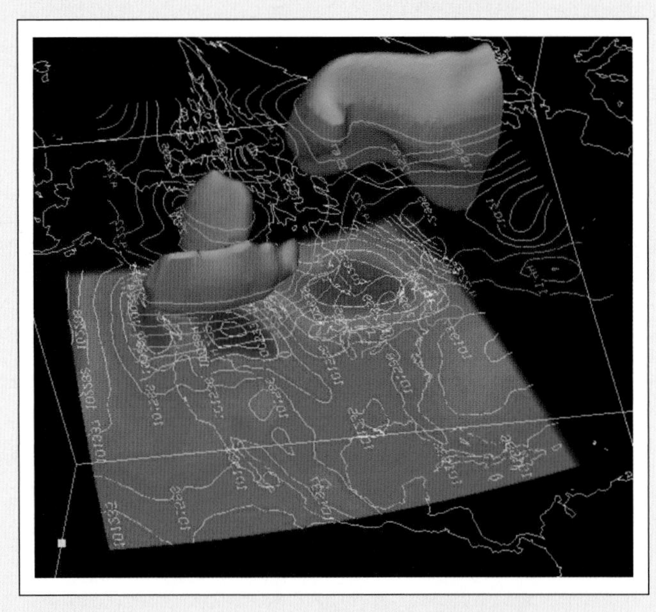

b

Plate 6

These screenshots were taken using two different VisAD applications. (a) Is a fully collaborative spreadsheet that can be used to view a wide variety of numerical data; (b) is from the Unidata Program Center's gridded data viewer for visualizing numerical weather simulations.

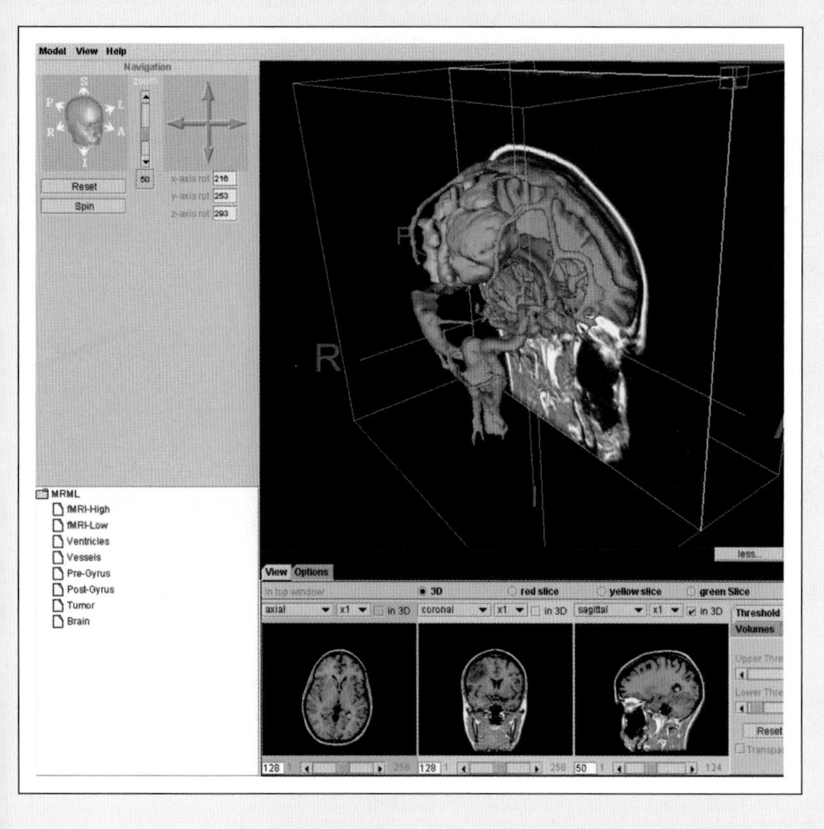

Plate 7
The brain tumor shown here is visualized with SPLViz, a Java 3D visualization toolkit developed by Brigham and Women's Hospital and Harvard Medical School.

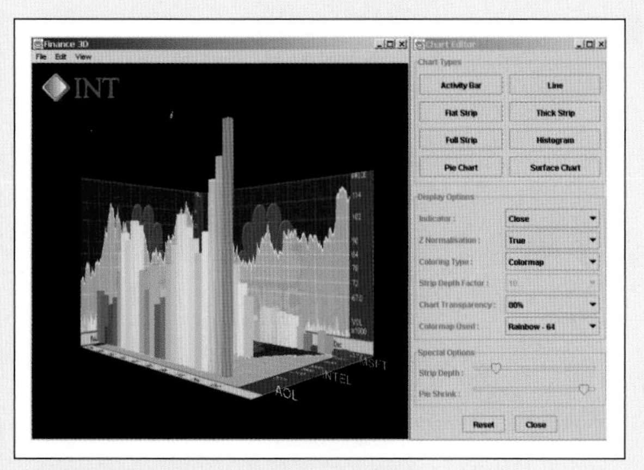

a

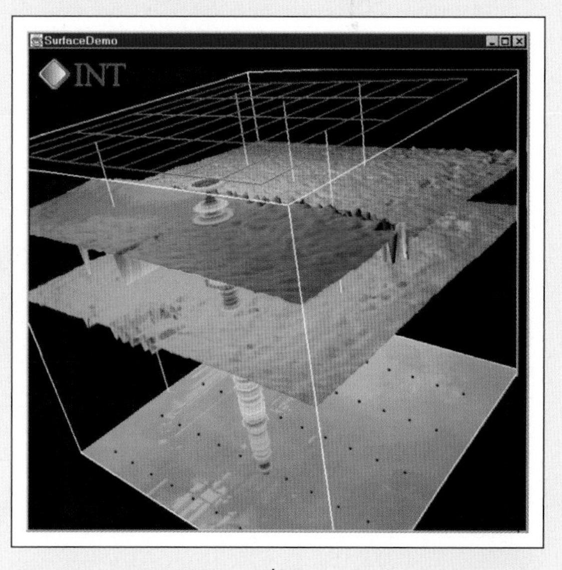

b

Plate 8
INT's J/View3Dpro product supports 3D visualization of various data types, including (a) financial data and (b) geological data.

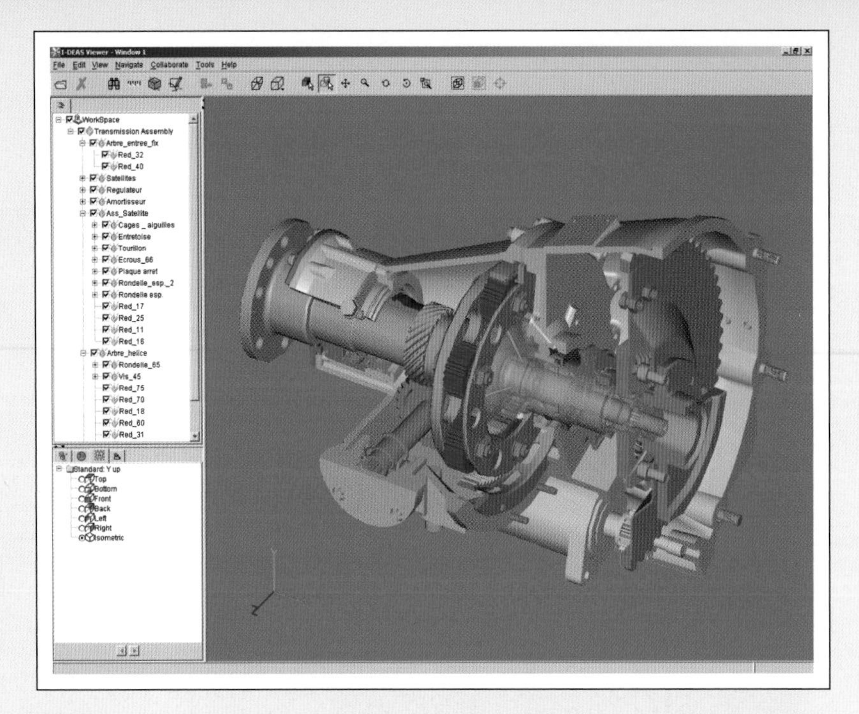

Plate 9

This screenshot shows an assembly loaded into SDRC's I-DEAS Viewer collaborative engineering product. Users can view product dimensions, a bill of materials, and other design data.

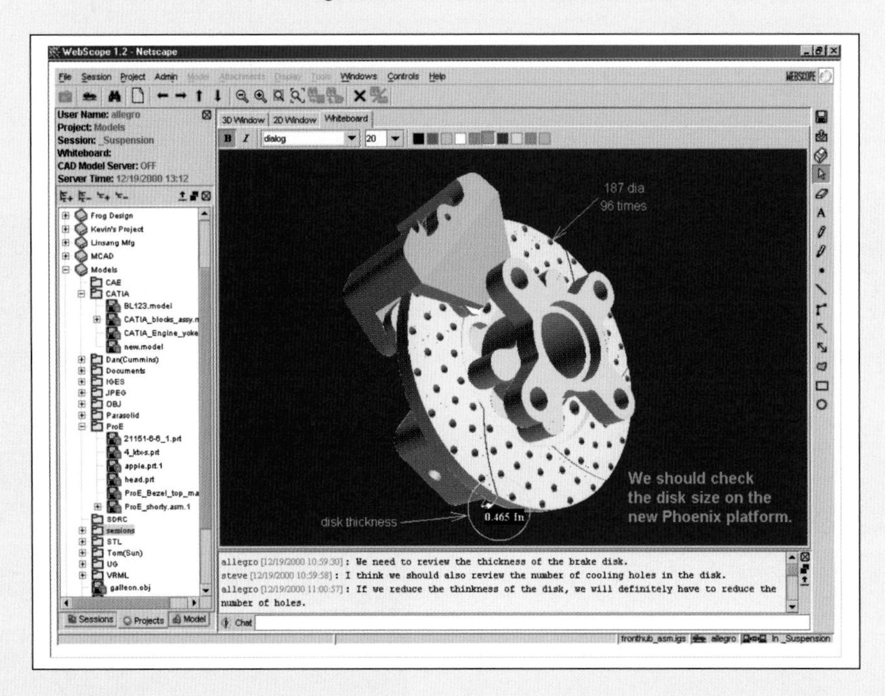

Plate 10

The WebScope collaborative engineering system allows engineers to view data from different design and analysis applications. Here we see an interactive discussion involving a part under development.

Plate 11

Above, an OpenFlight file was loaded using the Haze 3D Viewer, developed by Full Sail Real World Education.

a

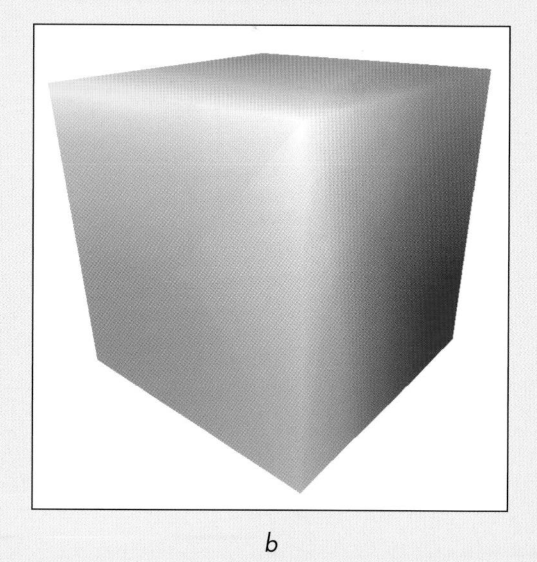

b

Plate 12

Shading modes: (a) SHADE_FLAT and (b) SHADE_GOURAUD.

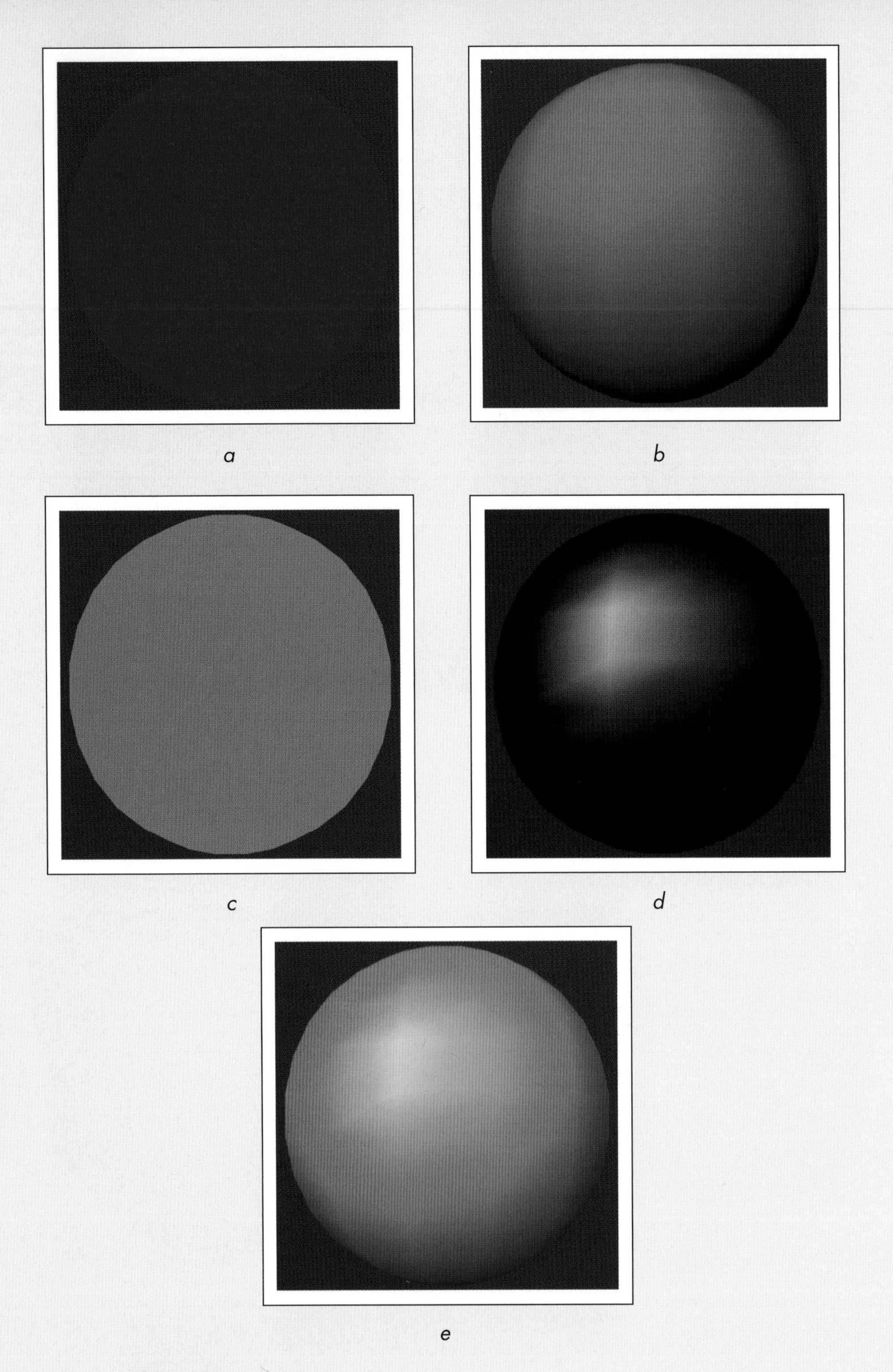

Plate 13
Lighting types: (a) ambient; (b) diffuse; (c) emmissive; (d) specular; and (e) ambient, diffuse, and specular combined.

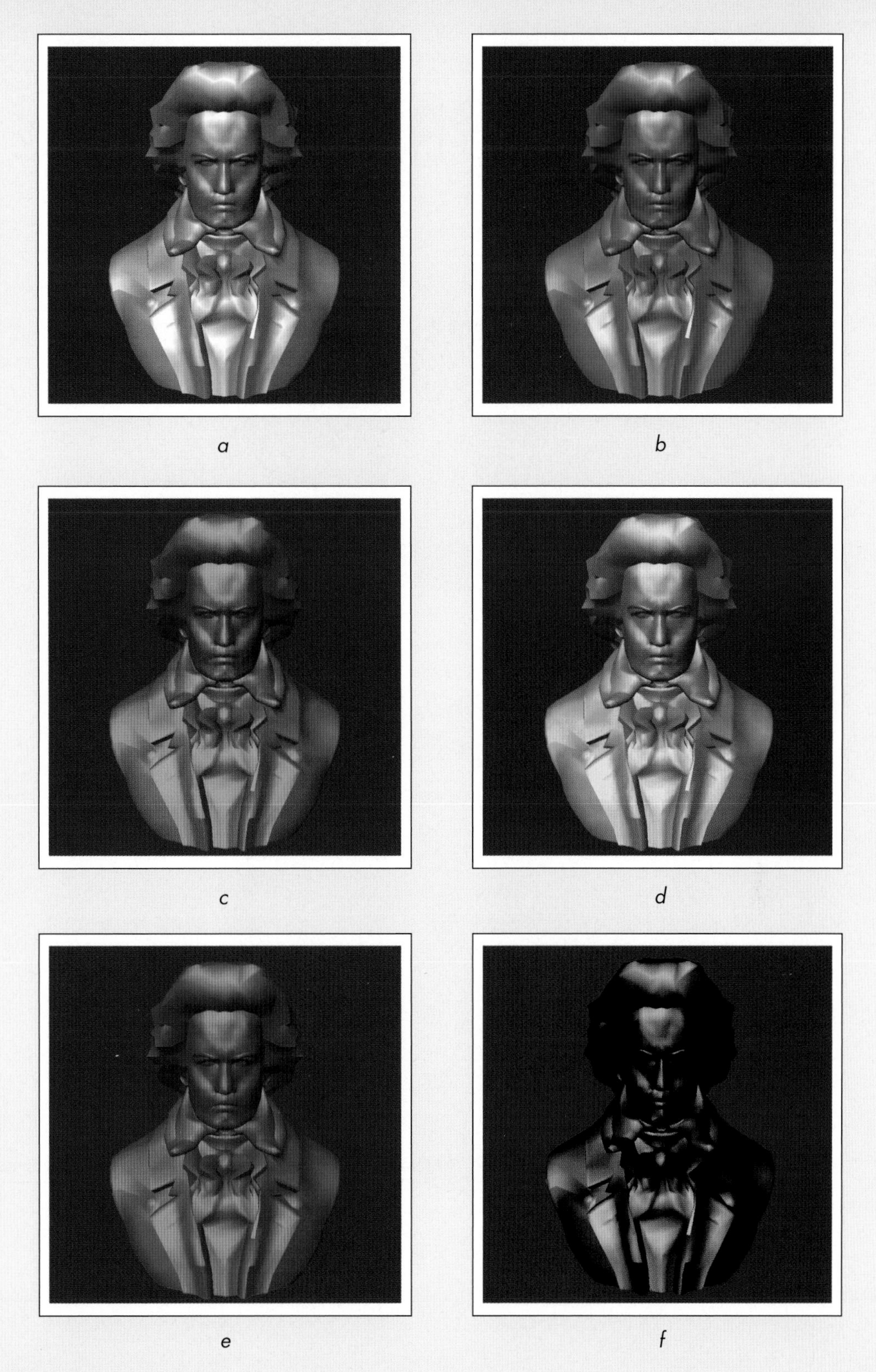

Plate 14
Material types: (a) aluminum, (b) red plastic, (c) copper, (d) gold, (e) red alloy, and (f) black onyx.

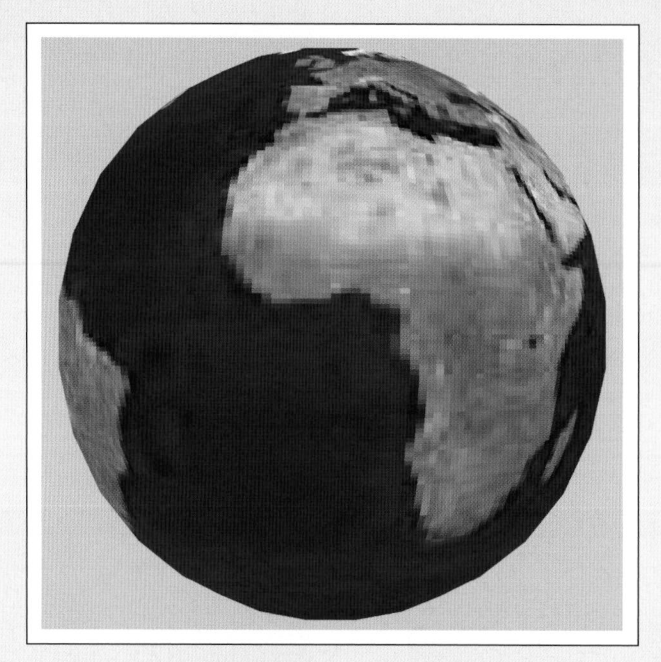

a

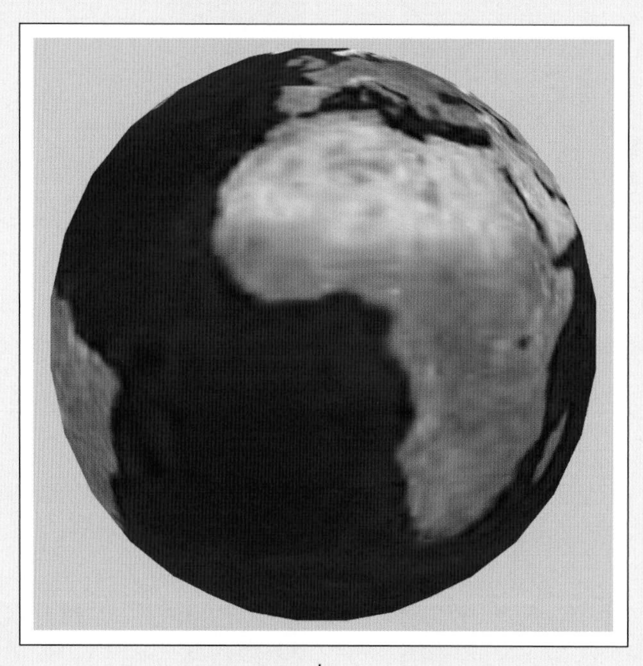

b

Plate 15

Texture Mag Filter: (a) BASE_LEVEL_POINT and (b) BASE_LEVEL_LINEAR.

a

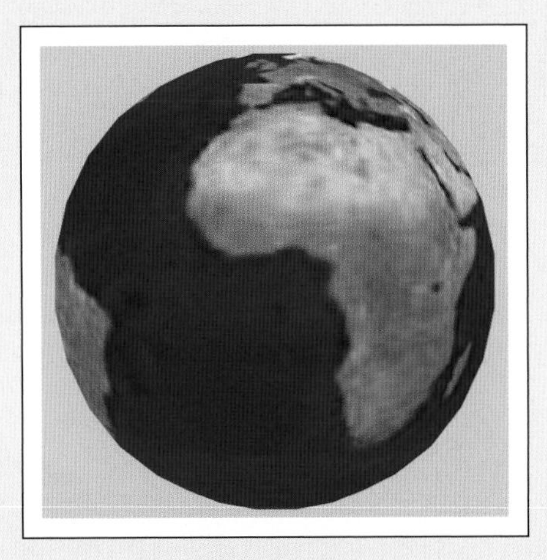

b

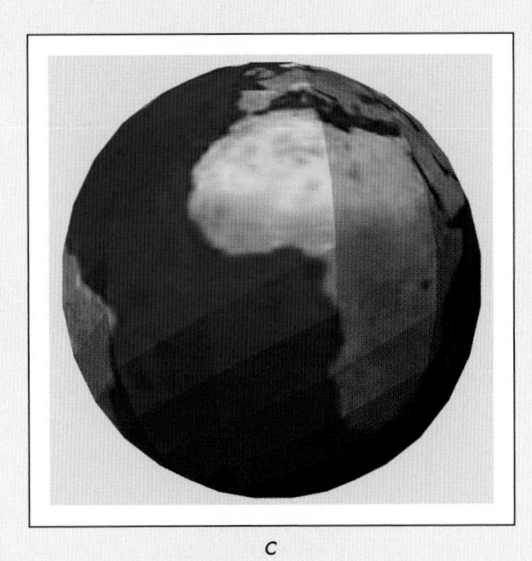

c

Plate 16
TextureAttributes Mode with opaque texture:
(a) no texture, (b) REPLACE, and (c) MODULATE.

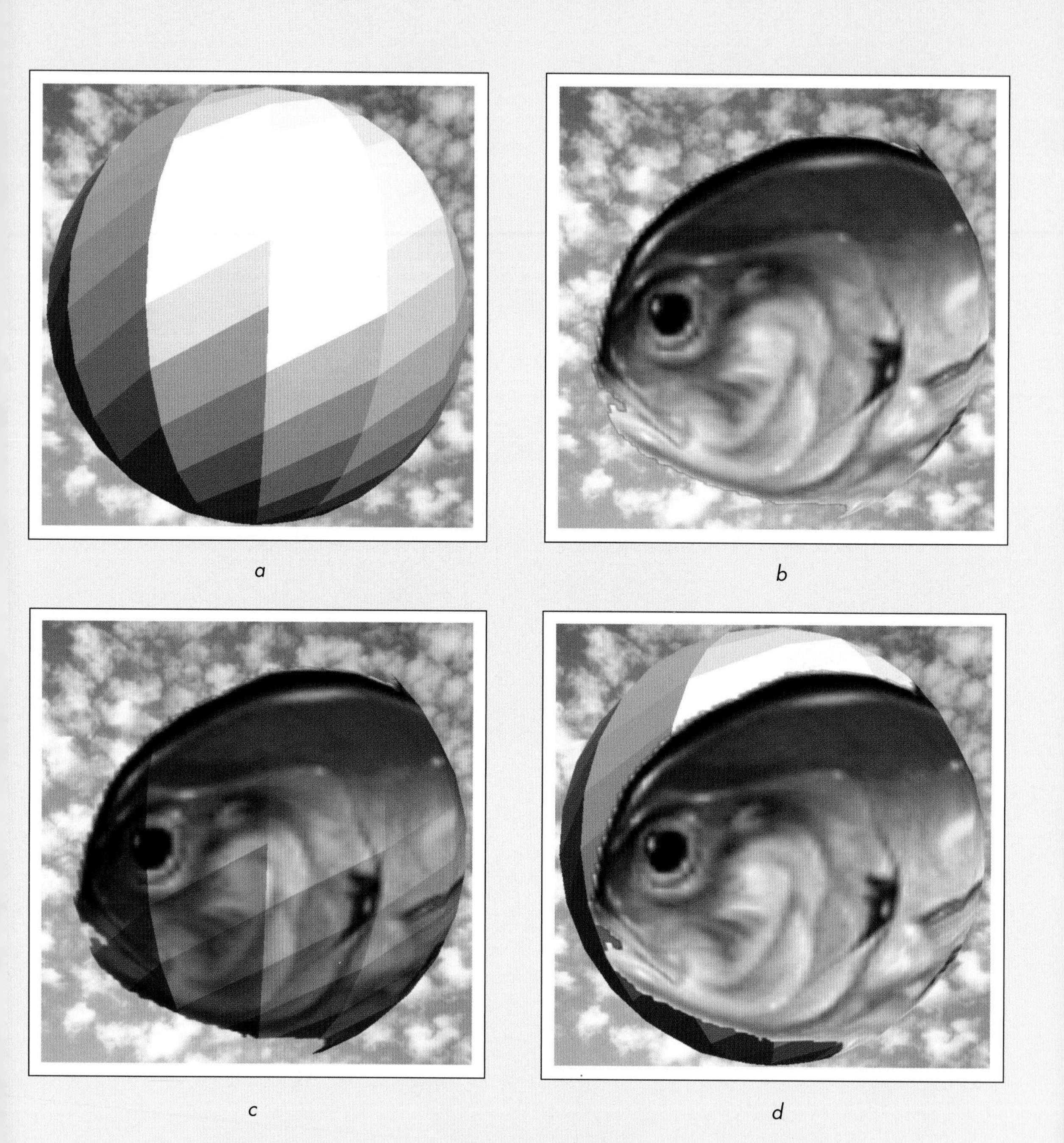

Plate 17

TextureAttributes Mode using a texture with a transparent background: (a) no texture, (b) REPLACE, (c) MODULATE, and (d) DECAL.

a

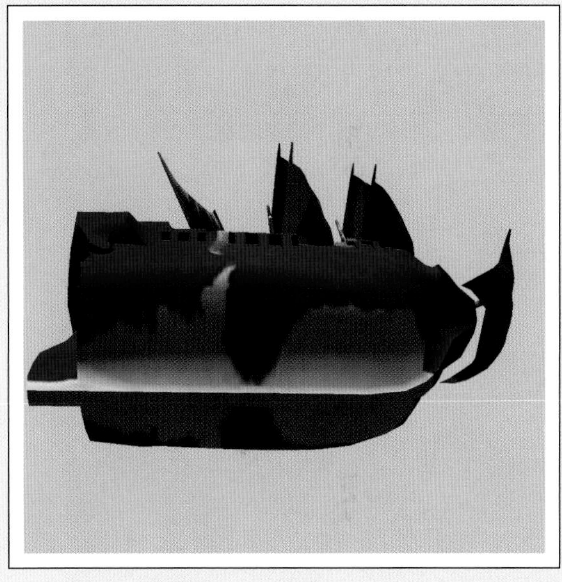

b

c

Plate 18

TexCoordGeneration: (a) OBJECT_LINEAR; (b) OBJECT_LINEAR, bottom view; and (c) SPHERE_MAP (notice the tail of the fish, "reflected" in the sails).

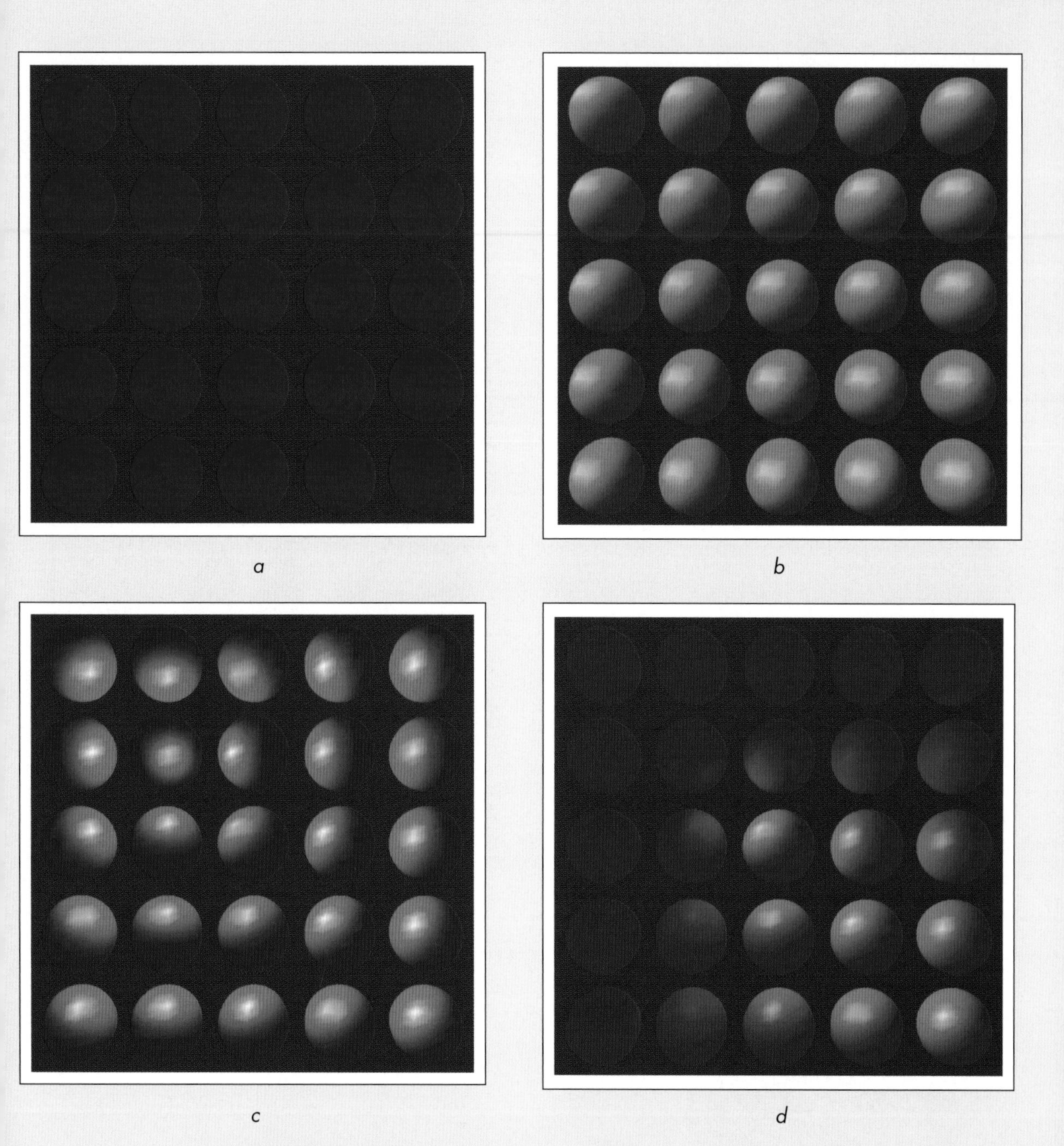

Plate 19
Light types: (a) ambient, (b) directional, (c) point, and (d) spot.

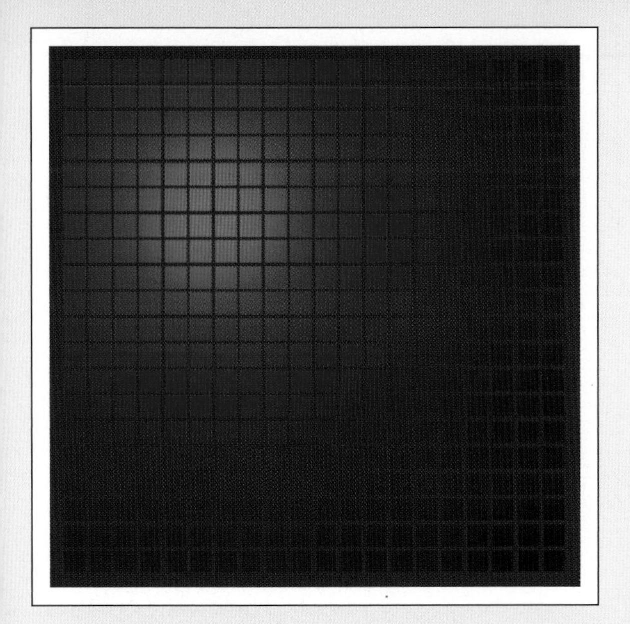

a

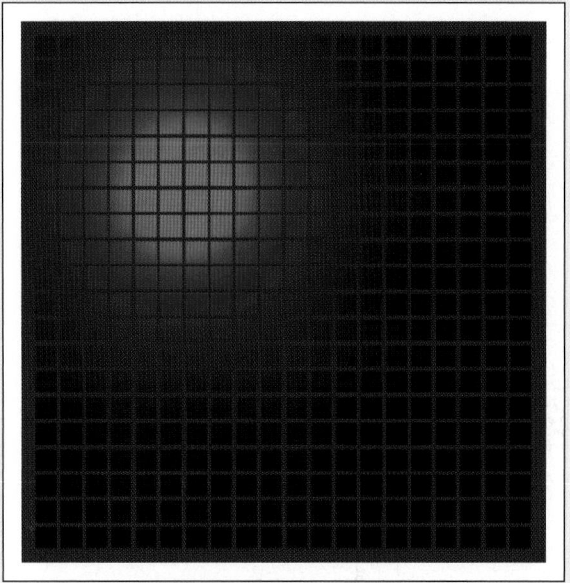

b

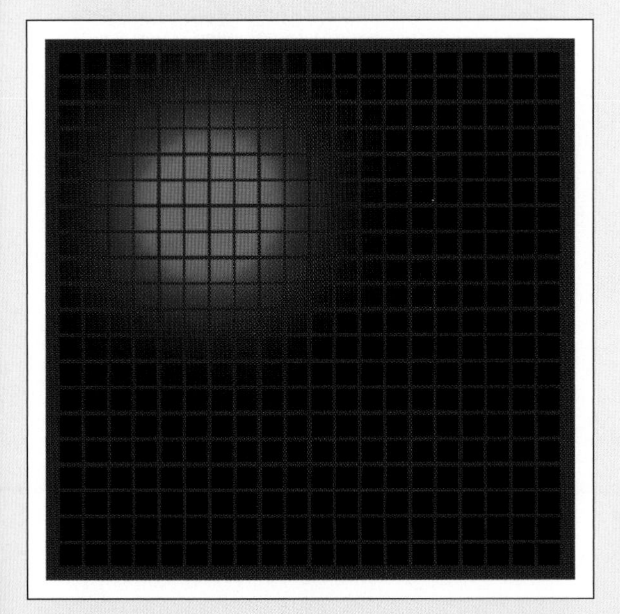

c

Plate 20

Point light attenuation: (a) constant (1, 0, 0) = 1 / 1 = 1.0, (b) linear (0, 1, 0) = 1/ d, and (c) quadratic (0, 0, 1) = 1 / d^2.

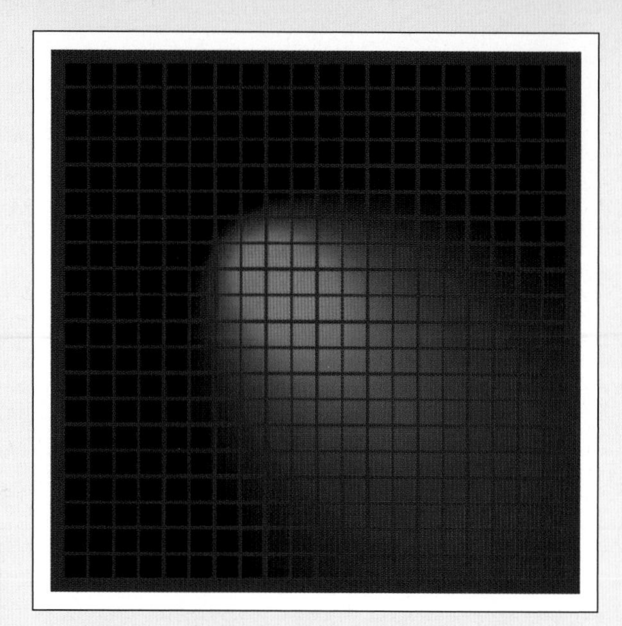

a

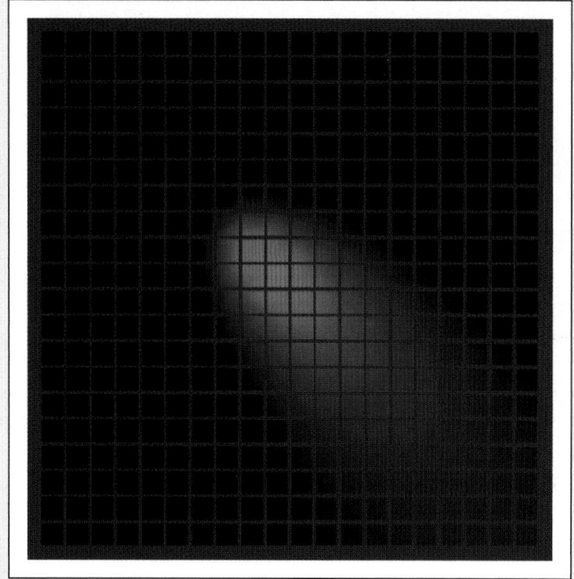

b

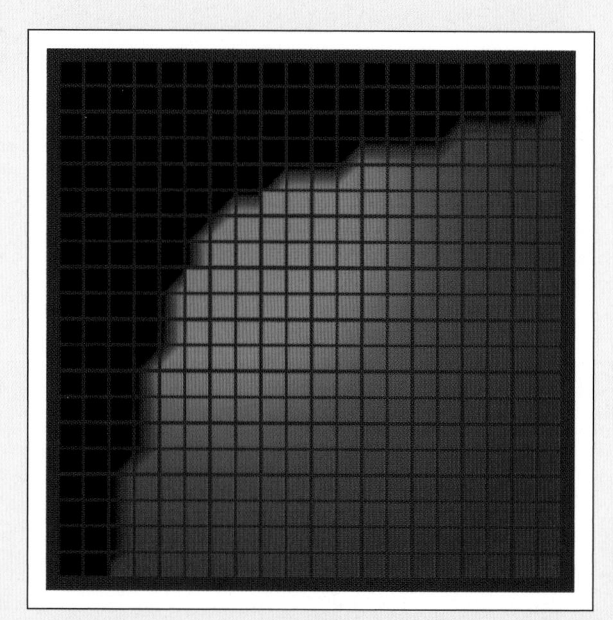

c

Plate 21
Spot light settings: spread angle 60 degrees (a) concentration 5, (b) concentration 15, and (c) concentration 0.

Line antialiasing controls whether the lines are drawn as smooth lines or with "jaggies." Figure 4–7 shows a close-up of aliased and antialiased lines.

FIGURE 4–7 Detail of (a) aliased and (b) antialiased lines.

By default, line primitives are one pixel thick, have a solid pattern (no dashes or dots), and do not utilize antialiasing. Note that antialiased lines are transparent: the smooth edges of the line are drawn by blending the color of the pixels along the edge of the line with the underlying image (see the note on transparent rendering later in this chapter).

Line width and antialiasing are not supported by DirectX.

PolygonAttributes

`PolygonAttributes` specify the attributes related to drawing polygon primitives. You can specify whether to render polygons as points, lines or polygons; whether to cull faces, specify the polygon offset, and whether to flip the normals of back-facing polygons.

The polygon mode tells what kind of primitive to use when rendering the polygon primitives:

```
POLYGON_POINT
POLYGON_LINE
POLYGON_FILL
```

`POLYGON_POINT` renders a point at each vertex of the polygon, `POLYGON_LINE` draws lines between the vertices of the polygon, and `POLYGON_FILL` (the default) renders the polygon as a filled primitive. Figure 4–8 shows a cube rendered using each of the polygon modes.

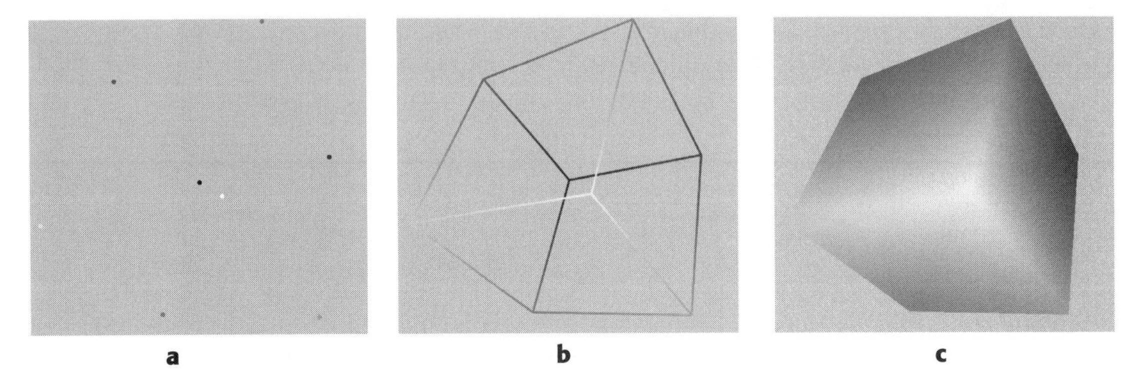

FIGURE 4–8 A polygon rendered in (a) POLYGON_POINT, (b) POLYGON_LINE, and (c) POLYGON_FILL modes.

The face-culling mode specifies if Java 3D should eliminate faces of the polygon based on whether they face toward or away from the viewer. `CULL_NONE` (the default) specifies that no faces should be culled. `CULL_BACK` removes faces that point away from the viewer. These faces are frequently hidden and can be removed without changing the picture. This can be useful to improve the performance or appearance of the scene; later we'll look at how this can be useful for transparency. `CULL_FRONT` removes the faces that point towards the viewer. This mode is included mainly for completeness: if you can remove back faces, why not front faces? This might be useful for a program that wants to show the interior of a box, for example. Figure 4–9 shows a wire-frame cube rendered with backface culling and frontface culling.

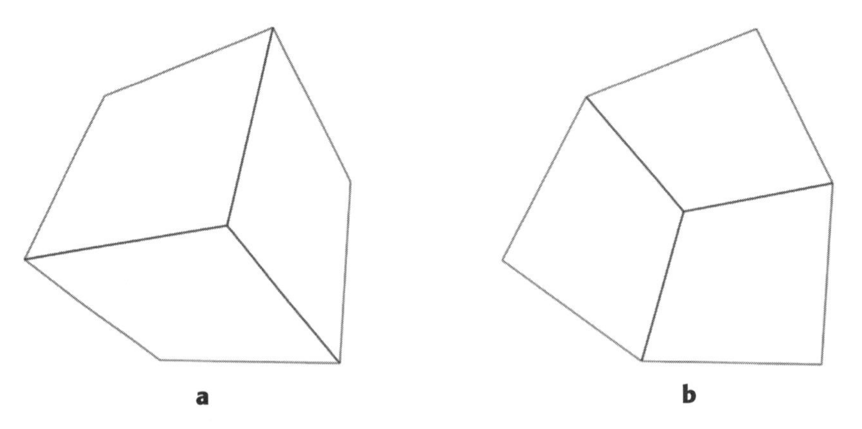

FIGURE 4–9 Wire-frame cube with (a) backface culling and (b) frontface culling.

Polygon offset is used to solve a specific problem: drawing lines on top of polygons. The typical usage of this is in drawing a "hidden line" display. This is a form of wire-frame display in which a solid object is drawn as lines so that the lines that are hidden by the foreground of the object are removed. The object is rendered using two shapes. The first draws the object in the background color without lighting or shading. The second draws the object using `POLYGON_LINE` mode (or using line primitives). The first shape hides the hidden lines using depth buffering, as seen in Figure 4–10.

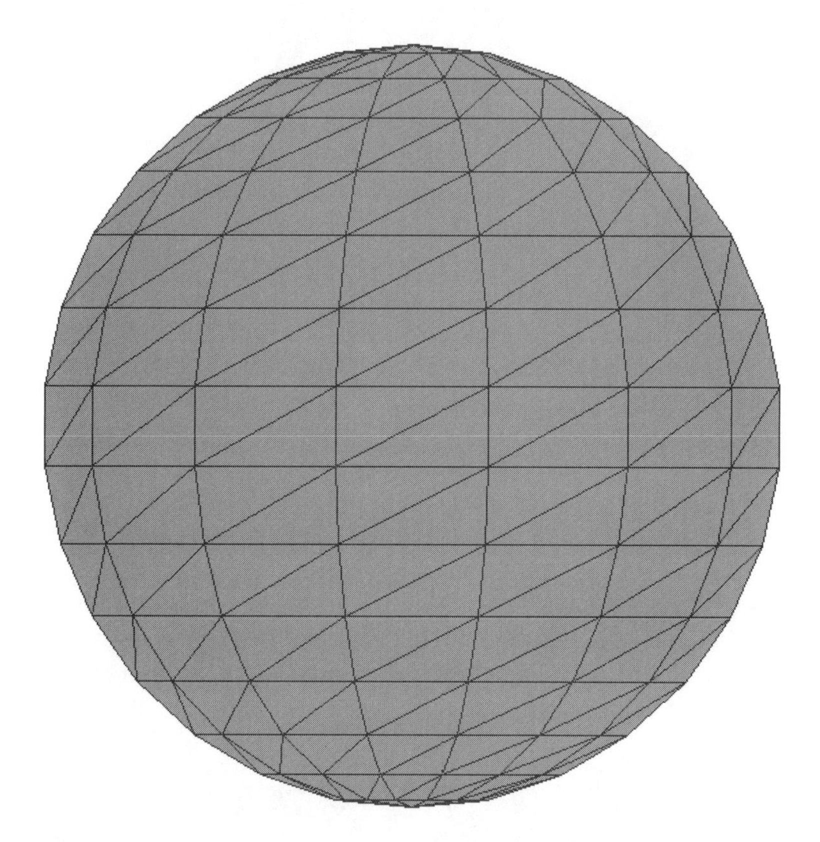

FIGURE 4–10 A "hidden line" display of a sphere.

Figure 4–11 shows an image from the Java 3D Explorer. Without using polygon offset, the lines and polygons interfere with each other in the depth buffer, leading to random gaps in the lines. Using polygon offset moves the lines closer to the viewer, eliminating the gaps. Figure 4–11 shows the same object without polygon offset.

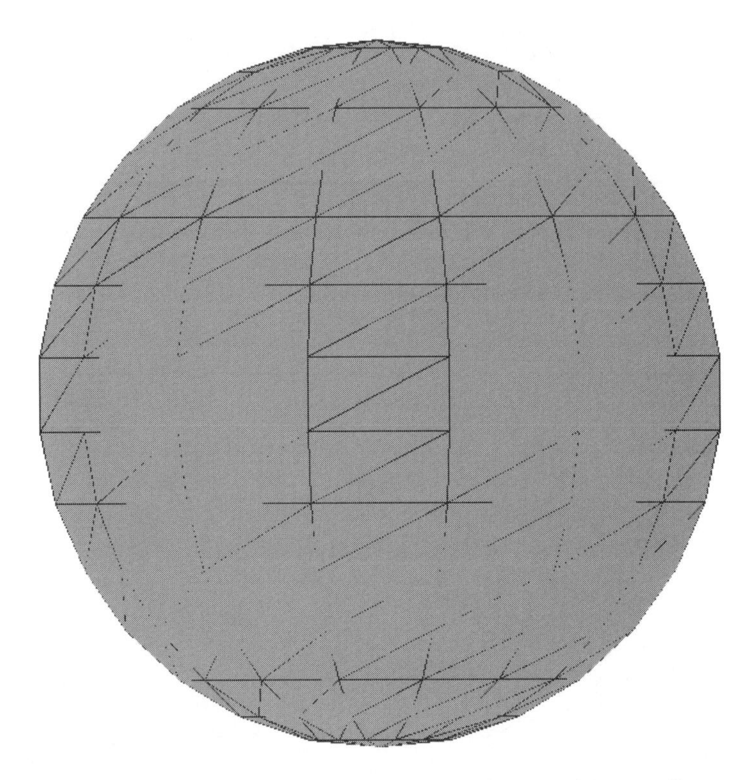

FIGURE 4–11 The hidden line sphere without polygon offset.

The offset is specified in two attributes, the bias, which is a static value applied to all of the polygons equally, and the factor, which is a dynamic value that applies more offset to the polygon faces which are turned more "on edge" to the viewer. You can use both factors for the best overall effect. Note, however, that using too much offsetting can result in edges that incorrectly "poke through" the solid polygons.

OpenGL supports both the bias and factor attributes, using positive or negative values for each. DirectX has a limitation that only allows negative bias values (internally, Java 3D combines the bias and offset on DirectX so you can still use both terms). If you want to deploy on both APIs, use negative offset values on the wire-frame shape. If you will be deploying only on OpenGL, you can use a positive offset on the solid shapes.

The backface normal flip attribute is used when you want to view the back of a surface with lighting. Normally, the back of a surface will be rendered without diffuse or specular lighting. If the backface normal flip is enabled, then normals for the backfacing polygons of the surface will be flipped or "negated," so that the back of the surface will be lit with diffuse and specular lighting.

Backface normal flip is not currently supported by Java 3D on DirectX.

RenderingAttributes

`RenderingAttributes` specify the attributes that apply to all shapes. These include several low-level controls for advanced applications. The attributes controlled by **`RenderingAttributes`** are:

- **alpha testing:** This is an advanced mechanism used to control rendering on a per-pixel basis. It uses the alpha value specified in RGBA colors and an alpha value and comparison function specified in the appearance to control whether each pixel gets drawn.
- **raster operation:** This controls the per-pixel rendering operation. It can be used by advanced applications to do XOR rendering, typically for rubber-banding user interfaces in immediate mode.
- **ignore vertex colors:** This allows an appearance to override the vertex colors specified with the geometry for a shape. This can be useful when the program wants to highlight the geometry by changing its color.
- **visibility flag:** This can be used to turn off the rendering of a shape without disabling the shape's pickability or collidability.
- **depth buffer control:** This allows depth buffering to be turned off for the shape.

TransparencyAttributes

`TransparencyAttributes` specify the attributes that control how transparent and antialiased shapes are rendered. The attributes are:

- **transparency value**, which is a floating-point number used to specify the overall transparency or opacity of a shape. Transparency values can range from `0.0f` to `1.0f`, where `0.0f` represents full opacity (solid; not transparent at all) and 1.0f represents complete transparency (an invisible shape).
- **transparency mode**, which is an integer value that specifies the rasterization technique to be used (if any) when rendering the transparency of a shape. Values are `NONE`, `BLENDED`, `FASTEST`, `NICEST`, or `SCREEN_DOOR`.

- **blend function,** which is used to specify the blending equations for transparent and antialiased primitives. This is an advanced attribute used to control how the color of the shape being rendered is combined with the background pixels.

The following snippet of code illustrates how to use the **TransparencyAttributes** `setTransparency()` and `setTransparencyMode()` mutator methods to specify the transparency value and transparency mode.

```
// Set up the transparency properties
TransparencyAttributes transpAttr = new TransparencyAttributes();
transpAttr.setTransparencyMode(TransparencyAttributes.BLENDED);
transpAttr.setTransparency(0.5f);
appearance.setTransparencyAttributes(transpAttr);
```

Figure 4–12 shows a sphere rendered using blended transparency with a value of 0.5.

FIGURE 4–12 A sphere with blended transparency.

As you can see from Figure 4–12, blended transparency mixes the color of the transparent shape with the color of the background pixels. Screen door transparency renders patterns of pixels with the color of the transparent shape, leaving holes where the background pixels show through. Blended transparency generally looks better, but sometimes screen door transparency is faster. Figure 4–13 shows the difference between the modes. The sphere on the left was rendered using `Transparency.BLENDED;` the sphere on the right was rendered using `Transparency.SCREEN_DOOR`.

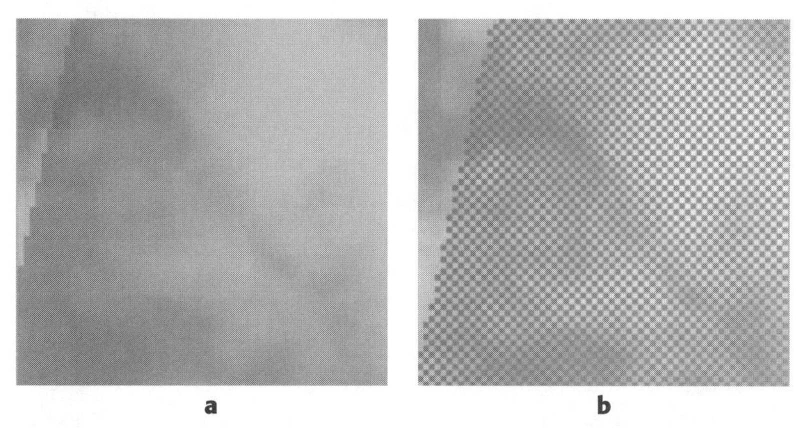

FIGURE 4–13 Closeup of a sphere with (a) blended and (b) screen door transparency.

The transparency mode `NICEST` is the same as `BLENDED`, and `FASTEST` corresponds to either `BLENDED` or `SCREEN_DOOR`, depending on the implementation.

Transparent Rendering

This is an advanced topic, but it can be an important factor to consider even as you get your feet wet with Java 3D because shapes drawn using blended transparency may have rendering problems or "artifacts" if they are drawn on top of other shapes.

To understand the problem, you first need to understand how depth buffering works for non-blended shapes. The window on the screen, called the "display," is a rectangular array of pixels, each of which maintains a color for its precise on-screen location. Similarly, the depth buffer is an array that holds (you guessed it!) the depth of the shape for each pixel in the display. At the beginning of rendering, the display is cleared to the background color (meaning the display area is painted with the current background color) and the depth buffer is cleared to the "back" depth. Each shape to be rendered is converted to pixels with depth values. For each pixel, the depth value is compared with the depth value currently stored in the depth buffer. If the pixel is in front of the existing value, the pixel replaces the current color for that pixel in the display and the depth value is written to the depth buffer. Using this algorithm ensures that only the pixels that are in front of the other pixels appear in the final image.

Transparent objects are difficult to depth buffer because they don't replace the pixel color when they are rendered. Instead, the pixel color is a blend of the transparent shape's color and the existing pixel color. In this case, the value stored in the depth buffer is a problem. If the transparent shape writes its depth value to the depth buffer, then a shape that is behind the transparent shape that is rendered after the transparent shape might not appear even though it should be visible "through" the transparent shape.

Java 3D solves this tricky transparency problem by rendering the scene in two passes. In the first pass, the opaque shapes are drawn with the depth buffer enabled for both testing and writing. In the second pass, the transparent shapes are drawn using the depth buffer test, but without writing to the depth buffer. This ensures that the opaque shapes that are visible through the transparent shapes are depth buffered correctly. Antialiased points and lines are drawn using the same mechanism; opaque shapes in the scene can obscure them, but they can't obscure other shapes in the scene through depth buffering.

However, there is another transparency-related problem that the Java 3D renderer must contend with. Since the transparent objects aren't written to the depth buffer, there can be rendering artifacts where there are several layers of transparent objects. This happens because the blending function that produces the best-looking transparent objects is dependent on the rendering order. Figure 4–14 shows how this can affect the final rendering of a scene.

FIGURE 4–14 A transparent sphere with blending artifacts.

The artifacts show up in Figure 4–14 because parts of the sphere's backside are drawn *after* parts of the sphere's front. Java 3D is expected to address this problem in release 1.3 by adding a mechanism to sort the transparent shapes and draw them from back to front.

In the meantime, there are several possible solutions for this problem. You can avoid these artifacts making sure that only one layer of transparent objects is drawn. For the sphere, turn on backface culling in the polygon attributes to remove the hidden faces. This is how the blended sphere in Figure 4–12 was drawn. You can also figure out the correct rendering order for the transparent objects and use an **OrderedGroup** to force the ordering. Finally, you can change the blend function to remove the order dependency.

Material

The **Material** appearance component specifies the color of shapes when lights are shining on them. Lighting is enabled if the geometry for the shape has normals, the **Appearance** has a **Material,** and the **Material** enables lighting. If any of these factors is not true, then lighting is disabled and the color is determined without lighting. If lighting is enabled, the colors specified by the **Material** are combined with the colors of the lights to produce the color of the shape. If this sounds confusing, don't panic: Lights are covered in detail in Chapter 5, "Environment Nodes." For now, we'll focus on the general capabilities of the **Material** node.

The **Material** node component encapsulates a variety of color settings. Specifically, this node gives us control over whether lighting is enabled; the ambient, emissive, diffuse and specular colors; and the shininess of the surface. In this section we'll look at each of these attributes in detail.

The **Material** node can be used to disable lighting using the following method:

```
void setLightingEnable(boolean);
```

If lighting is disabled it is as if the **Material** object was not associated with **Appearance**. The shape's color comes from its geometry or a **ColoringAttributes** appearance component. If no color is specified, the color comes from the default **ColoringAttributes** and the shape is rendered in white.

Now let's look at the material colors. The color produced by lighting is a combination of the color of the object and the color of the light. For example, a red light on a white surface produces a red highlight. The components of **Material** control the color contributed by the shape to the different kinds of lighting: ambient, diffuse, and specular.

Ambient Color

Ambient color settings specify the color of the object when it is illuminated by ambient light. The ambient light in a scene comes from **`AmbientLight`** sources, and is a rough approximation of how light is reflected off objects in the real world to "fill" the space. Ambient lights illuminate the shapes in the scene with light of constant intensity in all directions. Figure 4–15 shows a sphere with a white ambient color (`1.0, 0.0, 0.0`) lit by dark gray ambient light (`0.2, 0.2, 0.2`).

FIGURE 4–15 A sphere showing ambient lighting.

Many of the figures in this chapter are also reproduced in the color plates at the center of this book.

The use of ambient color and light in this example results in a sphere that has a constant dark red color (`0.2, 0.0, 0.0`). Ambient lights are often used to eliminate the "harshness" of lighting effects to simulate the way that light fills a room in the real world. The default ambient color is (`0.2f, 0.2f, 0.2f`).

Emissive Color

Emissive color is the color of the object independent of any light sources. It produces glowing colors that seem to emanate from within the shape itself. Whereas a diffuse color might be used to color a light bulb that has not been lit up, an emissive color can be used to render a light that is turned on; light appears to be emitted from within the bulb, making it glow. Figure 4–16 shows a sphere with a gray emissive color (`0.5, 0.5, 0.5`).

FIGURE 4–16 A sphere showing emissive color.

The result is that the sphere has a constant gray color (`0.5, 0.5, 0.5`). This is similar to the ambient coloring; the difference is that the emissive coloring is independent of any lights, while the ambient coloring is a combination of the ambient color and the ambient light color.

Although emissive colors seem to create shapes that emit lights, they do not actually illuminate objects around them (objects with emissive colors don't act as light sources). Since emissive coloring produces a constant color, a light source (such as a light bulb) usually has an emissive color in addition to other coloring. The default emissive color is (`0.0, 0.0, 0.0`).

Emissive colors only *appear* to cast light; they don't actually act as a light source. In other words, shapes created using emissive colors do not illuminate objects around them.

Diffuse Color

Diffuse color creates what we usually think of as the "true" color of an object. It is the color of the object when lit, excluding any light being reflected by the shininess of the object. Figure 4–17 shows a sphere with a red diffuse color (`1.0, 0.0, 0.0`) being lit by a white light (`1.0, 1.0, 1.0`).

FIGURE 4–17 A sphere showing diffuse lighting.

The diffuse color is the color produced by *diffuse reflection*, which is a term used to describe the light that bounces off objects in random directions. The intensity of diffuse lighting depends on the angle the light rays make with the surface of the object. If the light hits the surface of an object directly, it creates light at maximum intensity; the light intensity decreases as the angle increases. If the surface faces away from the light, then the light does not add any illumination to the surface.

In Figure 4–17 the brightest spot on the sphere faces directly toward the light. As a result, its color is pure red (`1.0, 0.0, 0.0`). The parts of the sphere that point away from the light have less intensity, while the part of the sphere in the lower right receives no light whatsoever and is consequently rendered in black (`0.0, 0.0, 0.0`). The default diffuse color is `white (1.0f, 1.0f, 1.0f)`.

Diffuse colors can be combined with other `Material` node properties to create shiny, glossy colors.

Specular Color

Specular color describes the color of a shape where it reflects light from shiny areas. Figure 4–18 shows a sphere with white specular color (`1.0, 1.0, 1.0`) being lit by a white light (`1.0, 1.0, 1.0`).

FIGURE 4–18 A sphere showing specular lighting.

The specular color comes from *specular reflection*, which is an approximation of the way a light bounces off a shiny object. Specular color is combined with shininess settings (see Shininess below) to create shiny highlights on the surface of shapes. The color of the highlight is a combination of the specular color and the light color. The maximum intensity is along the reflection of the light off the surface toward the viewer (the white part of the highlight in the figure). The intensity decreases as the reflection is directed away from the viewer (the darker parts of the highlight). The default specular color is white (`1.0f, 1.0f, 1.0f`).

Shininess

Shininess controls the size of reflective highlights created using specular colors. Shininess is a floating-point number in the range [`1.0, 128.0`], where `1.0` creates a surface that is not at all shiny and `128.0` creates an extremely shiny surface (values outside this range are clamped). The default shininess value is `64`. The sphere seen previously in Figure 4–18 has a shininess of `32`, while Figure 4–19 shows a sphere with shininess of `64`.

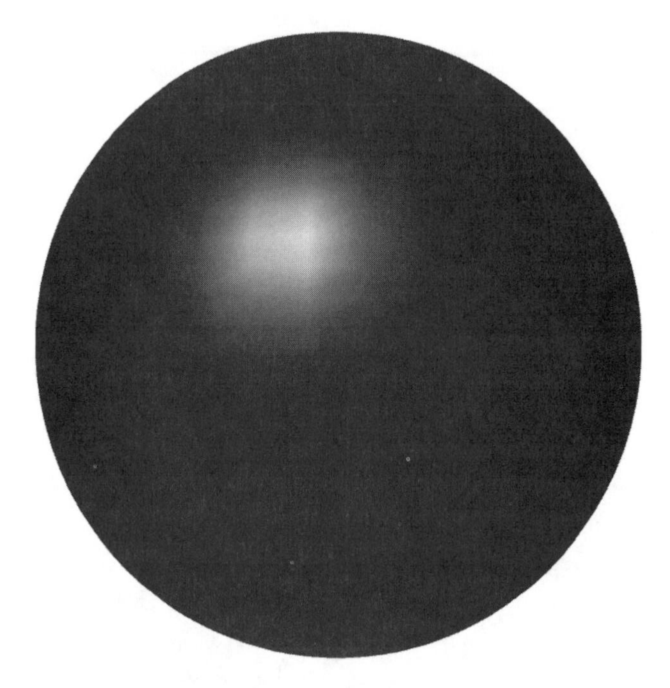

FIGURE 4–19 A sphere showing specular lighting with a shininess of 64.

Combining Colors to Create Realistic Surfaces

Colors can combine to produce realistic surfaces. Figure 4–20 shows our lovely sphere with red ambient, black emissive, red diffuse, and white specular coloring, being lit by a dark gray ambient light (`0.2, 0.2, 0.2`) and a white light from the upper left. The diffuse color provides the basic coloring, the ambient color fills in the unlit areas, and the specular color produces the shiny highlight.

The ambient and diffuse colors are usually set to the same value. If the geometry has vertex colors, they override the diffuse colors from the **`Material`**. In Java 3D 1.3 you will be able to specify which components get overridden by the colors in the geometry.

FIGURE 4–20 A sphere showing a combination of ambient, diffuse, and specular lighting.

Combinations of the material colors give the appearance of different surface types (see Table 4–1). The color plates show an object illuminated with these different materials.

TABLE 4–1 Material Colors

Surface	Diffuse Color	Specular Color	Shininess
Aluminum	.37 .37 .37	.89 .89 .89	17
Blue Plastic	.20 .20 .70	.85 .85 .85	22
Copper	.30 .10 0	.75 .30 0	10
Gold	.49 .34 0	.89 .79 0	17
Red Alloy	.34 0 .34	.84 0 0	15
Black Onyx	0 0 0	.72 .72 .72	23

Texture Mapping

Texture mapping changes the appearance of a shape by wrapping its surface with an image. The image, or *texture*, adds color detail, such as the ribbing of corduroy fabric or the rough bark of a tree trunk. For example, a surface textured with a wood grain image will look much more like a piece of wood than using a solid brown color. Textures are applied, or *mapped*, to the surface using data that relates each vertex of the geometry to a location in the texture. The locations in the texture are specified using *texture coordinates*. The texture is a rectangular array of color values called *texels*.

Texture Coordinates

Just as geometric coordinates are specified using `x`, `y` and `z` values, positions in a texture are specified using texture coordinates, which have `s` and `t` values. The `s` coordinate corresponds with the horizontal axis of the texture and the `t` coordinate corresponds with the vertical axis of the texture. The lower left hand corner of the texture is at `0,0` and the upper right corner of the image is at `1,1` (see Figure 4–21).

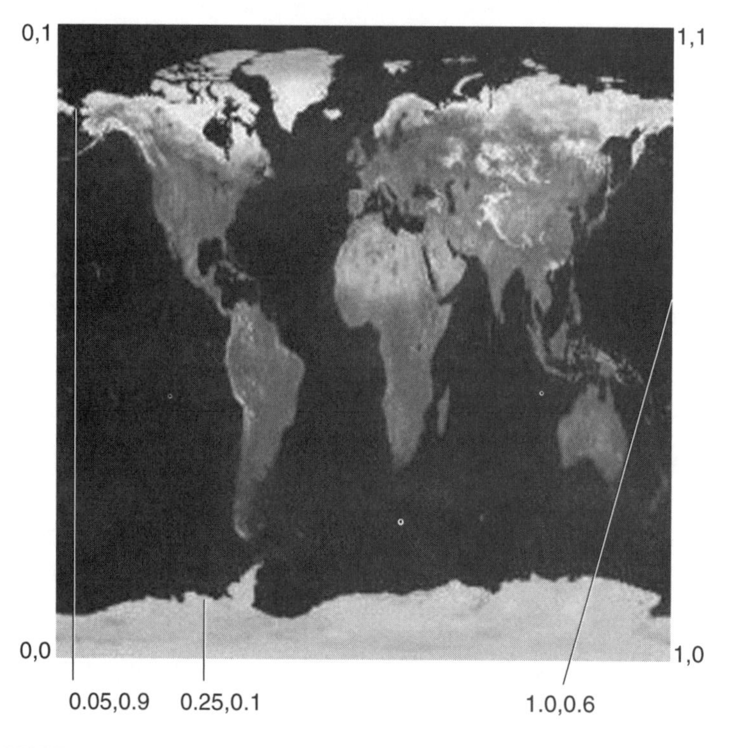

FIGURE 4–21 Texture coordinates.

Note that if the image is non-square the texture coordinates still have the same range. For example, if the texture is a 32x64 pixel image, the top of the image will be at `t = 1.0`, not `t = 0.5`.

Texture mapping stretches the texture to make the texture locations specified by the texture coordinates line up with the geometry. Figure 4–22 shows several triangles with different geometry that use the texture coordinates indicated in the figure above. Notice how the texture is stretched to fit the geometry.

FIGURE 4–22 Triangles with the same texture coordinates and different shapes.

Texture mapping is controlled by several components. The **`Texture`** appearance component controls the texture image. The **`TextureAttributes`** appearance component controls how the texture gets applied to the surface. The texture coordinates are specified by the **`Geometry`**; if the geometry does not have texture coordinates, a **`TexCoordGeneration`** appearance component can be used to generate texture coordinates from the geometric coordinates. In the following sections we'll look at each of these aspects of texturing.

Texture

The base class for textures is **Texture**; its subclasses are **Texture2D** and **Texture3D**. **Texture2D** specifies a 2D image, such as the example above. **Texture3D** specifies 3D or *volumetric* texture, which is an advanced form of texture mapping used for special cases like visualizing scientific data. In this book we'll work with 2D textures. When looking for the javadoc for **Texture2D** methods, look at the **Texture** class, since all the **Texture2D** methods except for the constructors are defined in the **Texture** class. The attributes of a **Texture2D** are the image itself and options that specify how the texture looks under different viewing modes. We'll look at setting up the image first, and then explore the other options.

Texture2D Images

The simplest way to create a **Texture2D** object is by using the **TextureLoader** utility class. The **TextureLoader** creates the **Texture2D** and sets up several basic properties. The input to the **TextureLoader** is typically a URL that refers to an image file:

```
TextureLoader(java.net.URL url, java.awt.Component observer);
TextureLoader(java.net.URL url, int flags,
                     java.awt.Component observer);
TextureLoader(java.net.URL url, java.lang.String format,
                     java.awt.Component observer);
TextureLoader(java.net.URL url, java.lang.String format,
                     int flags, java.awt.Component observer);
```

There are many variations on the constructor. For each of the URL constructors, there are corresponding constructors that take other references to images: a `String` containing a filename, or an image specified as a `java.awt.Image` or a `java.awt.image.BufferedImage`. See the javadoc for **TextureLoader** for details.

The first parameter to the constructor is a reference to an image. For the cases where the image is a file, the **TextureLoader** supports many types of images. Using the standard JDK, the GIF and JPEG file formats are supported. If you install the optional Java Advanced Imaging (JAI) package, then JAI will be used to load the image; the loader will also support BMP, FlashPix, PNG, PNM, and TIFF format files. Consult the JAI home page, java.sun.com/products/java-media/jai/, for more information on installing JAI.

The `flags` parameter is used for specifying options to the loader. The options that can be specified with the flags are integers that can be OR'd together:

```
GENERATE_MIPMAP
BY_REFERENCE
Y_UP
```

The GENERATE_MIPMAP flag tells the **TextureLoader** to create the texture with multiple levels of resolution called *mipmaps* that are used when the texture is viewed at a variety of scales. Mipmapping will be discussed in the **Texture2D** methods below. The BY_REFERENCE and Y_UP flags are advanced options that are used with a **BufferedImage** to allow the memory for the texture to be shared between the program and Java 3D. The default flags are 0, which specifies that a simple texture be created.

The format parameter is an advanced option that lets you specify the internal format of the image. The default format is RGBA, which represents your image using red, green, blue, and alpha components for each texel. Other formats let you load data with only parts of the RGBA data, such as ALPHA, which loads an image of transparency values.

The observer parameter is included in constructors where the image is not yet loaded into a **BufferedImage**. The *image observer* is a component that is used by the **ImageLoader** to monitor the progress of the image being loaded. You can specify any AWT component (if you are making an applet, a common choice is the applet itself, i.e., "this") use or null. Other than telling the **ImageLoader** what component to use for the observer, there is not much use for this parameter.

Once the **TextureLoader** has been created, a **Texture** or other data can be inquired from it. The methods that extract data out of a **TextureLoader** are:

```
Texture getTexture();
ImageComponent2D getImage();
ImageComponent2D getScaledImage(float xScale, float yScale);
ImageComponent2D getScaledImage(int width, int height);
```

The getTexture() method returns a **Texture** containing the image. For example, the code to create a **Texture2D** for the earth texture shown above is:

```
java.net.URL earthURL; // URL points to image file
TextureLoader texLoader = new TextureLoader(earthURL, null);
Texture2D texture = (Texture2D) texLoader.getTexture();
```

The other methods extract an **ImageComponent2D** from the **TextureLoader**. **ImageComponent2D** is used to represent images in Java 3D and is used for textures, background images (discussed in Chapter 5), and **Raster** primitives. The method getImage() returns the image in its original size. The getScaledImage() methods return images scaled by the specified scale factors, or scaled to the specified width and height.

The texture image can also be created without using the **TextureLoader**. This is an advanced usage, but the steps required are the same as what the **Texture-**

Loader does when `getTexture()` is called. The image is loaded into `java.awt.image.BufferedImage` (or the more general `java.awt.image.RenderedImage`). If the width or height of the image is not a power of two (i.e., 32, 64, 128, etc.), then the image is scaled to make its dimensions powers of two. The image is then loaded into an **ImageComponent2D** that is used to create the **Texture2D**. See the javadoc for **BufferedImage**, **ImageComponent2D,** and **Texture2D** for details.

Texture2D Methods

The texture image is the most important part of the texture. The other **Texture2D** attributes specify how the image appears when it is viewed. The texture can be enabled and disabled, the texture boundary mode specifies how the texture appears for texture coordinates outside the 0 to 1 range, and the texture filtering modes specify how the texture is drawn when it is larger or smaller than its original size.

Texture mapping is enabled in a way similar to lighting. Texture mapping is enabled if all three of the following are true: the shape has texture coordinates, either directly from the geometry or from a **TexCoordGeneration** component of the appearance; the appearance has a **Texture** associated with it; and the **Texture** is enabled. The **Texture** can be enabled and disabled using the method:

```
void setEnable(boolean state);
```

The `setEnable()` method has a "write" capability bit and can be called on a live scene graph if the capability bit is set. All the other **Texture** methods can only be called if the **Texture** is not yet live. You can change the other attributes on a live scene graph by making a new **Texture** and replacing the **Texture** associated with the **Appearance**.

The texture image specifies the texture for texture coordinates in the 0 to 1 range. If the coordinates are outside that range, the texture is specified by the boundary mode. The boundary modes are:

```
WRAP
CLAMP
```

The WRAP boundary mode repeats the texture for values outside the 0 to 1 range. The CLAMP boundary mode extends the color at the boundary of the texture for values outside the 0 to 1 range. Figure 4–23 shows a square with texture coordinates that range from –1 to 2 for both `s` and `t`. The `s` (horizontal) boundary mode is set to CLAMP while the `t` (vertical) boundary mode is set to WRAP.

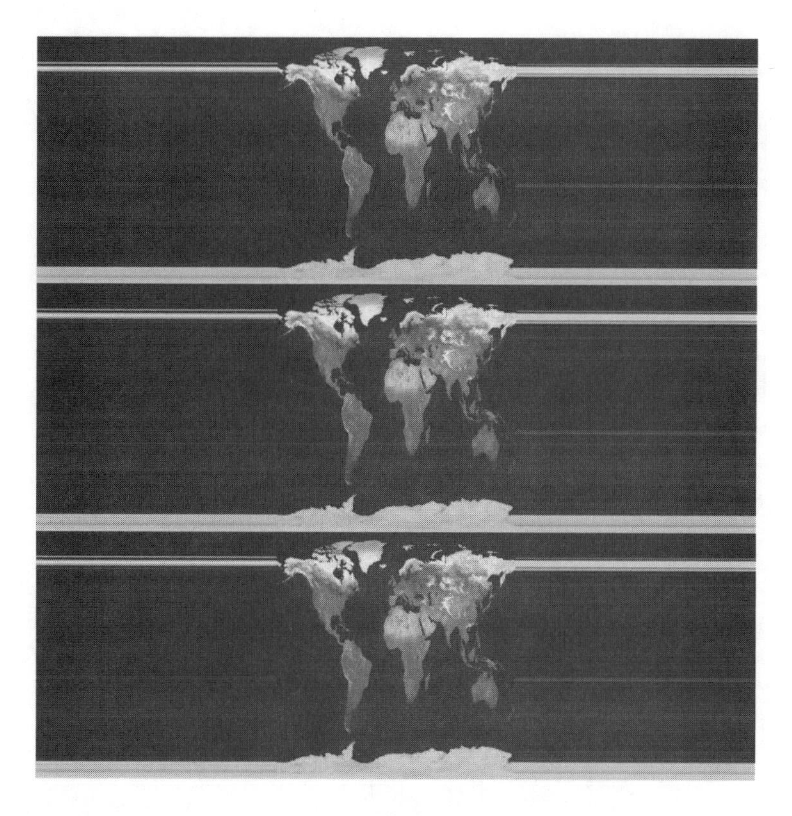

FIGURE 4–23 Texture boundary mode.

The methods to set the boundary mode are:

```
void setBoundaryModeS(int mode);
void setBoundaryModeT(int mode);
```

The texture filtering modes specify how the texture is made larger or smaller for viewing. When a texture is applied to a surface, the texels of the texture rarely correspond to the pixels of the shape. Instead, a single pixel of the shape can correspond to anything from a small portion of a texel, *magnification*, to an area of the texture, *minification* (see Figure 4–24).

The texture-filtering modes specify the quality of the process used to magnify or minify the texture. Lower-quality filter modes render the texture more "blocky" or "grainy." Higher-quality filtering modes render the texture smoothly.

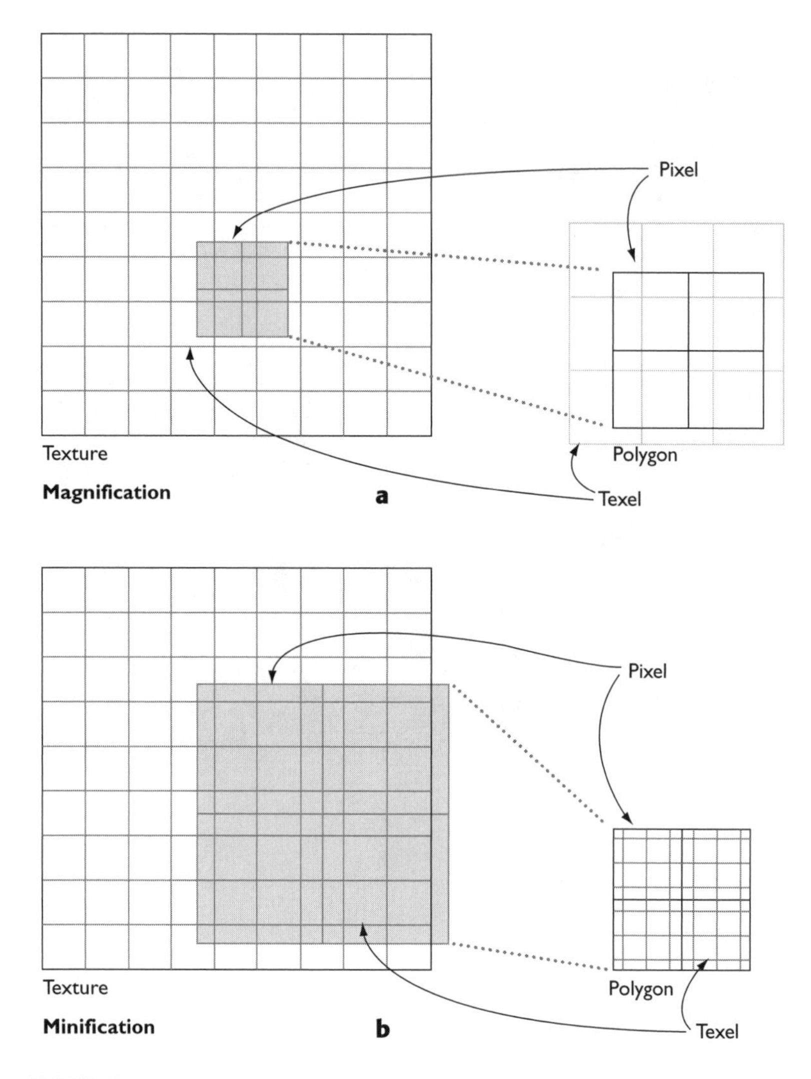

FIGURE 4–24 Texture magnification (a) and (b) minification.

Magnification is the simpler case. The method to set the magnification filter is:

```
void setMagFilter(int filter);
```

The filter values are:

```
BASE_LEVEL_POINT
BASE_LEVEL_LINEAR
FASTEST
NICEST
```

The BASE_LEVEL_POINT filter selects color for the pixel using the texel closest to the texture coordinate, while BASE_LEVEL_LINEAR selects the color for the pixel using a weighted average of the 2x2 array of texels around the texture coordinate. Figure 4–25 shows the difference between these modes:

a

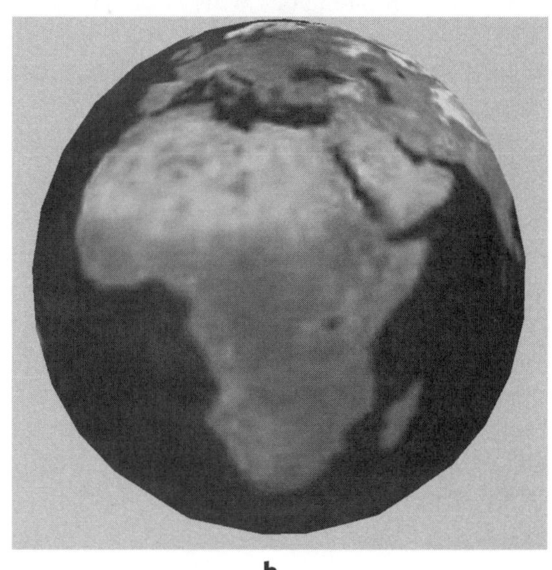

b

FIGURE 4–25 Textured sphere rendered with (a) BASE_LEVEL_POINT and (b) BASE_LEVEL_LINEAR.

BASE_LEVEL_POINT magnifies the texture by replicating the texels, which gives a "blocky" appearance. BASE_LEVEL_LINEAR magnifies the texture by finding color values that transition from each texel to the next, giving a "smooth" appearance. The FASTEST and NICEST modes have their usual meanings, with FASTEST corresponding to BASE_LEVEL_POINT and NICEST corresponding to BASE_LEVEL_LINEAR.

Minification is a bit more complex. The method to set the minification filter is:

```
void setMinFilter(int filter);
```

The filter values are:

```
BASE_LEVEL_POINT
BASE_LEVEL_LINEAR
MULTI_LEVEL_POINT
MULTI_LEVEL_LINEAR
NICEST
FASTEST
```

The minification filter is used when pixels of the rendered texture are smaller than the texels. Using BASE_LEVEL_POINT, the closest texel to the pixel is rendered. The problem with this mode is that, as the shape with the texture is slowly moved, the texture-mapped pixels "shimmer" as the nearest texel changes. Using BASE_LEVEL_LINEAR, the problem goes away because the four texels nearest to the texture coordinate are combined to produce the pixel, smoothing out the shimmering. However, when the texture is rendered even smaller, the flickering returns when the texture gets small enough that each pixel maps to blocks of four texels, so that the filter can't smoothly move from each texel to the next. At that point BASE_LEVEL_LINEAR looks about the same as BASE_LEVEL_POINT.

The solution is to extend the minification filtering using a technique called *mipmapping*. In mipmapping, lower resolution versions of the texture map are computed to use when the texture is rendered to a smaller area. The **TextureLoader** can automatically calculate the extra textures using a flag in the constructor. For example, to generate mipmaps for the earth texture above, create the texture using the GENERATE_MIPMAP flag:

```
TextureLoader texLoader = new TextureLoader(earthURL,
      TextureLoader.GENERATE_MIPMAP, null);
Texture2D texture = (Texture2D) texLoader.getTexture();
```

The MULTI_LEVEL_POINT mode selects the correct resolution for the texture map and then does filtering using the BASE_LEVEL_POINT filter. Using the

MULTI_LEVEL_LINEAR mode, the color for the pixel comes from eight texels: the four closest texels on each of the closest texture maps. Using MULTI_LEVEL_LINEAR ensures that the texture won't shimmer as the texture moves from full resolution down to a single pixel and back.

Again, NICEST and FASTEST let you make a speed versus quality tradeoff. NICEST corresponds to MULTI_LEVEL_LINEAR and FASTEST corresponds to BASE_LEVEL_POINT.

TextureAttributes

The **TextureAttributes** appearance component controls how the texture gets applied to the surface. The attributes in **TextureAttributes** are the texture mode, which controls how the texture's colors are combined with the surface colors; the texture map transform, which allows the texture coordinates to be modified before the texture mapping is applied; and the perspective correction mode, which is used to specify the quality versus speed tradeoff when texture mapping.

Texture Mode

The most often used attribute is the texture mode. This controls how the colors in the texture are combined with the color of the non-textured surface. The method to set the texture mode is:

```
void setTextureMode(int mode);
```

The values for the mode are integer fields:

```
REPLACE
MODULATE
DECAL
BLEND
```

In order to show the different texture-mapping modes, we'll apply textures to a shaded sphere. The untextured version of the sphere is show in Figure 4–26.

The REPLACE texture mode pastes the texture directly onto the object, overriding the shape's underlying color. The default texture mode is REPLACE. This mode is useful when the texture completely specifies the object's coloring. Note that lighting is not applied to the texture colors. Figure 4–27 shows the sphere texture mapped in REPLACE mode.

The MODULATE texture mode mixes the texture's colors with the coloring of the underlying surface. This mode makes it possible to use lighting with texture mapping. Figure 4–28 shows the sphere texture mapped in modulate mode.

FIGURE 4–26 A shaded sphere with no texturing.

FIGURE 4–27 The sphere with REPLACE mode texturing.

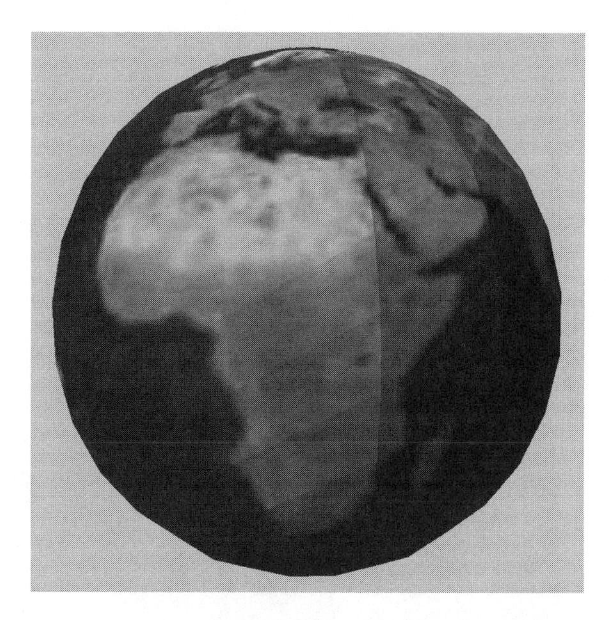

FIGURE 4–28 The sphere with MODULATE mode texturing.

Note that the color of the underlying surface is used, not just the lighting intensity. If the untextured sphere were colored red, then the texture-mapped sphere would be colored with a combination of the shaded red coloring and the colors of the texture map. Use white materials with `MODULATE` mode to make the lighting appear to affect the textured object.

The textures we have been looking at so far have been opaque. Each texel has had an RGBA color associated with it, with the alpha component set to 1.0. This makes the texel opaque. If the alpha were 0.0, then the texel would be transparent. Different file formats have different levels of support for transparent textures. The GIF file format allows each texel to be either transparent or opaque. Figure 4–29 shows a fish texture from a GIF file.

FIGURE 4–29 A GIF texture with a transparent background.

The background of the texture is transparent, with an alpha of 0.0. The transparent areas of the texture apply to the surface in the REPLACE and MODULATE modes in the same way as the color. Figure 4–30 shows the sphere with the fish texture in the REPLACE and MODULATE modes with a background image, blended transparency enabled, and backface culling enabled (see the earlier note on transparent rendering).

FIGURE 4–30 The sphere with the transparent background fish texture in (a) REPLACE and (b) MODULATE modes.

Note how the background shows through the transparent areas. The opaque areas either ignore lighting (REPLACE mode) or appear lit though mixing with the underlying color (MODULATE mode).

The DECAL texture mode uses transparent textures in a different way. This mode uses the texture's transparency values to indicate where the texture should be drawn and where the underlying material should show through. This technique is similar in nature to applying a decal to a model airplane in real life: the opaque areas of the decal replace underlying colors entirely, while the transparent areas show the underlying colors. To use the DECAL mode, the texture must have an alpha component (using an RGB texture will make the texture opaque and produce the same effect as REPLACE mode). Figure 4–31 shows the sphere with the fish texture applied to it.

FIGURE 4–31 The sphere with the transparent fish texture in DECAL mode.

Note that in the places where the texture is transparent, the underlying shaded colors are drawn; where the texture is opaque, the fish image is drawn as in the REPLACE mode, without lighting.

The BLEND texture mode is an advanced technique. In this mode, the texture color specifies the blending between the surface color and the texture blend color (another attribute in **TextureAttributes**). For each color component, R, G, B, and A, the texture color specifies the blending between the texture blend color and the surface color. If the texture color component is 1.0, then the blend color component is used; if it is 0.0, then the surface color component is used; if the value is in between, then a combination of the surface color and the blend color is used. This technique can be used to create a variety of colored texture maps from the same texture image. The default texture blend color is transparent black (0, 0, 0, 0).

Texture Map Transform

The texture map transform allows the texture coordinates for the shape to be translated, rotated, and scaled before being applied to the texture mapping. The transformation is specifed using a Transform3D object:

```
void setTextureTransform(Transform3D trans)
```

The `s` and `t` values of the texture coordinates are altered by the transform in the same way as the `x` and `y` values of a coordinate would be (see Chapter 6, "Tools: Transformation, Viewing, and Picking" for more information on working with Transform3D objects.)

Perspective Correction Mode

The perspective correction mode specifies how Java 3D should handle the rendering of textures when the shape is affected by a perspective viewing. When a textured shape is viewed at an angle, the shape appears to get smaller as it gets farther from the viewer. The rendering of the texture may have errors where the texture gets smaller. These errors can be avoided by applying *perspective correction* to the texture mapping. The default perspective correction mode is `FASTEST`. You can, however, change this mode to `NICEST` at the expense of processing power. Many graphics cards automatically apply perspective correction even in `FASTEST` mode, while software rendering is typically quite a bit slower in `NICEST` mode, so the default is usually acceptable.

Assigning Texture Coordinates

Texture coordinates tell what locations on the texture correspond with the verticies of the geometry. Texture coordinates can be either specified with the geometry for the shape or generated automatically using a **TexCoordGeneration** attribute component.

Texture coordinates can be specified with the geometry when the shape node is created (see Chapter 3, "Creating and Loading Geometry"). The `s` and `t` coordinates are specified at each vertex. For **GeometryArray** primitives, this is done by calling the `setTextureCoordinates()` methods. For the **Primitive** shapes (such as the **Sphere** used in this section), the texture coordinates are specified using the GENERATE_TEXTURE_COORDS flag to the constructor.

Texture mapping is enabled only for surfaces with texture coordinates, so you must either specify the coordinates with the geometry or use **TexCoordGeneration**.

TexCoordGeneration

The **TexCoordGeneration** attribute component lets you automatically generate texture coordinates. The simplest usage of generated coordinates is to attach a texture to a surface in a manner similar to specifying texture coordinates with the geometry. Generated coordinates can also be used for special effects, such as making a surface appear to be mirrored or generating contour lines. We'll look at the simple case first and then explore the special effects.

TexCoordGeneration uses equations to generate the texture coordinates from the geometry. For the simplest case, called OBJECT_LINEAR mode, the texture coordinates come from multiplying the coordinates of the geometry [x, y, z] with a set of values called the generation *planes*, planeS and planeT, which are **Vector4f** objects:

```
s = x * planeS.x + y * planeS.y + z * planeS.z + planeS.w;
t = x * planeT.x + y * planeT.y + z * planeT.z + planeT.w;
```

The default planes are planeS = [1, 0, 0, 0] and planeT = [0, 1, 0, 0], which make the generation equations as follows:

```
s = x;
t = y;
```

Figure 4–32 shows a square rendered using these coordinates.

The square goes from –1 to 1 in x and y, which makes the texture coordinates have the same range. The result is that texture repeats twice in each direction. To make the texture fit the square, we need to set up the planes so that the geometry coordinates [-1, -1, 0] and [1, 1, 0] correspond to the texture coordinates [0, 0] and [1, 1]. This can be done using the equations:

```
s = x * 0.5 +0.5
t = y * 0.5 +0.5
```

which can be specified using planeS = [0.5, 0, 0, 0.5] and planeT = [0, 0.5, 0, 0.5]. The result is that the texture is now aligned with the square as shown in Figure 4–33.

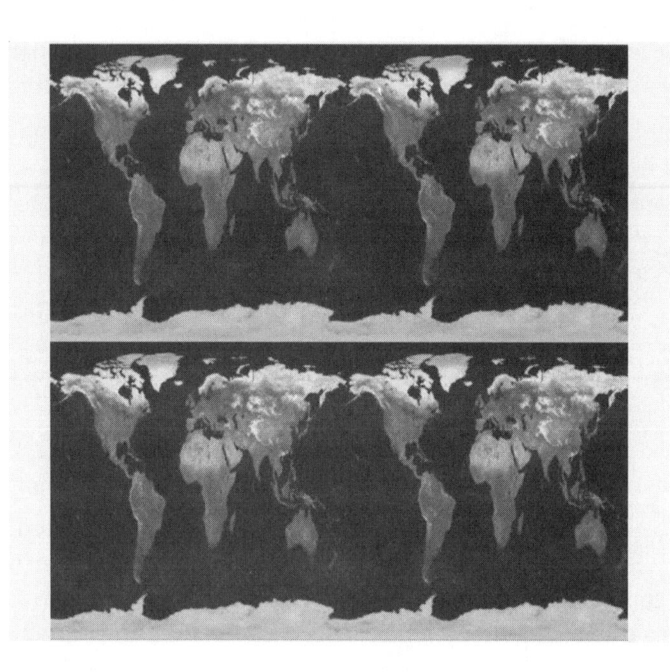

FIGURE 4–32 A square with automatically generated texture coordinates.

FIGURE 4–33 Square with texture coordinates that align with the boundaries of the square.

Here is the interesting part. If instead of the square we use the "galleon" part (loaded from a file, see Chapter 3, "Creating and Loading Geometry") which has coordinates in the –1 to 1 range, the generated coordinates have the same effect (see Figure 4–34).

FIGURE 4–34 The galleon with generated texture coordinates.

The generated coordinates apply to the surfaces of the galleon, attaching the texture with a minimum of effort. The only problem is that the texture is sort of "stamped" on the surface. All the parts of the surface with the same [`x`, `y`] value get the same texture coordinate. This can be seen if we rotate the galleon up so that we can see the hull, as in Figure 4–35.

The texture is stretched along this hull instead of being "wrapped" around the hull. This limits the effect you can achieve with this technique, but there are many cases where the generated coordinates work well.

The constructors for **`TexCoordGeneration`** set up the parameters for the generation:

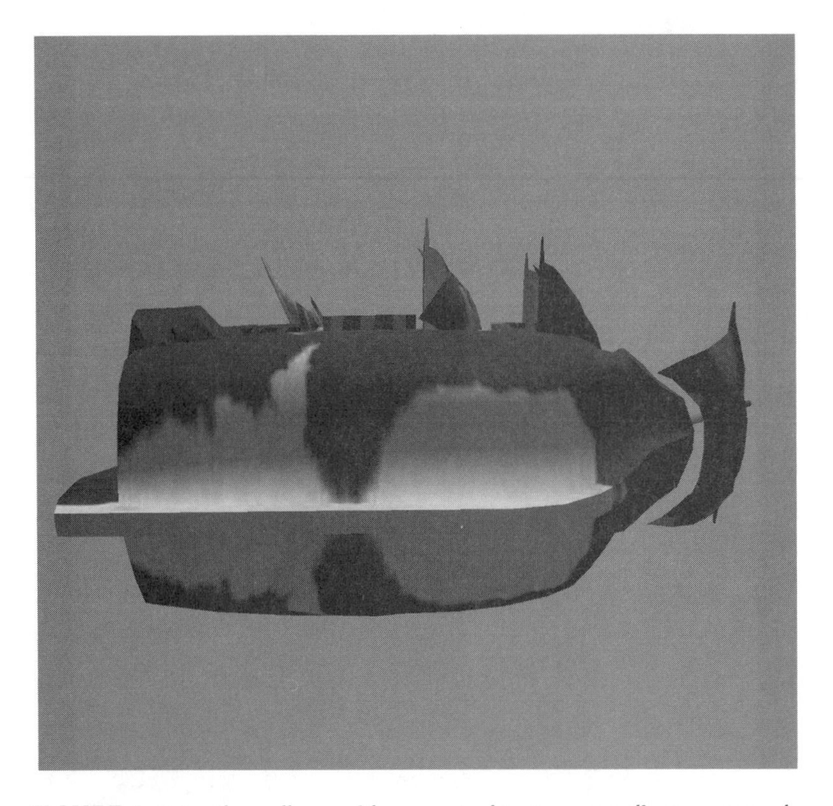

FIGURE 4–35 The galleon with generated texture coordinates, rotated to show the bottom.

```
TexCoordGeneration()
TexCoordGeneration(int genMode, int format);
TexCoordGeneration(int genMode, int format, Vector4f planeS,
       Vector4f planeT);
```

The `genMode` parameter specifies the generation mode. The modes are:

```
OBJECT_LINEAR
EYE_LINEAR
SPHERE_MAP
```

We've looked at `OBJECT_LINEAR`, which is the default, above. `EYE_LINEAR` is an advanced mode, similar to `OBEJCT_LINEAR`, except that the shape's coordinates are transformed to the viewer's coordinate system before the texture coordinates are generated. `SPHERE_MAP` is used to generate coordinates, which make the surface appear to be reflecting. We'll now look at how `EYE_LINEAR` and `SPHERE_MAP` modes are used.

The format parameter tells how many coordinates to generate. The formats are:

```
TEXTURE_COORDINATE_2
TEXTURE_COORDINATE_3
```

These correspond to 2D and 3D texture mapping; TEXTURE_COORDINATE_2 is the default.

The planeS and planeT parameters specify the planes as described above. The defaults are [1, 0, 0, 0] and [0, 1, 0, 0], respectively.

The methods for **TexCoordinateGeneration** include:

```
void setEnable(boolean enable);
void setGenMode(int genMode);
void setPlaneS(Vector4f planeS);
void setPlaneT(Vector4f planeT);
```

The setEnable() method turns the texture coordinate generation on and off. Note that the generated coordinates override any texture coordinates specified with the geometry. The rest of the methods set the corresponding attributes. In addition, there is the usual assortment of inquires, plus methods for 3D texture mapping. See the javadoc for a complete listing. Only the setEnable() method can be called on a live scene graph (if the ALLOW_ENABLE_WRITE capability bit is set); to change any of the other parameters a new **TexCoordinateGeneration** must be set on the **Appearance**.

The code to set up the texture coordinate generation for the galleon is:

```
Vector4f planeS = new Vector4f(0.5f, 0.0f, 0.0f, -1.0f);
Vector4f planeT = new Vector4f(0.0f, 0.5f, 0.0f, -1.0f);
TexCoordinateGeneration texGen = new TexCoordinateGeneration();
texGen.setPlaneS(planeS);
texGen.setPlaneT(planeT);
```

This sets up texGen with the default OBJECT_LINEAR and TEXTURE_COORDINATE_2 values and then sets the plane equations.

A simple special effect that can be achieved with generated texture coordinates is to make the surface appear to be mirrored. For this effect, use the SPHERE_MAP mode. See Figure 4–36 for an image of the galleon rendered using this mode.

The galleon now appears to be made of chrome, reflecting the image of a fish texture map. In this mode the texture coordinates are generated using the viewer's location and the vertex coordinates and normals (planeS and planeT are not used). The effect is that the texture coordinates are calculated to point to where the reflection of the surface would point. The texture map is interpreted as a

FIGURE 4–36 The galleon with texture coordinates generated with SPHERE_MAP.

sphere around the viewer. This technique needs the texture map to be an image from a "spherical camera" for really accurate results, but as the image shows, any image with dark areas can be used since the reflections come out pretty distorted.

An advanced use of generated coordinates is to make contour lines. These are places where the surface passes through a particular value. For example, in maps, contour lines are used to indicate elevation, with contour lines at 100 feet, 200 feet, etc. The same effect can be achieved using generated texture coordinates. The texture is a simple square with a stripe. The texture generation is set up so that the stripe corresponds with the value being studied. For example, contour lines on a map would set it up so that the stripe was at each 100 feet of elevation. Using `OBJECT_LINEAR` mapping the contour lines are generated using the object's coordinates. Using `EYE_LINEAR`, the contour lines are generated using the coordinates of the object relative to the viewer, which could be used to generate contour lines that indicate the distance of the object from the viewer. The OpenGL Programmers Guide has examples of generating contour lines.

Multitexturing

The texture options we have been looking at thus far have applied a single texture to a surface. Java 3D supports multitexturing, a feature where several layers of textures are applied to a surface. This is an advanced feature, useful for special applications. For example, some kinds of lighting and shadows can be efficiently implemented using multitexturing. Multitexturing uses separate texture coordinates and texture attributes for each layer of texturing to be applied to the surface.

The texture-mapping attributes for multiple layers of texture mapping are specified using **TextureUnitState** objects for each layer of texture mapping. A **TextureUnitState** holds the **Texture**, **TextureAttributes,** and **TexCoordGeneration** objects that apply to each layer of the texturing. The `setTextureUnitState()` methods on the **Appearance** are used to set the texture attributes for each layer.

Several texture coordinates can be associated with each vertex of a **GeometryArray** primitive. The mapping of the texture coordinates to the **TextureUnitStates** is indicated in the constructor to the **GeometryArray.** For example, for a **TriangleArray**, the constructors are:

```
TriangleArray (int vertexCount, int vertexFormat);
TriangleArray (int vertexCount, int vertexFormat, int texCoordSetCount,
        int [] texCoordSetMap);
```

The first constructor is used to specify a single set of texture coordinates. The second is used to specify multiple sets of coordinates. The `texCoordSetCount` parameter specifies the number of coordinates associated with each vertex. The texture coordinates are assigned using methods like:

```
void setTextureCoordinates (int texCoordSet, int index,
                TexCoord2f [] texCoords) ;
```

The program calls `setTextureCoordinates` () for each set of texture coordinates associated with each vertex, using `texCoordSet` to indicate the set of texture coordinates being assigned. For example, if `texCoordSetCount = 2`, the first set would be assigned by calling `setTextureCoordinates` () with `texCoordSet = 0`, and the second set with `texCoordSet = 1`.

The `texCoordSetMap` parameter in the constructor indicates the texture coordinate set to use for each **TextureUnitState.** The array is indexed by the **TextureUnitState** and indicates the texture coordinate set index to use for that **TextureUnitState** with the value –1 indicating that no texture coordinates are specified for that **TextureUnitState.**

For example, a program might have an **Appearance** with three **TextureUnitStates** and a **TriangleArray** with two sets of texture coordinates per vertex. In the constructor for the **TriangleArray** the program might use texCoordSetMap = [0, 1, –1]. This indicates the texture coordinates to be used by each **TextureUnitState**. **TextureUnitState** 0 would use the texCoordSet = 0 texture coordinates. **TextureUnitState** 1 would use the texCoordSet = 1 texture coordinates. The
–1 entry indicates that there are no texture coordinates specified in the **TriangleArray** for **TextureUnitState** 2, perhaps because the texture coordinates will be specified by a **TexCoodGeneration** object in the **TextureUnitState**. Generated texture coordinates override any coordinates specified in the geoometry. If the number of **TextureUnitStates** is greater than the size of the texCoordSetMap the value –1 (no coordinates specified is assumed).

See the javadoc for **Appearance**, **TextureUnitState**, or the **GeometryArray** for more details. The example program, TextureTest/MultiTextureTest, shows an example of multitexturing.

Summary

Appearance node components tell Java 3D how to render your shapes. **Appearances** collect many different kinds of appearance components. **ColoringAttributes** specify the basic color information for shapes. **PointAttributes**, **LineAttributes**, and **PolygonAttributes** specify the attributes of the corresponding types of shapes. **RenderingAttributes** specify the basic drawing control for shapes. **TransparencyAttributes** control how transparent and antialiased shapes are rendered. **Materials** specify the coloring of shapes when lighting is active. Texture mapping wraps the shapes with an image. Texture mapping is controlled by a **Texture** component that specifies the image, **TextureAttributes** that control how the texture is applied to the surface, and a **TexCoordGeneration** that can be used to generate texture coordinates.

Summary of URLs Found in This Chapter

Java 3D Explorer **web3dbooks.com/java3d/jumpstart/**

Java Advanced Imaging (JAI) **java.sun.com/products/java-media/jai/**

CHAPTER

5 Environment Nodes

TOPICS IN THIS CHAPTER

- LIGHTING SCENES WITH DIRECTIONAL, POINT, AND SPOTLIGHT SOURCES
- CREATING BACKGROUND COLORS AND IMAGES
- CREATING LINEAR AND EXPONENTIAL FOG EFFECTS
- ADDING POINT AND BACKGROUND SOUND SOURCES TO SCENES
- PREDEFINED BEHAVIORS
- USER-DEFINED BEHAVIORS
- USING BOUNDING REGIONS TO OPTIMIZE PERFORMANCE

In this chapter you'll learn how to work with Java 3D's *environment nodes*. As the name implies, environment nodes affect the environment in an area of your virtual world. Specifically, environment nodes enable you to control the lighting, sound, background, and other properties of your virtual world. In the sections that follow we'll show you how to enhance your worlds by adding lights, fog, backdrops, sound sources, and behaviors.

Environment Nodes in the Java 3D Explorer

As with previous chapters, the examples and images presented here come from the Java 3D Explorer created specifically for Java 3D Jump-Start readers. The freely available Java 3D Explorer is available online at web3dbooks.com/java3d/jumpstart/.

For each section of this chapter there is a corresponding area in the Java 3D Explorer. In this chapter we present the most important sections of the Java 3D Explorer source code for each topic, although the complete source code is available online.

Java 3D Explorer is freely available to Java 3D Jump-Start readers online at web3dbooks.com/java3d/jumpstart/. You can more closely examine the topics discussed in this chapter by running the Java 3D Explorer and experimenting with the application as we walk through the topics discussed in the sections that follow.

Bounding Regions

Environment nodes affect the virtual world around them. Light nodes, for example, shine on shapes, while sound nodes create audible content that you can hear. In the real world, however, if you get far enough away from a light or a sound you can't see it or hear it anymore. Real-world *attenuation* properties of light and sound are based on physics; these items have less impact on the world around you as the distance between you and the source of the effect increases. The farther away you are from a light or sound, the less you'll be able to see or hear its effect on your immediate world. Eventually, they'll have no effect whatsoever if you're far enough away from the source.

Java 3D employs a similar concept when it comes to nodes that affect the virtual environment. Java 3D's environment nodes specify the area, or *bounding region*, of the world that they affect. If you don't specify a bounding region for your node, Java 3D will consider it inactive. Consequently, that node doesn't change the environment for *any* area in the world (this is a well-known problem when working with environment nodes). For environment nodes that should always be active, you can specify an "infinite" bounding region as follows:

```
BoundingSphere infiniteBounds =
  new BoundingSphere(new Point3d(), Double.MAX_VALUE);
```

This creates a bounding region in the shape of a sphere. The region starts at the origin of the scene, and extends out as far as you can throw a double (the maximum value for a double precision floating point number). Simple programs in which all of the nodes should always be active can use a single infinite bounding region for environment nodes. The examples presented in this chapter use infinite bounds as defined above. Later in this chapter we'll take a closer look at bounding regions.

Lighting

Light nodes illuminate shapes in your virtual world. Java 3D supports four basic types of lights:

- **Directional lights** provide a simple, fast light type that simulates light from a distant source, such as the sun.
- **Point lights** position the light at a point in space like the light from a bare light bulb.
- **Spot lights** are like a point light which can be focused in a particular direction.
- **Ambient lights** simulate the diffused light that fills a room, lighting areas that are not directly illuminated.

Each of these Java 3D light nodes is derived from the same **`Light`** base class. As a result, all lights support the following basic methods defined by **`Light`**:

```
void setEnable(boolean state);
boolean getEnable();
void setColor(Color3f color);
void getColor(Color3f color);
```

These methods allow you to turn the light on and off (enable/disable) and to set its color. As with all Java 3D nodes, there are capabilities that must be enabled to allow these methods to be called when the light is part of a live scene graph (see the section on capability bits in Chapter 2, "Scene Graph Basics"). The `setEnable()` method requires the ALLOW_STATE_WRITE capability bit, while the `setColor()` method requires the ALLOW_COLOR_WRITE bit. The corresponding get() methods, meanwhile, require the corresponding READ capability bits.

The Java 3D Explorer uses a grid of spheres to illustrate the effects of the different light types. The grid is useful since it shows the same object at a variety of locations, so that differences in the lighting types are more clear.

Turn to the color plate section of this book to see color screen shots of the Java 3D topics discussed in this chapter.

Directional Lights

A directional light source produces light similar to that from a distant source, such as the sun. The light appears to come from the same direction no matter where the surface is located. The rays of light are parallel, striking surfaces from a particular direction but with no particular source, as shown in Figure 5–1.

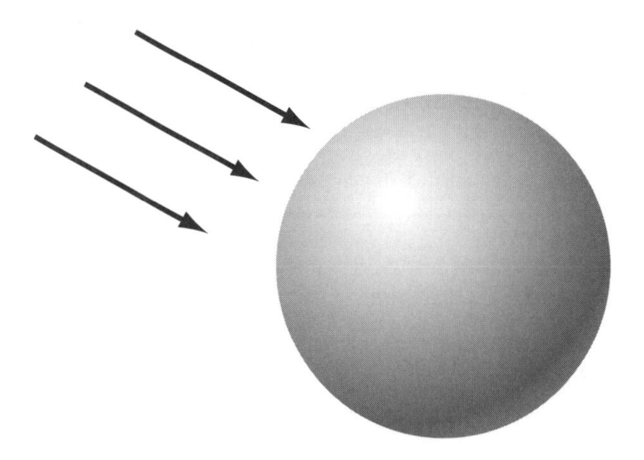

FIGURE 5–1 DirectionalLight emits parallel rays that strike illuminated surfaces from a specific direction.

In other words, the location of a **DirectionalLight** is irrelevant—it has the same effect no matter where it's located in your scene. The only properties that you can set with a directional light source are the direction it's pointing in, and the color of the light and whether it is on or off.

The effect of a directional light is shown in Figure 5–2. Here we see a directional light shining along the –Z axis.

Note that the diffuse effect (the colored shading) is the same for all the spheres, but the specular highlight is different for each sphere because the highlight is a reflection of the light off the sphere to the viewer (see the section on lighting in Chapter 4, "Appearances").

Creating a directional light source is easy. First, we create a vector that gives the direction the light should point in, like so:

```
Vector3f lightDirection =
  new Vector3f(0.65f,-0.65f,-0.4f);
```

This points the light so that it appears to come from the upper left. Next, specify the color of light you want:

```
Color3f white = new Color3f(1f, 1f, 1f);
```

FIGURE 5–2 A DirectionalLight shining on the grid of spheres.

After that, create the light itself:

```
DirectionalLight lightDirectional =
  new DirectionalLight(white, lightDirection);
```

Next, set its influencing bounds:

```
lightDirectional.setInfluencingBounds(infiniteBounds);
```

This tells Java 3D in what area of the universe the light is active, which in this case is everywhere since we are using the infinite bounds. You can then set the ALLOW_STATE_WRITE capability to allow the light to be turned on and off while the scene graph is live:

```
lightDirectional.setCapability(Light.ALLOW_STATE_WRITE);
```

Finally, add the light to the environment:

```
group.addChild(lightDirectional);
```

This connects the light to the scene graph so that it can light the spheres. The direction of the light can also be changed while the scene graph is live by setting the ALLOW_DIRECTION_WRITE capability and calling the method:

```
void setDirection(Vector3f direction);
```

Although directional lights provide simple, effective illumination, their light doesn't work well in cases where you want to have the light source be part of the scene, such as a lamp in a room. For more complex lighting cases you need to use point or spot lights. We'll explore each, starting with point lights.

PointLight

A directional light can be compared to the sun; a point light source is more like a light bulb. Unlike directional lights, which shine light in a specific direction (hence, the name *directional* light), point lights emit light in all directions. As a result, **PointLight** has a specific point of origin, as illustrated in Figure 5–3.

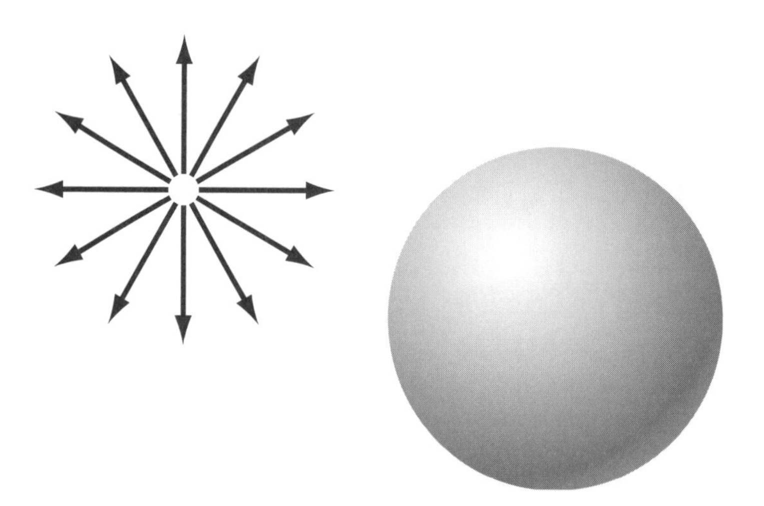

FIGURE 5–3 Point lights emit rays from a central point.

Placing a positional light just above one of the spheres in the grid shows how the positional light differs from the directional light. See Figure 5–4. The light is located over a sphere in the upper-right corner of the grid; notice how the lighting changes on the other spheres in the grid.

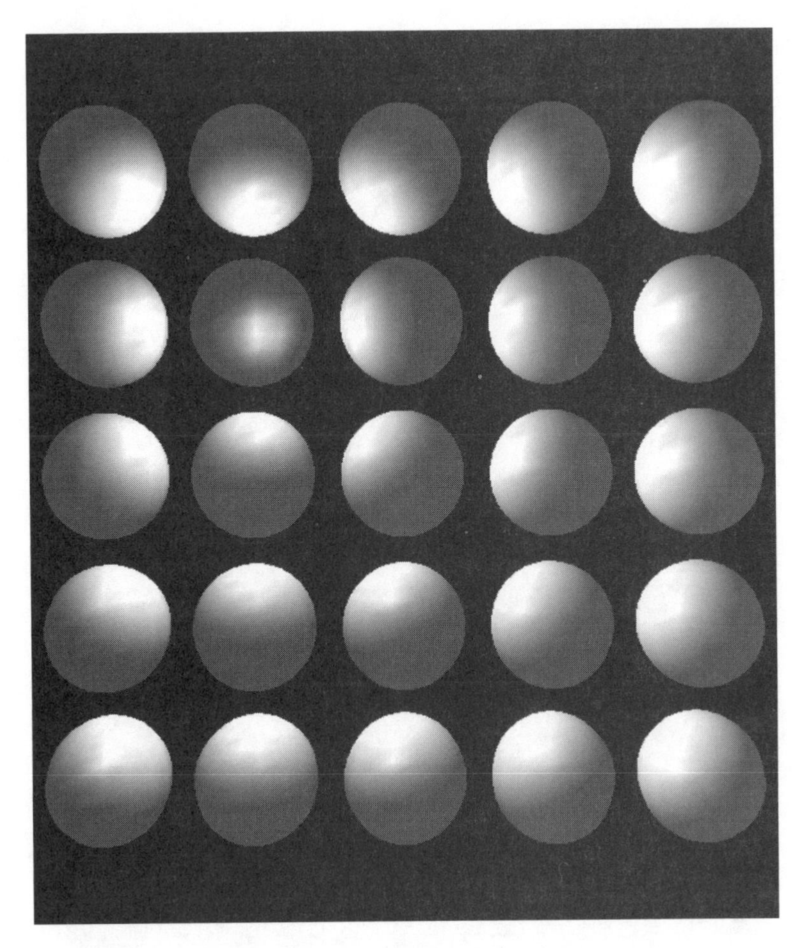

FIGURE 5–4 A PointLight located just above a grid of spheres.

Note that the light node does not appear in the scene, just the light that it casts.

Point lights have positions like lights in the real world. They also support a realism factor not available for directional lights. Specifically, point lights support *attenuation*. Attenuation is a fancy word for "weakening" or "petering out." In the real world, all light is attenuated by a variety of factors. Simple distance causes the light from a source to be spread out over a larger area as you get farther from the light source in an inverse square relationship. In other words, if you move twice as far from the light source, it'll seem only one-fourth as bright.

Java 3D supports a full inverse quadratic for attenuation based on the following formula:

```
brightness = intensity / (const + lin * d + quad * d²)
```

where d is the distance from the light source to the object being illuminated, const is the constant coefficent, lin is the linear coefficient, and quad is the quadratic coefficient. The three factors (constant, linear, quadratic) are stored in a Point3f. The x component of the Point3f stores the constant factor, the y component stores the linear factor, and the z component stores the quadratic factor. A perfect light source in the real world would have an attenuation factor of (0, 0, 1), or $1/d^2$, but in practice computer graphics lights look better with constant and linear factors. The default light attenuation is (1, 0, 0), which is the same as:

```
brightness = intensity
```

Switching the data to a grid of quads we can see the effect of this attenuation (see Figure 5–5).

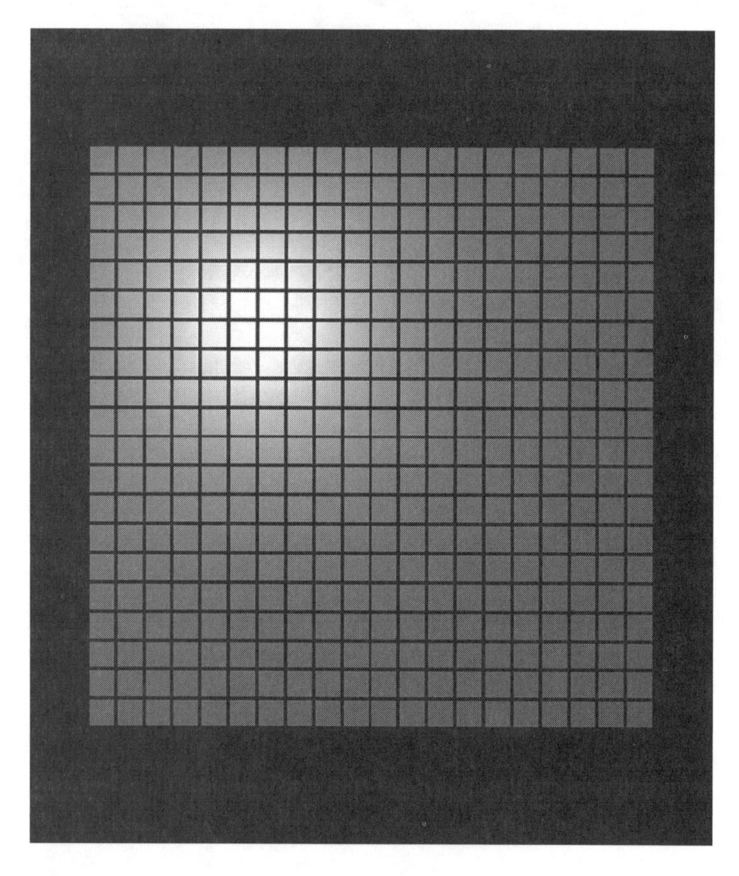

FIGURE 5–5 A PointLight over a grid of quads.

The lighting shows some variation due to the different angles the light rays make with the quads, but the distant areas have about the same brightness as the close areas. Figure 5–6 shows an attenuation of (0, 1, 0) or 1/d.

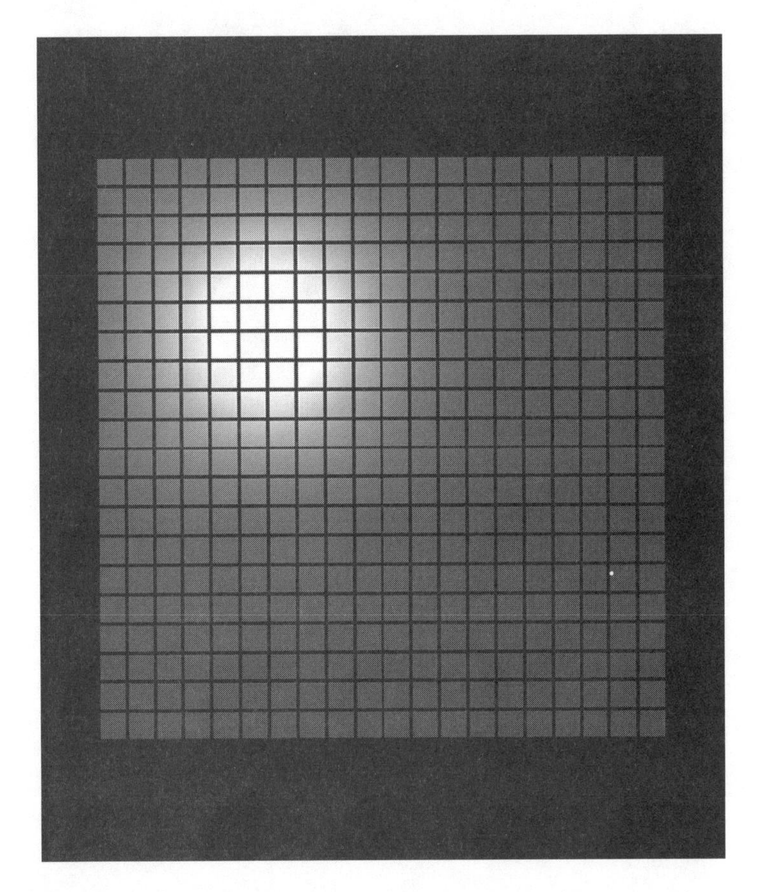

FIGURE 5–6 A PointLight with an attenuation of (0, 1, 0) or 1/d.

The brightness falls off for the more distant quads, giving a more realistic appearance. Figure 5–7 shows an attenuation of (0, 0, 1) or $1/d^2$.

While mathematically accurate, this attenuation quickly drops off in intensity as the distance increases. Experiment with a variety of factors to find the attenuation that looks best for your program.

To add a point light source to the scene, we start by defining its location and attenuation factors:

```
Point3f lightPosition = new Point3f(-1f, 1f, 0.6f);
Point3f lightAttenuation = new Point3f(0.0f, 1.0f, 0f);
```

FIGURE 5–7 A PointLight with an attenuation of (0, 0, 1) or $1/d^2$.

This will put the light source near the upper-left corner of the grid of spheres, with an attenuation of 1/d.

Next, we'll define the color of our light source:

```
Color3f white = new Color3f(1f, 1f, 1f);
```

Our next step is to create the point light source itself and set its influencing bounds.

```
PointLight pointLight =
  new PointLight(white, lightPosition, lightAttenuation);

PointLight.setInfluencingBounds(bounds);
```

Finally, of course, we need to add it to the scene graph:

```
group.addChild(pointLight);
```

All of the parameters for point light can be modified by calling individual methods, such as `setPosition(Point3f newPosition)`, and can be changed in a live scene graph if the proper capability bits are set.

SpotLight

Java 3D's **`SpotLight`** can be compared to a spotlight in the real world. In both cases the light has a position, a direction that it is pointing toward, and controls for how focused the light beam is. Figure 5–8 illustrates these concepts. Returning the attenuation to (1, 0, 0) and changing the light type to a spot light show the difference between a point light and spot light.

FIGURE 5–8 A SpotLight with attenuation (1, 0, 0), a spread angle of 60 degrees, and a concentration of 5.0.

The spot light casts the same light as the point light along its direction vector, with the light intensity dropping off the farther the light is from the direction vector.

A **SpotLight** has a direction (similar to that for the **DirectionalLight**), a spread angle, and a concentration factor (a **SpotLight** class is a subclass of the **PointLight** so it adds on to the **PointLight**'s attributes). The concentration controls how strongly the light shines along the direction. A concentration of 0 (the default) makes the light have equal intensity in all directions, like a **PointLight**. A concentration of 128 makes the light only shine along a very narrow beam along the direction. The concentration falls off smoothly, giving a soft edge to the light beam. The spread angle controls the width of the beam. It is a hard edge: light inside the spread angle is not affected by the spread angle; light outside the spread angle is completely blocked.

FIGURE 5–9 A SpotLight with a spread angle of 60 degrees and a concentration of 1.5.

Figure 5–9 shows the light from a **`SpotLight`** with a spread angle of 60 degrees and a concentration of 5.0. Figure 5–10 shows a light with a spread angle of 60 degrees and a concentration of 1.5.

Note that the light is shining in a tighter beam. Figure 5–10 shows a **`SpotLight`** with a spread angle of 60 degrees and a concentration of 0.

FIGURE 5–10 A SpotLight with a spread angle of 60 degrees and a concentration of 0.

Note the "hard" edge to the light. The edge has a "staircase" effect since the lighting is computed at each vertex of the quad. If the lighting were computed at each pixel, the edges would be smooth.

To create our **`SpotLight`**, we're going to reuse the position, direction, color, and attenuation variables. Next, we'll set up the spread angle and concentration:

```
float lightSpotSpreadAngle = 60;    // degrees
float lightSpotConcentration = 5.0;
```

Finally, we'll create our **`SpotLight`**:

```
SpotLight lightSpot =
    new SpotLight(lightColor, lightPosition,
                 lightAttenuation, lightDirection,
        (float) Math.toRadians(lightSpotSpreadAngle),
                 lightSpotConcentration);
```

We use the `MathtoRadians()` method to convert the spread angle to radians.

Finally, we set the influencing bounds and add the spotlight to the scene graph:

```
lightSpot.setInfluencingBounds(bounds);
group.addChild(lightSpot);
```

Ambient Light

Ambient light has no source and is non-directional. It doesn't emanate from any specific location, and it doesn't point in any particular direction. In the real world, ambient light is actually the result of light reflecting off objects, and then being reflected off other objects, and so on, until it completely fills a space. In Java 3D, an ambient light does the same thing. It provides a source of light that fills the room and shines equally on all objects from all directions. Ambient light is used to give some illumination to the shapes that are not lit by other lights. Figure 5–11 shows a scene lit with ambient light.

For our example, we'll create an ambient light that fills in the darkest areas of the grid. Let's begin by creating a gray color:

```
Color3f gray = new Color3f(0.1f, 0.1f, 0.1f);
```

Next, we create the ambient light, set its influencing bounds, and add it to our environment:

```
AmbientLight ambLight = new AmbientLight(lightColor);
ambLight.setInfluencingBounds(sceneBounds);
environment.addChild(ambLight);
```

That's all there is to it. If only the ambient light is enabled, the grid is drawn in dark red. Try combining the ambient light with the other light types. Observe the difference with the ambient light on and off.

FIGURE 5–11 A scene lit with AmbientLight.

Ambient lights decrease the "harshness" of the other light types. You can use ambient lights to give your scenes a sense of warmth that is similar to lighting in the real world.

Backgrounds

The **`Background`** node specifies visual content that appears behind the scene, such as a background color, clouds in the sky, or perhaps objects in the distance that form the backdrop for your world. The **`Background`** class gives you a choice of a solid color, a static background image, or a sphere of geometry that is drawn "around" the world.

The default display has no background: the screen is cleared to black before the scene is drawn. If a **Background** node is present in the scene and the view platform is inside its activation region (more about this later), then the **Background** node specifies the background for the scene.

The Background is drawn behind your scene so that all the other elements of the world appear on top of it.

For example, a **Background** that changes the background color to a light blue is shown in Figure 5–12. The code that sets up the color background is:

FIGURE 5–12 The sphere grid with a constant color background.

```
Color3f skyBlue = new Color3f(0.6f, 0.7f, 0.9f);
Background bgColor = new Background(skyBlue);
bgColor.setApplicationBounds(infiniteBounds);
bgSwitch.addChild(bgColor);
```

This snippet of code creates a sky blue color and then creates the **Background** specifying this color. The `infiniteBounds` is used to make the **Background** always active and the **Background** is connected to the scene graph to make it active (`bgSwitch` is a **Switch** group which the Java 3D Explorer uses to switch between the backgrounds).

We can replace the sky blue background with an image showing clouds in the sky using an image with the background. Figure 5–13 shows such a scenario.

FIGURE 5–13 The sphere grid with an image background.

Using an image instead of a solid color is simple once we get the image loaded. For that, we need to use the **TextureLoader** utility class to load the image from a URL. The **TextureLoader** was discussed in more detail in Chapter 4, "Appearances."

```
URL bgImageURL; // URL of the background image
TextureLoader bgTexture  =
            new TextureLoader(bgImageURL, null);
```

This tells the **TextureLoader** to open the URL and begin loading the image. Next, we create the background using the image from the TextureLoader:

```
Background bgImage = new Background(bgTexture.getImage());
bgImage.setApplicationBounds(infiniteBounds);
bgSwitch.addChild(bgImage);
```

This gets the **ImageComponent2D** from the **ImageLoader** and creates the **Background** using it. We set the bounding region of the background to infinite bounds, and then add the background to the switch group.

In this particular case, the image is larger than the window. If it were smaller than the window then the image would be drawn in the upper-left corner of the window with black outside the range of the image. Changes have been proposed for Java 3D 1.3 to allow the image to be scaled so that either the entire image is displayed or the entire window is filled.

If you're not up to creating your own textures, you can always use the freely available Universal Media textures. Available through the Web3D Consortium at web3d.org/WorkingGroups/media/, and the Web3DMedia.com site, Universal Media contains hundreds of professional-level textures, sounds, and 3D objects that you can use free of charge in your own worlds.

As the viewer moves around the scene, the background image remains static. We can make the clouds in the background move as the view changes by using geometry with the background (see Figure 5–14).

The background shown in Figure 5–14 is actually a sphere that surrounds the scene. As you can see, the texture mapped to this sphere is an image of sky and clouds. This sphere is being drawn as if it were an infinite distance away, so that everything else in your scene will appear in front of it. Setting up the background with geometry uses the same **TextureLoader**. This time, however, a **Texture2D** is extracted instead of an **ImageComponent2D**:

FIGURE 5–14 The sphere grid with background geometry: a sphere texture mapped with the cloud texture.

```
Background bgGeo = new Background();
bgGeo.setApplicationBounds(bounds);

BranchGroup beGeoBG = new BranchGroup();

Appearance bgGeoApp = new Appearance();
bgGeoApp.setTexture(bgTexture.getTexture());

Sphere sphereObj =
   new Sphere(1.0, Sphere.GENERATE_NORMALS,
            Sphere.GENERATE_NORMALS_INWARD |
            Sphere.GENERATE_TEXTURE_COORDS, 45,
            bgGeoApp);

bgGeoBG.addChild(sphereObj);
bgGeo.setGeometry(bgGeoBG);
bgSwitch.addChild(bgGeo);
```

The geometry is a sphere with texture coordinates. The appearance for the sphere applies the texture and the sphere is put into a **BranchGroup**. The **BranchGroup** is attached to the background using the `setGeometry()` method and the background is added to the switch group. If you rotate the view you'll notice that the texture has places where it doesn't match up. This is because the texture we are using was not intended to texture-map onto a sphere. For best results, you should use a texture intended to map to a sphere, such as an image taken in from a "spherical" camera.

Universal Media contains a number of seamless textures, including sky and clouds, that are designed to be mapped to 3D surfaces. Visit web3d.org/WorkingGroups/media/ or Web3DMedia.com to get your hands on these freely available textures.

Fog

Fog nodes simulate the way in which real-world objects appear to fade into the background when viewed from a distance. Fog is a surprisingly useful feature that can not only increase the realism of your scenes, but can also improve overall performance by allowing you to reduce the amount of detail required for objects positioned far away from the viewer. In the real world, distant objects seem to fade somewhat because the light reflected from them has to travel farther through the earth's atmosphere to reach your eyes. Depending on atmospheric conditions, this fading effect can be quite extreme. This fog effect is sometimes called "depth cueing" because it gives the brain a visual cue as to the depth of an object in the scene. Fog is implemented in Java 3D by blending the fog color with the color of the objects in the scene based on distance from the viewer. The farther away an object is from the viewer, the more it gets blended with the fog color, as illustrated in Figure 5–15. In this case the spheres are fogged to fade into the blue background.

Java 3D supports the following two basic types of fog:

- **LinearFog** has a constant density, so that an object that is twice as far away appears to be twice as "fogged."
- **ExponentialFog** has a density that approximates the way fog appears in the real world.

Generally speaking, linear fog is useful for depth cueing and exponential fog is best for simulating atmospheric effects.

Linear fog has a pair of distance values that define the "fog bank." Anything closer than the front distance is not fogged at all, anything beyond the back dis-

FIGURE 5–15 Spheres with fog that matches the background color.

tance is completely obscured by the fog (that is, it is drawn in the fog color), and anything in between the two distances is fogged depending on the distance (see Figure 5–16). This shows the same fog as we saw previously in Figure 15–5, although in this case the background is set to black. As you can see, the spheres positioned in the front of the scene are not fogged at all, whereas the spheres at the back are completely fogged.

Adding fog to a scene is easy. We simply add the following lines of code to our example program:

```
Color3f skyBlue = new Color3f(0.6f, 0.7f, 0.9f);
LinearFog fogLinear = new LinearFog(skyBlue, 7.5f, 15.0f);
BoundingSphere bounds = new BoundingSphere(new Point3d(), 100.0);
fogLinear.setInfluencingBounds(InfiniteBounds);
fogSwitch.addChild(fogLinear);
```

FIGURE 5–16 LinearFog with a black background.

This creates a sky blue linear fog where the fog starts to be applied at 6 meters from the viewer, and objects are completely fogged at 12 meters from the viewer. As usual, the bounds are set to the infinite bounds. Finally, the fog is added to the environment.

You can set your far fog distance to correspond with the back distance in a Clip node, so that anything that would be completely obscured by fog will be clipped out and not rendered. See the javadoc for Clip.

Exponential fog simulates real-world fog and haze using a density value that relates distance to fog intensity using an exponential equation. Nearby objects will hardly be fogged at all, but a distant object will be exponentially more heavily fogged, as shown in Figure 5–17.

FIGURE 5–17 ExponentialFog with a black background.

Using exponential fog is not much different than linear fog. Instead of setting the distances, however, we now set an exponent value that controls the fog density:

```
ExponentialFog fogExp =
  new ExponentialFog(skyBlue, 0.3f);

fogExp.setInfluencingBounds(bounds);
fogSwitch.addChild(fogExp);
```

This sets the fog to use the sky blue color and a density of 0.3. The higher the density, the "thicker" the fog appears.

For maximum effect, the fog color and the background color should be the same. When fog and background color are the same, objects that are far away and heavily fogged appear to blend into the background color and disappear.

Sound

Java 3D provides extensive support for the use of 3D sound. Sounds are represented by audio data files, typically stored in the ".au" or ".wav" file format. Most sound editing programs (such as CoolEdit) are able to read and write sounds in a variety of formats, including ".au" and ".wav."

Like lights, sound nodes have a base class, **Sound**, which defines the properties common to all sound nodes. A **BackgroundSound** defines an "ambient" sound with no particular source location. A **PointSound** defines a sound source that has a position in the virtual world. A **ConeSound** class is like a **SpotLight**; it is a **PointSound** that is directed in a particular direction.

Java 3D provides some sense of spatialization as sounds are played. While a sound source moves around the virtual world (relative to the listener), Java 3D's sound subsystem modifies the volume, left and right balance, and the interaural delay of the sounds in order to create the illusion that the sound is coming from a different direction. As the sound moves closer to the listener, it gets louder. As it moves off to the left, the sound is panned over to the left speaker. As it moves around the listener, a delay is added between the left channel and the right channel. Although Java 3D's sound subsystem does not yet support 3D sound hardware, you can create a very effective illusion of spatialized audio by using a few simple techniques.

Common Sound Elements

There are a number of things that are common to using **BackgroundSound**, **PointSound,** and **ConeSound** nodes. For starters, the audio device must be explicitly created, based on the **Viewer** object for the universe. As with other environment nodes, sound sources must be assigned a bounding region that defines when they're audible. In addition, all sound sources must have a **MediaContainer** node component associated with them to hold, or contain, the actual sound. Sounds must also be enabled, and additionally they must be instructed on how often to loop (if at all). Finally, a sound source can be made the child of some other object in the scene, so that it moves in tandem with that object. For example, you might create a transistor radio object and attach a sound source to it so that the sound travels with the radio whenever it moves.

The simplest way to work with sound is to use the **SimpleUniverse** class. We need to create an audio device and associate it with the **Viewer**. After creating the **SimpleUniverse**, we can use the `getViewer()` method to find the **Viewer**. The **Viewer** itself has a method for creating an audio device and initializing it:

```
// create an audio device
universe.getViewer().createAudioDevice();
```

Now any sound nodes that we add to our scene will make audio come out of your speakers.

All of the sound nodes extend the methods from the **Sound** base class:

```
void setEnable();
void setSoundData(MediaContainer data);
void setInitialGain(float amplitude);
void setLoop(int loopCount);
```

These methods turn the sound on and off, specify the sound using a **MediaContainer** to hold the sound, set the initial volume for the sound, and set the number of times to loop the sound. A loop count of `Sound.INFINITE_LOOPS` means that the sound should play continuously.

BackgroundSound

We'll start our audio exploration with the simplest kind of sound source, the **BackgroundSound**. This creates a background, or "ambient," sound that has no apparent source. The following code snippet illustrates how to use **BackgroundSound**. First, we'll set up a **MediaContainer** with the URL that points to the sound file:

```
URL  soundURL; // holds location of sound file
MediaContainer soundMC = new MediaContainer(soundURL));
```

Next, we create the **BackgroundSound** and set the scheduling bounds to the infinite bounds to ensure that the sound is always active:

```
BackgroundSound soundBg = new BackgroundSound();
soundBg.setSchedulingBounds(infiniteBounds);
```

Finally, we set up the parameters for the sound:

```
soundBg.setLoop(Sound.INFINITE_LOOPS);
soundBg.setEnable(false);
soundBg.setInitialGain(0.25f);
```

```
soundBg.setCapability(Sound.ALLOW_STATE_WRITE);
group.addChild(soundBg);
```

This sets up the sound to loop continuously at 0.25 of its maximum volume. In this case the sound is initially disabled. You can make the sound active at any time by calling `setEnable(true)`.

PointSound

Now let's look at the **`PointSound`**. This form of sound radiates uniformly in all directions from a specific location in the scene, much like a **`PointLight`** radiates light. **`PointSound`** also has attenuation factors similar to those offered by **`PointLight`**.

We begin by creating the **`PointSound`** itself:

```
// create a new point sound:

PointSound soundPoint = new PointSound();
soundPoint.setSchedulingBounds(infiniteBounds);
soundPoint.setSoundData(soundMC);
soundPoint.setLoop(Sound.INIFINTE_LOOPS);
soundPoint.setPosition(-5.0f, 5.0f, 0.0f);

Point2f[] distGain = new Point2f[2];
// set the attenuation to linearly decrease volume from
// max at the source to 0 at a distance of 5 meters:
distGain[0] = new Point2f(0,0, 1.0f);
distGain[1] = new Point2f(5.0, 0.0f);
soundPoint.setDistanceGain(distGain);
group.addChild(soundPoint);
```

In the Java 3D Explorer, this locates the sound at the upper sphere of the grid of spheres. Move the view by dragging the mouse with the first button pressed and notice how the sound changes as the upper left sphere gets closer to the **`ViewPlatform`**.

The attenuation uses a set of distance-attenuation pairs. These set up an attenuation value at each distance. The distances in each value must form an increasing sequence. If the distance is less than the first value, the first attenuation is used. If the distance is greater than the last distance, the last attenuation is used. If the distance is between two values, the attenuation is calculated as a linear interpolation of the attenuation values for the values.

Also, like a **`PointLight`**, **`PointSound`** has a subclass that adds directional control. A **`ConeSound`** is a **`PointSound`** with a direction vector and attenuation that makes the sound intensity lessen when the listener is not in the direction of the sound.

See the javadoc for ConeSound to learn more about the features offered by this type of sound.

Behaviors

Behaviors are nodes that make changes to the scene graph in response to events, such as user input or the passing of time. In other words, **Behaviors** are a general event handling mechanism for Java 3D. A **Behavior** indicates interest in a set of events, called the **Behavior**'s *wakeup criterion*. When an event occurs that matches the criterion, Java 3D calls a method on the **Behavior** to process the event. The **Behavior** processes the event, making changes to the scene graph (or performing any other task the program requires) to handle the event.

Java 3D programs make use of both predefined and custom **Behaviors**. We'll look at the predefined behaviors offered by Java 3D, and then review the basic structure of **Behavior** nodes. Finally, we'll create a simple **Behavior** class of our own.

First, let's look at the basic methods that all behaviors use. **Behavior** is an abstract base class that defines the methods:

```
void setEnable(boolean state);
void setSchedulingBounds(Bounds region);
```

These control whether or not the behavior is enabled, and the area where the **Behavior** is active. Like other environment nodes, behaviors are only active in a specific area of your virtual world. If the **ViewPlatform** is inside the scheduling bounds, the **Behavior** is considered active.

Predefined Behaviors

Java 3D defines several useful behaviors. In this section we'll look at the behaviors defined as part of the Java3D core—**DistanceLOD**, **Billboard,** and **Interpolator**. In the next chapter we'll look at other predefined behaviors with transformations and viewing.

A **DistanceLOD** node controls a **Switch** node to provide a level of detail (LOD) control. The **DistanceLOD** node uses the distance from the **ViewPlatform** to a reference point to control which child of the **Switch** to display. The constructors specify the reference point and distance values:

```
DistanceLOD();
DistanceLOD(float[] distances);
DistanceLOD(float[] distances, Point3f postion);
```

DistanceLOD is activated with each frame and calculates the distance from the **ViewPlatform** to the reference point, which defaults to [0,0,0]. The current distance, *d*, is used to select a value for the **Switch** nodes associated with the **DistanceLOD** using the *n* distance values in `distances` with the equations:

```
0, if d <= distances[0]
i, if distances[i-1] < d <= distances[i]
n if d > distances[n-1]
```

The **Switch** nodes associated with the **DistanceLOD** are controlled using the following methods:

```
void addSwitch(Switch node);
void insertSwitch(Switch node, int index);
void removeSwitch(int index);
void setSwitch(Switch node, int index);
int numSwitches();
Switch getSwitch(int index);
java.util.Enumeration getAllSwitches();
```

The list of **Switches** is managed in the same way as are children of a group or the elements of a **Vector**.

A **DistanceLOD** can be used to draw a low-resolution version of an object when the **ViewPlatform** is far away and a high-resolution version of the object when the **ViewPlatform** is close.

A **Billboard** node controls a **TransformGroup** to keep the children of the **TransformGroup** oriented towards the viewer. The **Billboard** can rotate around a fixed point or an axis. The constructors for the Billboard specify the **TransformGroup** and alignment:

```
Billboard();
Billboard(TransformGroup tg);
Billboard(TransformGroup tg, int mode, Point3f point);
Billboard(TransformGroup tg, int mode, Vector3f axis);
```

The values for the mode are:

```
ROTATE_ABOUT_AXIS
ROTATE_ABOUT_POINT
```

These indicate how the children of the **TransformGroup** should be rotated. `ROTATE_ABOUT_AXIS` indicates that the rotation should be around the vector specified by `axis`. `ROTATE_ABOUT_POINT` indicates that the rotation should be about the point specified by `point`.

A **Billboard** is useful for objects, such as signs, that should always be oriented toward the user.

The **OrientedShape3D** node provides the same kind of functionality as **Billboard**, except that only a single **Shape3D** is affected. **OrientedShape3D** is generally faster than **Billboard** and should be used where possible. See Chapter 3 for an example of **OrientedShape3D**.

Interpolators

Interpolators are nodes that perform animations by changing a transform or attribute over time. Interpolators can be used to change the color, transparency, position, rotation, or scale for nodes. They can also alter a transformation to make an object travel along a path. Although details of **Interpolators** are beyond the scope of this book, we'll discuss the basic concepts necessary to jump-start your use of them.

Specifically, interpolators change a property between one or more *key values*. For example, a **ColorInterpolator** changes a color between a starting color and an ending color. The value of the interpolator is controlled by an **Alpha** node component. The **Alpha** component converts the current time into an *alpha* value in the range (0,1). The alpha selects the amount of the key values to combine into the output value. For example, for a **ColorInterpolator**, an alpha of 0.25 will produce a color that is a mix of 0.25 of the start color and (1 – 0.25) = 0.75 of the end color.

Simple interpolators have a start and end value, while **PathInterpolators** let you specify a set of values and move through the values. Each value has a *knot* associated with it that indicates the alpha value associated with the interpolator value. The knots form an increasing sequence, starting with 0.0 and ending with 1.0. For each alpha value, the **PathInterpolator** selects the knots that are close to the alpha value and interpolates between the values associated with those knots.

The **Alpha** node component generates alpha values over time. The **Alpha** object can generate repeating patterns of alpha values that increase and decrease in a complex waveform. A simple constructor for an Alpha is:

```
Alpha(int loopCount, long increasingAlphaDuration);
```

The `loopCount` specifies the number of times the **Alpha** should generate values. A `loopCount` of –1 indicates that the **Alpha** should loop indefinitely. The `increasingAlphaDuration` specifies many milliseconds the **Alpha** should take to go from 0 to 1. For example, here is an **Alpha** object that generates alpha values that go from 0 to 1 each second and repeats indefinitely:

```
Alpha alpha = new Alpha(-1, 1000);
```

The increasing alpha duration is 1,000 milliseconds, or one second. For an **Alpha** that doesn't loop indefinitely, the starting time for the **Alpha** is specified using the methods:

```
void setStartTime(long startTime);
void setTriggerTime(long triggerTime);
```

The `startTime` is a system time value, which is returned from `System.currentTimeMillis()`. The default start time is 0, which corresponds to midnight, January 1, 1970 UTC. The trigger time is an offset after the start time, which defaults to 0. The **Alpha** produces values if the current time (as returned from `System.currentTimeMillis()`) is greater than or equal to `startTime + triggerTime`. For example, to start an **Alpha** right now, set the start time:

```
alpha.setStartTime(System.currentTimeMillis());
```

To start the alpha one second from now, set both the start time and the trigger time:

```
alpha.setTriggerTime(1000);
alpha.setStartTime(System.currentTimeMillis());
```

This will start the alpha in 1,000 milliseconds, or one second from now.

The **Alpha** component can be used to produce complex waveforms, as shown in Figure 5–18.

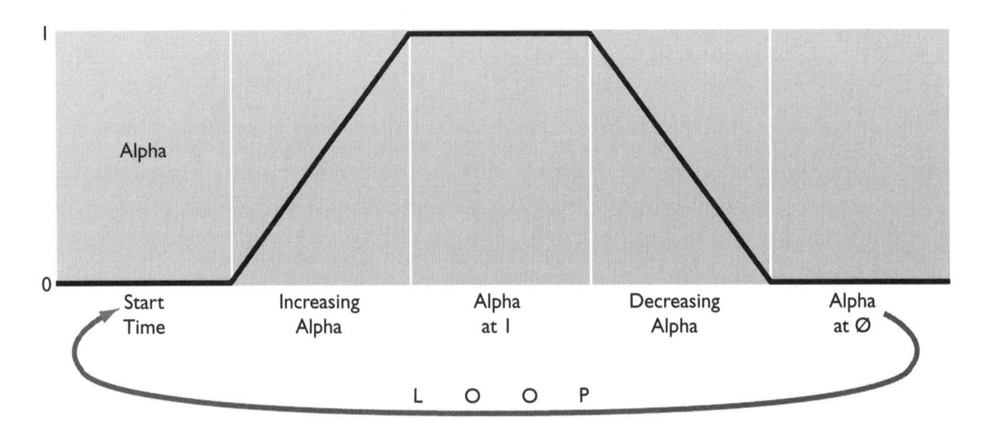

FIGURE 5–18 Alpha phases.

The phases specify how long the **Alpha** takes to reach 1.0, how long it stays at the 1.0, how long it takes to decrease to 0.0, and how long it stays at 0.0 before looping. The waveform can be smoothed out using an alpha ramp, which slowly increases the rate of change in the alpha, making the change from constant alpha to changing alpha less abrupt.

The following excerpt from Sun's sample **HelloUniverse** Java 3D program gives us a simple but effective example of a **RotationInterpolator** in action:

```
// make alpha go from zero to one every four seconds,
// repeating forever
Alpha rotationAlpha = new Alpha(-1, 4000);

// set up the Behavior object that will do
// the animation
Transform3D yAxis = new Transform3D();
RotationInterpolator rotator =
      new RotationInterpolator(rotationAlpha, objTrans,
            yAxis, 0.0f, (float) Math.PI*2.0f);
// add the rotator to the scene graph
BoundingSphere bounds =
  new BoundingSphere(new Point3d(0.0, 0.0, 0.0), 100.0);
rotator.setSchedulingBounds(bounds);
objRoot.addChild(rotator);
```

The `yAxis` parameter to the **RotationInterplorator** specifies the transformation for the rotation axis. By default, the rotation is around the Y axis. This **Transform3D** uses the default transformation, which doesn't change the rotation axis, leaving it around the Y axis. The parameters to the **RotationInterpolator** constructor specify that the interpolator should use `rotateAlpha` for the alpha values; affect the transform for `objTrans` (a **TransformGroup** defined earlier); transform the rotation axis using the `yAxis` transform; and use 0.0f and `Math.PI` * 2.0 for the beginning and ending rotation values. This makes the interpolator rotate 360 degrees around the Y axis as alpha goes from 0 to 1.

User-Defined Behaviors

So far we've only explored Java 3D's predefined behaviors. Now it's time to look at how to set up your own custom behaviors. There are two main reasons for using behaviors to hold your program's logic. First, you can set up automatic behaviors that are only active when the viewer is nearby, letting Java 3D turn off your behaviors when the viewer is far away. Second, you can use behaviors to group sets of changes to the scene graph. By default, Java 3D does not specify when a change to the scene graph will show up. If you are making a set of changes, some of the changes may show up in one frame, with other changes showing up in a later frame. On the other hand, all of the changes made by a behavior within one wakeup will show up in the same frame, so using behaviors can ensure that your changes are grouped together in the same frame.

When you use subclasses of **Behavior,** you specify the action of the **Behavior** by implementing the methods:

```
void initialize();
void processStimulus(java.util.Enumeration criteria);
```

The `initialize()` method is called when the behavior is first made live. It initializes the behavior, including telling Java 3D which events should cause the **Behavior** to wake up. The `processStimulus()` method is called when there is an event for the **Behavior** to process. The `Enumeration` passed to `processStimulus()` contains the events which were requested by the **Behavior**.

The `wakupOn()` method is used to indicate the events that should wake the **Behavior**:

```
void wakeupOn(WakeupCondition criteria);
```

A **WakeupCondition** is a combination of one or more **WakeupCriterion**. The subclasses of **WakeupCriterion** define the events that a **Behavior** can register an interest in. The `wakupOn()` method must be called by `initialize()` to register interest in the events, and by `processStimulus()` to register continued interest in the event.

Be sure to call wakeupOn() from your processStimulus() method or your behavior will only be woken once.

Many kinds of wakeup criterion can wake the **Behavior**, such as:

- **WakeupOnElapsedFrames**: Generated when a specific number of frames have elapsed. Specifying zero frames causes a wakeup to be generated after each frame.
- **WakeupOnElapsedTime**: Generated after a specific time interval has elapsed. For example, this can generate a wakeup once a second.
- **WakeupOnBehaviorPost**: This is a "manual" wakeup, generated either by the program or another **Behavior**. The event is generated when the `postId()` method is called on the **Behavior**. All behaviors with a **WakeupOnBehaviorPost** criterion may then get a wakeup. The criteria can filter the wakeups based on the **Behavior** generating the wakeup or the integer id passed to `postId()`.
- **WakeupOnAWTEvent**: Generated when an AWT event, such as a key press or mouse movement, occurs on the **Canvas3D**.

- **WakeupOnActivation**: Generated when the **Behavior** becomes active. This happens when the **ViewPlatform** moves inside the **Behavior's** scheduling bounds.
- **WakeupOnDeactiviation**: Generated when the **Behavior** becomes inactive. This happens when the **ViewPlatform** moves outside the **Behavior's** scheduling bounds.
- **WakeupOnTransformChange**: Generated when a **Transform3D** changes.
- **WakeupOnViewPlatformEntry**: Generated when the **ViewPlatform** enters a specific region.
- **WakeupOnViewPlatformExit**: Generated when the **ViewPlatform** exits a specific area.
- **WakeupOnCollisionEntry:** Generated when two objects begin to collide.
- **WakeupOnCollisionMovement:** Generated when objects that are colliding move.
- **WakeupOnCollisionExit:** Generated when two objects that were colliding are no longer colliding.

For example, a **Behavior** can be woken by an AWT event using the **WakeupOnAWTEvent** class. The constructors specify the AWT events:

```
WakeupOnAWTEvent(int AWTid);
WakeupOnAWTEvent(long eventMask);
```

The first constructor takes a specific event id, such as **java.awt.KeyEvent.KEY_ PRESSED**; the second takes an event mask, such as **java.awt.AWTEvent.KEY_ EVENT_MASK**. Multiple event masks can be OR'd together.

More than one **WakeupCriterion** can be combined using the classes **WakeupAnd**, **WakeupOr**, or other classes that specify even more complex combinations (see the javadoc for **WakeupCondition**).

Here is a simple example of a **Behavior**. This class prints out the keys that are pressed on the **Canvas3D**:

```
public class KeyPrintBehavior extends Behavior {
   // this tells what events should wake the
   // behavior
   WakeupCondition wakeup = new
   WakeupOnAWTEvent(java.awt.KeyEvent.KEY_PRESSED);
```

```
    // set up the initial wakeup
    public void initialize() {
    wakeupOn(wakeup);
    }

            // called when an event that matches happens
            public void processStimulus(Enumeration criteria) {
                while(criteria.hasMoreElements()) {
                    wakeup = (WakeupCriterion)
                                        criteria.nextElement();
                    // in this case we know the type of wakeup,
                    // but in general we have to check
                    if (wakeup instanceof WakeupOnAWTEvent) {
                        AWTEvent[] evt = ((WakeupOnAWTEvent)
                                        wakeup).getAWTEvent();
                        for (int i = 0; i  < evt.length; i++) {
                            // we know it is KeyEvent,
                            // but in general we have to check
                            if (evt[i] instanceof KeyEvent) {
                                KeyEvent keyEvt =
                                        (KeyEvent) evt[i];
                                System.out.println("Key: '"
                                 + KeyEvt.getKeyChar() + "'");
                            }
                        }
                    }
                }
            }
}
```

Notice that the behavior narrows the general objects such as **WakeupCriterion** using `instanceof`. Most behaviors have to do this to sort through the different kinds of events which can cause the wakeup.

Another commonly used **WakeupCondition** is **WakeupOnElapsedFrames**. This condition can be used to do actions for every frame that is rendered. The constructors in this condition are:

```
WakeupOnElapsedFrames(int frameCount);
WakeupOnElapsedFrames(int frameCount, boolean passive);
```

The wakeup occurs after `frameCount` frames have elapsed. Specifying a `frameCount` of zero will generate a wakeup on each frame. The `passive` flag controls the effect of the behavior on rendering. If `passive` is true, or if the constructor without the `passive` parameter is used, then the **WakeupOnElapsed-**

`Frames` behavior will cause the renderer to run continuously so that the wakeup will be generated. This can be used to drive animations or other actions which should cause Java 3D to generate frames as quickly as possible. However, this can also cause Java 3D to render the scene again and again even if the scene is not changing. Setting `passive` to true will make the **`WakeupOnElapsedFrames`** not affect the rendering status. Frames will be generated when a scene graph changes or other events occur.

Bounding Regions

A common trait of environment nodes is that they affect a specific area of the virtual world. The area can be set to be the whole universe, but typically a more specific area is specified. This area is called the node's *bounding region*. A bounding region is a volume of space that contains objects that are affected by a particular background, light, sound, or fog. By associating the environment node with a bounding region, we can easily limit the range of their effect on the scene. So far, we have been using a simple bounding sphere that has made the environment nodes everywhere. More advanced uses need to employ different boundary regions.

To see why boundary regions could be important, consider the following hypothetical example. You've built a small virtual house three stories high with a number of rooms. Your living room is well lit with a number of floor lamps and an overhead light. The basement, right below it, is quiet and dark, lit by a single candle. The television is on in the living room, while upstairs a small portable radio is playing. The kitchen is full of smoke from a roast that's burning in the oven.

Sounds great, but it won't work! Without bounding regions, the lights from the living room will illuminate the basement as well, the transistor radio right overhead would be louder than the television across the room from you, and the smoke from the kitchen would fill the house. This is because, without bounding regions, the light, sound, and fog nodes would have no limits to their effect aside from plain old distance, and the result is a virtual world that's not very much like our real one.

The way to get around these problems is to use bounding regions. You would set up regions such that your television could be heard only within the living room, and the radio could be heard only upstairs. The bounds around the kitchen would contain the fog for the smoke, and the lights from the living room wouldn't affect the basement.

There are three basic types of bounding volume in Java 3D:

- **BoundingBox** defines a rectangular box aligned with the X, Y, and Z axes.
- **BoundingSphere** defines a sphere with a center point and radius.
- **BoundingPolytope** defines a set of mathematical planes that enclose a convex region of space, which is useful for enclosing an arbitrary volume.

Which shape to use depends on your program. A **BoundingBox** is simple to calculate (just find the X, Y, and Z limits of your geometry) and can be handy if the space you want to bound is a rectangular volume, such as the rooms of the house above. A **BoundingSphere** is a common choice since it is simple to describe and similar to how real lights and sounds work. Put the center of the sphere at the source and set the radius to be the distance where the source is no longer visible or audible. A **BoundingPolytope** is a more advanced case. It is useful when you want to enclose an arbitrary volume, such as triggering a cheer when the **ViewPlatform** crosses the plane of the goal line in a football game simulation.

Every light, sound, background, and fog node must have a bounding region associated with it. By default, the bounding regions are null and the nodes have no effect, leading to one of the most common problems encountered by programmers new to Java 3D. A programmer new to Java 3D, for example, will create a fog bank and then wonder why it has no effect on their scene. To remedy the situation, a bounding region must be set.

By default, bounding regions are null, and the nodes have no effect. In order to use bounding regions you must actually *set* them as seen in the code examples.

The usage of the bounding region depends on the node type. A shape will be affected by a light or fog node if it is inside the nodes's influencing bounds. A background or sound will be active if the viewing platform is within the node's bound.

Boundary regions are important for maximizing the performance of very large worlds since they limit the environment nodes that are active.

Light and fog nodes have an additional mechanism that provides another mechanism for limiting the area where the nodes are active. These nodes can be made active only for groups that have been associated with the node via the methods:

```
void addScope(Group scope);
void insertScope(Group scope, int index);
void removeScope(int index);
void setScope(Group scope,. int index);
java.util.Enumeration getAllScopes();
int getNumScopes();
```

These methods set up a list of scopes associated with the node. If the scope list is not empty, only shapes included in a group in the scope and within the influencing bounds for the light or fog will be affected by the node.

Summary

Environment nodes affect an area of a virtual world. **Lights** illuminate shape nodes. **DirectionalLights** are simple and fast. **PointLights** more closely approximate real-world lights, with controls that let you decrease the effect of the light with distance. **SpotLights** extend **PointLights** with the ability to direct the light in a particular direction. **AmbientLights** fill in your scene with a constant light which simulates the way light fills a room. **Background** nodes change the image rendered behind your scene. **Backgrounds** can have a constant color, a static image, or geometry such as a texture-mapped sphere that provides a dynamic image. **Fog** nodes make your shapes "fade" into the background. **LinearFog** provides a "depth cue," while **ExponentialFog** simulates the effect of real-world fog and haze. **Sound** nodes let your user hear your world. **BackgroundSounds** have no apparent source, **PointSounds** appear to come from a particular source, and **ConeSounds** come from a source and are directed in a particular direction. **Behaviors** make changes to the scene graph in response to events such as user input or the passing of time. Predefined behaviors include **DistanceLOD**, which controls a **Switch** to provide level of detail control, and **Billboard**, which controls a **TransformGroup** to keep the children of the **TransformGroup** oriented toward the viewer. **Interpolators** perform animations by changing a transform or attribute over time. **Interpolators** are controlled by **Alpha** components, which map time values to interpolator settings. User defined behaviors can be used to change the scene graph in response to a variety of events called **WakeUpCriterion**. Bounding regions specify the area of the virtual world affected by the environment node.

Summary of URLs Found in This Chapter

Java 3D Explorer **web3dbooks.com/java3d/jumpstart/**

Universal Media **www.web3d.org/WorkingGroups/media/**

Web3DMedia.com **web3dmedia.com/**

CHAPTER

6 Tools: Transformation, Viewing, and Picking

TOPICS IN THIS CHAPTER

- THE BASIC TRANSFORMATION OPERATIONS: TRANSLATION, SCALING, AND ROTATION
- HOW TO SPECIFY TRANSFORMATIONS WITH A TRANSFORM3D
- HOW TO MAKE COMPOUND TRANSFORMATIONS
- WORKING WITH OBJECT HIERARCHIES
- BASIC VIEWING
- ADVANCED VIEWING
- BASIC PICKING

This chapter covers tools that most Java 3D programs use: transformations, viewing, and picking. Transformations change the position, orientation, and size of objects in your virtual world. Viewing renders your 3D world into 2D images from the point of view of a virtual observer. Picking finds the shapes in your world that are being pointed to by the mouse.

Transformations, viewing, and picking are related. Transformations are used to move, orient, and scale objects in the virtual world, including the ViewPlatform. Viewing is a form of transformation, converting shape data from the 3D virtual world to a 2D representation in the physical world. Picking reverses the viewing operation, using the 2D screen location pointed to by the mouse to select objects in the 3D virtual world. In this chapter we'll look at each of these tools.

Transformations

By default, every virtual object in a Java 3D scene is initially stationary and unchanging. Every light source, view platform, sound source, and shape remains at its starting location unless you write code that specifies otherwise. In this chapter you'll learn how to change the position, size, and orientation of these objects. These three basic operations are known as "translation," "scaling," and "rotation." These operations, as well as combinations of these operations, are called "transformations," or "transforms" for short.

Transformations with Java 3D Explorer

Most of the figures found in this chapter come from the example program Java 3D Explorer, which is freely available at web3dbooks.com/Java 3D/jumpstart/. You can try out the transforms discussed in the sections that follow by running the Java 3D Explorer application while you read the topic. Look at the source for the Java 3D Explorer to see how the explorer changes the attributes as you interact with the user interface.

Basic Transformations

Let's explore the basic transformations: translation, scaling, and rotation. The subgraph used for the cone in these examples is very simple. It is just a **TransformGroup** that holds the cone (see Figure 6–1).

FIGURE 6–1 A simple scene graph with a TransformGroup holding a cone.

All of the operations that change the transformation on the cone simply call the method:

```
void setTransform(Transform3D transform);
```

with different transformations.

The `setTransform` () method copies the **Transform3D** to the **TransformGroup**. Since the **Transform3D** is copied, changing the **Transform3D** does not affect the **TransformGroup** unless `setTransform` () is called again.

Translation

Translation simply means moving an object from one location in space to another. It adds an offset to each of the X, Y, and Z components of the object's location. For example, if an object is located at [7, 15, 2] (that is, seven meters along the X axis, 15 meters up the Y axis, and 2 meters forward along the Z axis) and you add a translation of [2, 0, 5], the object will end up at [9, 15, 7].

Figure 6–2 shows the effect of translation on a cone. The initial location of the cone is at the origin [0, 0, 0]. Applying a translation of [1, 0, 0] moves the cone to the right.

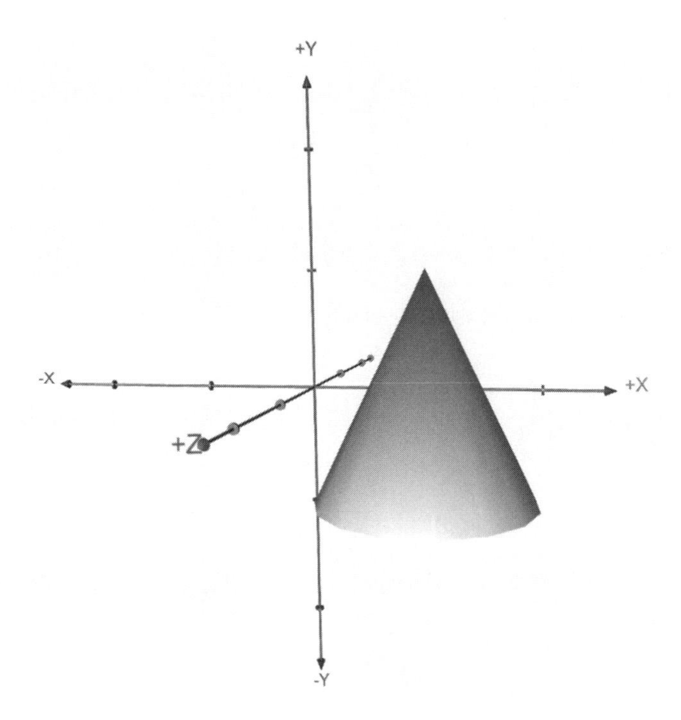

FIGURE 6–2 The cone is translated by [1, 0, 0].

The cone has moved 1 meter along the X axis. Changing the translation to [0, 1, 0] moves the cone up, as shown in Figure 6–3.

Changing the translation to [0, 0, 1] moves the cone towards the viewer, as shown in Figure 6–4.

Scaling

Scaling an object means changing its size. There are two different types of scaling: uniform and nonuniform. A uniform scale changes the size of an object but

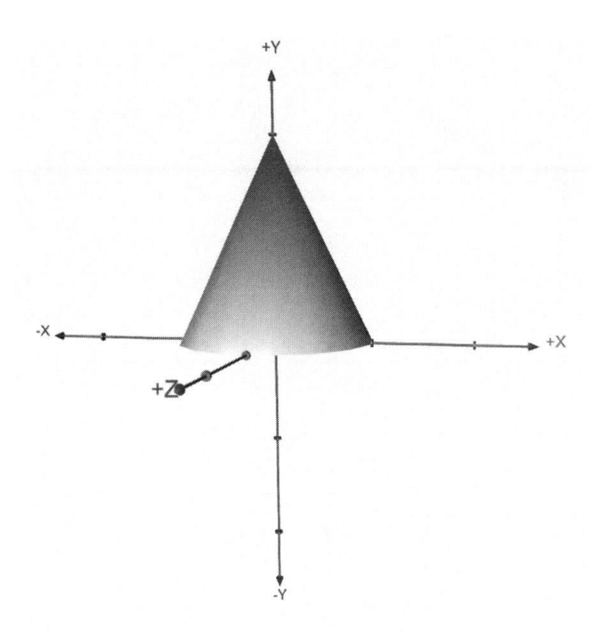

FIGURE 6–3 The cone is translated by [0, 1, 0].

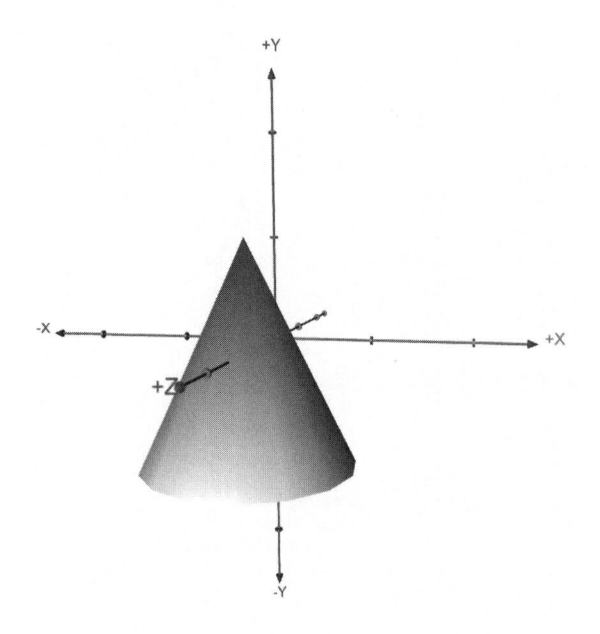

FIGURE 6–4 The cone is translated by [0, 0, 1].

not its shape, making it larger or smaller in all directions. A nonuniform scale changes the scale of the object by different amounts in each direction, stretching the object and changing its proportions.

For example, setting a uniform scale of 2.0 makes the cone bigger as shown in Figure 6–5.

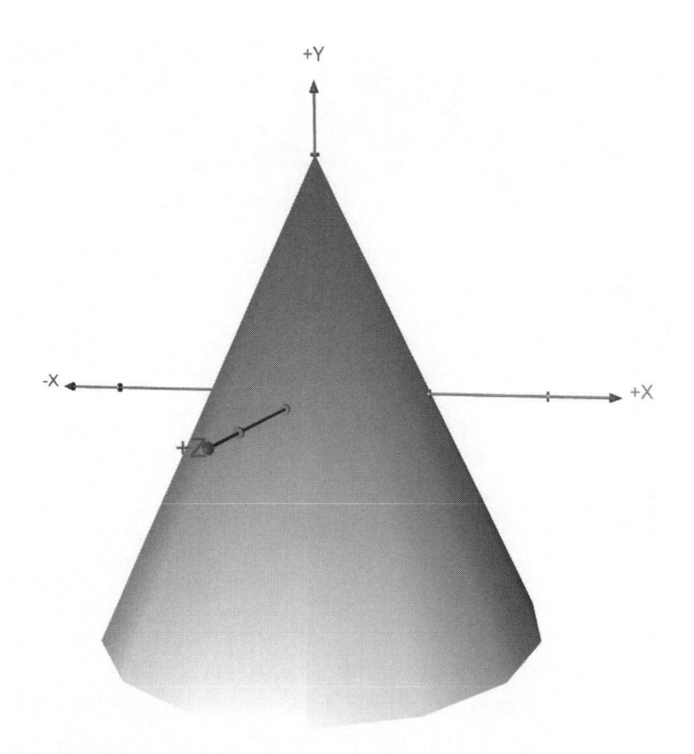

FIGURE 6–5 The cone, scaled by a uniform scale of 2.0.

The cone has been scaled 2x, making it twice as large in each direction. The cone has retained its shape; only the size has changed: the bottom is still a circle and the height is the same as the diameter.

With a nonuniform scale of [2.0, 0.5, 1.0] the size and shape of the cone are changed, as shown in Figure 6–6.

The base of the cone was a circle; now it is an ellipse. Nonuniform scaling changes the proportions of objects; circles become ellipses and squares become rectangles.

FIGURE 6–6 The cone, scaled by the nonuniform scale [2.0, 0.5, 1.0].

Uniform scaling multiplies the X, Y, and Z of the vertices of an object by a single value. Nonuniform scaling uses three different values, one for the X direction, one for the Y direction, and one for the Z direction. A box that gets scaled more along the X axis than along Y or Z will become oblong, and a sphere that gets scaled more along Y than along X or Z will become an ellipsoid, as shown in Figure 6–7.

In general, you should use uniform scaling whenever possible; nonuniform scaling is more computationally expensive. For example, it is better to make a cone that has a radius of 1.0 and a height of 2.0 than to use nonuniform scaling to create the same cone from a cone with a height of 1.0.

You should avoid nonuniform scaling because it is much more mathematically complex than uniform scaling. This is particularly true for lit shapes. Nonuniform scaling operations increase the complexity graphics operations, which may slow down your program.

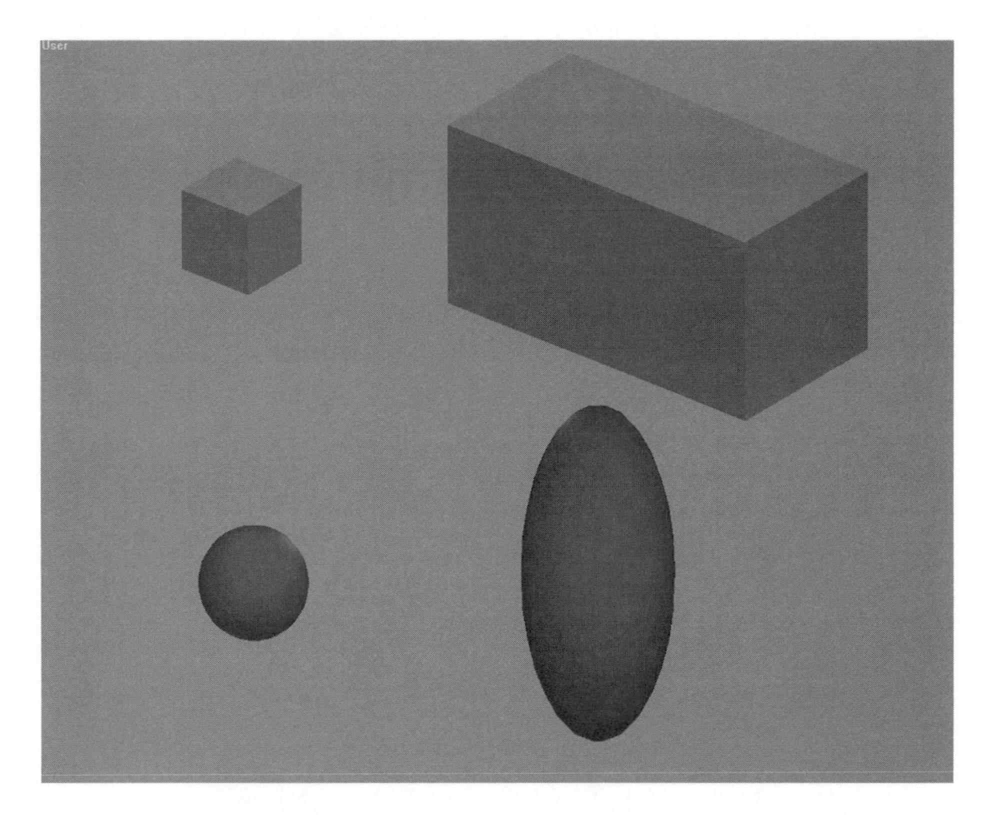

FIGURE 6–7 Where uniform scaling merely changes the size of an object, nonuniform scaling is used to resize an object along a specific axis (or any combination of axes) so it can alter its shape.

Rotation

Rotation changes the orientation of an object. An object can be rotated around any combination of the X, Y, and Z axes, which can result in every point on the object's surface getting moved to a different location.

For example, in Figure 6–8 the cone has been rotated by 45 degrees around the X axis, [1, 0, 0].

Changing the rotation axis to [0, 0, 1] rotates the cone around the Z axis (Figure 6–9). Notice that the rotation is around the origin, [0, 0, 0]. Rotation is around the origin unless a translation is used to move the rotation point. We'll look at this more in detail later.

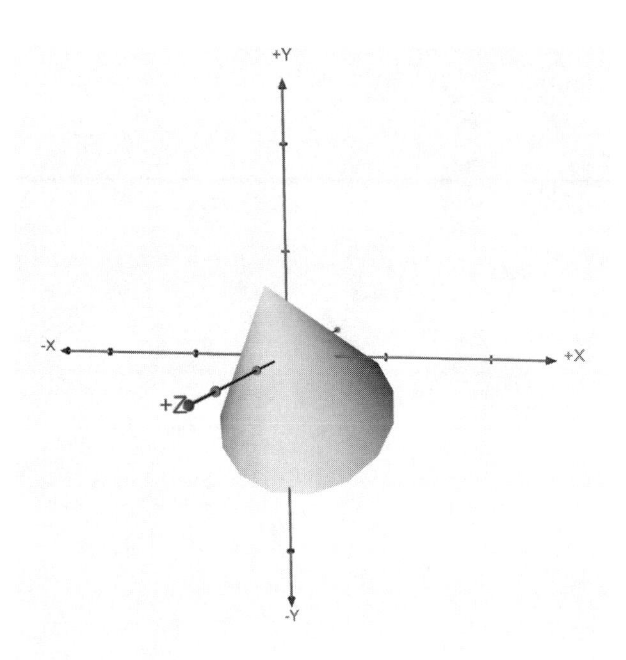

FIGURE 6–8 The cone, rotated by 45 degrees around the X axis.

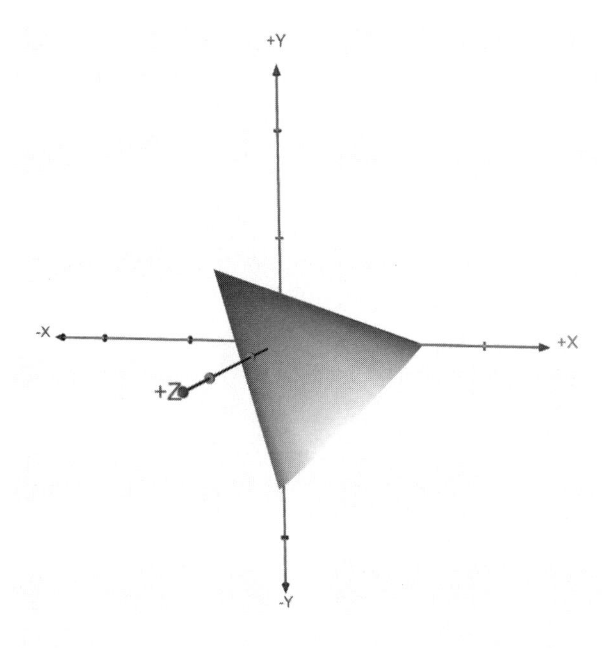

FIGURE 6–9 The cone, rotated by 45 degrees around the Z axis.

Transform3D

Transformations are represented in Java 3D by the **Transform3D** class (`javax.media.j3d.Transform3D`). A single **Transform3D** object can represent a translation, a rotation, a scaling, a combination of the three, or more complex transformations.

Transform3D Methods

There are many methods to create and modify **Transform3D** objects. These include methods to make a **Transform3D** have a translation, scale, or rotation. A **Transform3D** can also express combinations of these operations. These combinations can do complex transformations, which you will explore later. However, all transformations that are made from combinations of translation, scale, and rotation operations can be broken up (or "decomposed") into translation, scale, and rotation "components."

When you modify a **Transform3D**, the method will either modify only the specific component of the transformation, leaving the other components intact; or will replace the transformation with one that does only the specified component, resetting the other components. For example, calling `setTranslation(Vector3f translation)` changes just the translation part of the matrix, leaving any existing rotation and scale intact. Meanwhile, calling `set(Vector3f translation)` changes the entire matrix, resetting the rotation and scale to make the transformation have only the translation. You'll see both kinds of methods as we look at the specifics for setting transformations on a **Transform3D**.

In general, it is better to use the `set()` methods, since they can be quickly applied to the **Transform3D**. The methods which set only the component may require the matrix to be decomposed to apply the operation, resulting in much more processing than the `set()` methods.

In this section you'll learn about the basic **Transform3D** methods, translation, scaling, and rotation methods, and then look at how to build up more complex transformations from combinations of the basic transformations.

Most of the time you will create a **Transform3D** using the constructor:

```
Transform3D()
```

This creates a Transform3D with an identity matrix. You also can initialize the **Transform3D** with another **Transform3D**:

```
Transform3D(Transform3D t1)
```

You can also initialize the **Transform3D** with arrays of floats or doubles to manually specify the 4x4 matrix, but these are only useful if you have a matrix produced by an application.

You can initialize a **Transform3D** using a combination of translations, scales, and rotations. You'll learn about these when we talk about combination methods below.

To return a matrix to the initial identity transformation, call the method:

```
void setIdentity();
```

The mathematical details of transformations are covered in Appendix A.

Translation

Translation adds an offset to the X, Y, and Z coordinates of an object. The methods that set a **Transform3D** for translation are:

```
void set(Vector3d trans);
void set(Vector3f trans);
```

For example, you could move the cone in the Java 3D Explorer to [1.0, 0.0, 0.0] by changing the transform for its **TranformGroup**, `coneTG`:

```
tmpVector.set(1.0f, 0.0f, 0.0f);
tmpTrans.set(tmpVector);
coneTG.setTransform(tmpTrans);
```

This stores the translation in the vector `tmpVector`, which is used to set the transformation for the Transform3D `tmpTrans, which` is used to set the internal transform in `coneTG`.

There are corresponding `setTranslation()` methods:

```
void setTranslation(Vector3d trans);
void setTranslation(Vector3f trans);
```

These set only the translation components of the transformation, leaving the rotation and scaling intact.

The Java 3D Explorer uses the `setTranslation()` method when the translation changes so that the scaling and rotation are preserved. The **TransformGroup** for the cone is `coneTG`. When the translation is changed, the user interface code changes the **Vector3f** variable `coneTranslation` and then calls:

```
void setConeTranslation() {
    coneTG.getTransform(tmpTrans);
    tmpTrans.setTranslation(coneTranslation);
    coneTG.setTransform(tmpTrans);
}
```

The variable `tmpTrans` is a **`Transform3D`** that is reused for all of the transformation changes. When `setConeTranslation()` is called, it inquires the current transformation for the cone, updates the translation part of the transformation, and sets the transformation on the **`TransformGroup`**.

Scaling

Scaling changes the size of an object. Uniform scaling changes the size equally in all directions; nonuniform scaling changes the size differently in the X, Y, and Z directions. Uniform scaling is set using the methods:

```
void set(double scale);
void setScale(double scale);
```

The set() method sets the scale and resets the rotation and translation. The `setScale()` method updates only the scaling portion of the transform retaining the rotation and translation.

Nonuniform scaling is set using the method:

```
void setScale(Vector3d scale);
```

The X, Y, and Z components of the vector set the X, Y, and Z scale factors. This sets the scale while retaining the rotation and translation. There is no `set()` method for nonuniform scale (you can use `setIdentity()` followed by `setScale()` instead).

The Java 3D Explorer updates the scaling like it updates translation. There are variables for the uniform and nonuniform scaling and, when they change, a method inquires the current transform, applies the scale, and sets the current transform.

Rotation

Rotation changes the orientation of an object. There are several ways to specify rotation; the simplest is to specify the axis of rotation and the angle to rotate. So far, we have looked at rotation around the X and Z axes, but the rotation can be around any axis. For example, a 45 degree rotation around the axis [0.5, 0, 0.5] is shown in Figure 6–10. The cone is rotated along the axis shown by the white arrow.

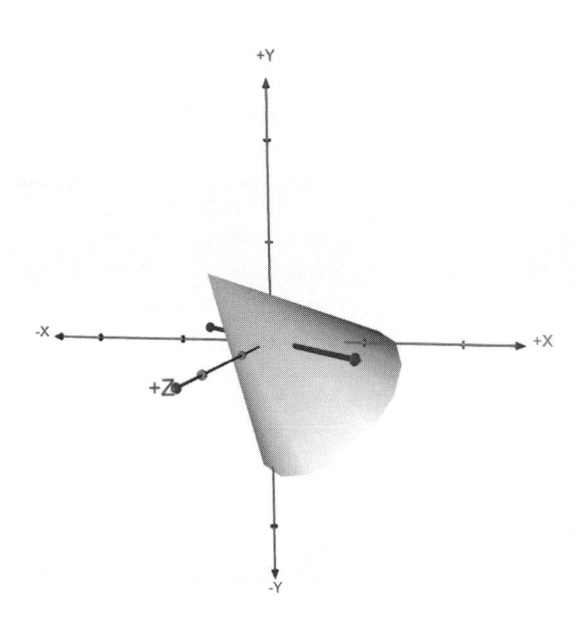

FIGURE 6–10 The cone is rotated by 45 degrees around the axis [0.5, 0.0, 0.5].

The angle of rotation tells how much to rotate the object around the axis. The direction of rotation is determined by the "right hand rule," as shown in Figure 6–11.

To visualize the direction your rotation will take, imagine grabbing the X axis of rotation with your right hand. Your thumb should point in the positive direction of the axis. Now, close your fingers around the axis. The direction your fingers curl is the direction of positive rotation around the axis.

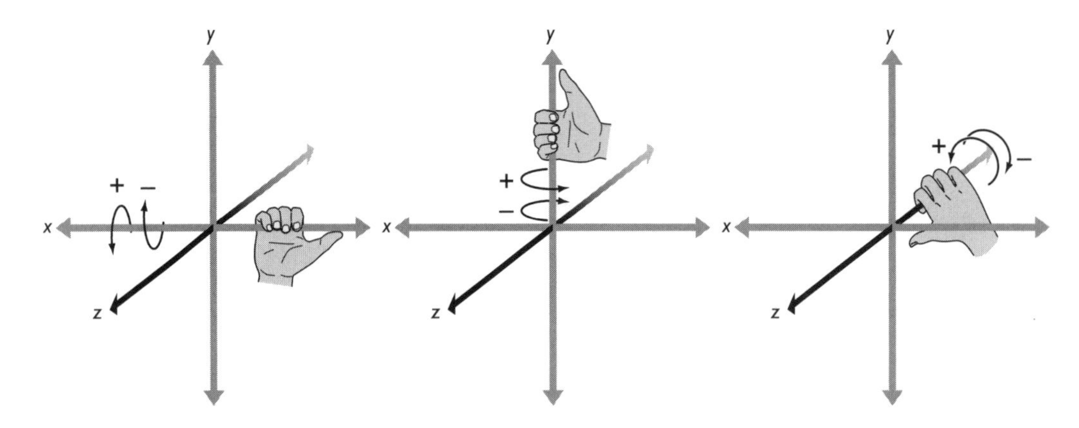

FIGURE 6–11 Positive rotation is the way your right-hand fingers curl around the axis.

The axis is specified using a vector. For example, the rotation you have just visualized is along a vector on the positive X axis, [1, 0, 0]. To rotate around the minus X axis (to the left), the vector is [–1, 0, 0]. The vector can be any combination of `x`, `y`, and `z` values. Since the axis vector is specifying a direction, it is useful to make its length be one unit; this is called "normalizing" the vector. The Java 3D Explorer shows the normalized vector alongside the unnormalized values. For example, the normalized version vector [1, 1, 0] is [.707, .707, 0]. When specifying rotations, the axis vector does not have to be normalized, but other cases (such as surface normals—see Chapter 3, "Creating and Loading Geometry") do require normalized vectors.

The **`Transform3D`** methods that set up a rotation transform using an axis and angle are:

```
void set(AxisAngle4d a1)
void set(AxisAngle4f a1)
```

These specify the axis and angle using `javax.vecmath` objects **`AxisAngle4d`** and **`AxisAngle4f`**. These are the `float` and `double` versions of objects with fields that hold the `x`, `y`, and `z` components of the axis vector and the angle much the same way as a **`Vector3f`** holds the translation values for `setTranslation()`.

There are corresponding methods that set only the rotation component of the transform:

```
void setRotation(AxisAngle4d a1)
void setRotation(AxisAngle4f a1)
```

The angle is specified in radians (see the Radians Versus Degrees section that follows). Use `Math.toRadians()` to convert between degrees and radians.

Radians versus Degrees

Java 3D expresses rotation angles in radians. Although degrees are generally easier for people to deal with than radians, computers prefer radians when doing calculations with angles. Fortunately, the formula for converting from degrees to radians isn't terribly difficult:

```
radians = (degrees / 180) * Math.PI
```

To convert 45 degrees into radians, for example, divide 45 by 180 and then multiply the result by 3.142. The answer, .785, is the number of radians in 45 degrees. To convert radians to degrees, the formula is applied in reverse:

```
degrees = (radians / Math.PI) * 180
```

An even easier way to deal with this is to use the utility routines from the java.lang.Math class:

```
double toRadians(double degrees)
double toDegrees(double radians)
```

The `toRadians()` method takes a degree value and returns its radian equivalent, and `toDegrees()` takes a radian value and returns its degree equivalent.

Following are a few of the more common angles you'll use in Java 3D, expressed in both degrees and radians (see Table 6–1).

TABLE 6–1 Converting Degrees to Radians

DEGREES	RADIANS
0	0.000
10	0.175
45	0.785
90	1.571
18	3.142
270	4.712
360	6.283

Java 3D supports other ways of specifying rotations. There are methods which rotate around the coordinate axes:

```
void rotateX(double angle)
void rotateY(double angle)
void rotateZ(double angle)
```

These are the equivalent of rotating around the positive X, Y, or Z axes. These are `set()` style methods: they reset the translation and scaling.

The method:

```
void setEuler(Vector3d euler)
```

sets all three of coordinate axis rotations in a single method, using the components of a **`Vector3d`** to specify the rotations.

Quaternions

Another powerful mechanism for specifying rotations is "quaternions." These are one of those great mathematical concepts that are useful even though they are hard to visualize. Employing quaternions is a somewhat advanced Java 3D usage, but they are necessary for some situations, so here is a brief description. Quaternions are like specifying rotations using an axis and angle, only they are better for interpolating, which is the process of calculating intermediate values between two values. For example, if we had two rotations for an object and we wanted to make a smooth transition between the rotations, we could use quaternions to find the intermediate rotations. This doesn't work if we try to calculate the intermediate rotations using axis-angle notation. Say the axis-angle rotations were [1, 0, 0, 80] and [–1, 0, 0, –100]. If you plug these values into the Java 3D Explorer, you'll find that these rotations are very close to the same result: [1, 0, 0, 80] rotates the cone to point toward the viewer with the tip slightly up; [–1, 0, 0, –100] rotates the cone toward the viewer with the top slightly down. If we wanted to find a rotation which was halfway between these rotations (perhaps as part of an animation which was moving from one rotation to the other), the usual method would be to average each component of the rotations: [(–1 + 1) /2, 0, 0, (80 + –100)/2] = [0, 0, 0, –10]. This is plainly wrong; [0, 0, 0] is a vector that doesn't point anywhere and –10 isn't the correct angle around any axis. The problem here is that axis-angle representations don't interpolate. This is where quaternions come in. A quaternion is a collection of four values like an axis-angle. The values are called x, y, z, and w. The way an axis-angle turns into these four values isn't important. The useful piece is that once the rotation is in quaternion form, the quaternion values can be interpolated to produce intermediate rotations.

Quaternions are represented in Java 3D using classes in the `javax.vecmath` package with the prefix **`Quat`**. As usual, there are float and double versions and conversion methods to convert between quaternions and axis-angles. For example, for **`Quat4f`** there is the method:

```
void set(AxisAngle4f a)
```

which sets the **`Quat4f`** to the rotation specified by the **`AxisAngle4f`**. **`AxisAngle4f`** has the corresponding method:

```
void set(Quat4f q)
```

which sets the **`AxisAngle4f`** to have a rotation that is equivalent to the **`Quat4f`**.

So, in our example, quaternions can be used to find the rotation halfway between the two rotations. The axis-angle [1, 0, 0, 80] is equivalent to the quaternion [.643, 0, 0, .766] and the axis-angle [–1, 0, 0, –100] is equivalent to the quaternion [.766, 0, 0, .643]. The quaternion halfway between these rotations is [.704, 0, 0, .704], which is equivalent to the axis-angle [1.0, 0, 0, 90], which is indeed halfway between the two rotations.

The quaternion methods on **Transform3D** are:

```
void set(Quat4d)
void set(Quat4f)
void setRotation(Quat4d)
void setRotation(Quat4f)
```

As you might expect, **Quat4f** uses floats; **Quat4d** uses doubles. The `set()` methods set the rotation and reset the translation and scale; the `setRotation()` methods set the rotation and preserve the translation and scale.

Combination Methods

The translation, scale, and rotation methods have versions that set the transform component and preserve the other components. There are also methods that allow you to set more than one component in the same call, as follows:

```
void set(double scale, Vector3d v)
void set(float scale, Vector3f v)
void set(Quat4f rot, Vector4d trans, double scale)
void set(Quat4f rot, Vector4f trans, float scale)
```

These methods reset any components they don't set.

There are other methods that set the translation and scaling, only the operations are made in reverse order:

```
void set(Vector3d v, double scale)
void set(Vector3f v, float scale);
```

In these methods the translation is applied before the scaling, so that the translation is scaled along with the object.

In equation form, the first set of methods apply the transformation:

```
x' = x * scale + v.x
y' = y * scale + v.y
z' = z * scale + v.z;
```

While the second set of methods apply the transformation:

```
x' = (x + v.x) * scale  = x * scale + v.x * scale
y' = (y + v.y) * scale  = y * scale + v.y * scale
z' = (z + v.z) * scale  = z * scale + v.z * scale
```

In the second case, the scale applies to the translation along with the coordinates. This brings us to our next topic, creating complex transformations.

Compound Transformations

So far we have been letting Java 3D create our combinations of transformations. The problem is that sometimes you will need a transformation that Java 3D doesn't provide. A common case is where you want to rotate an object around a point other than 0, 0, 0 in the local coordinate system. For example, if we rotate the cone around the point [0, 1, 0], the rotation is around the top of the cone instead of the center of the cone (see Figure 6–12).

To rotate around a reference point, we need to use a "compound" transformation. This is a combination of transforms. The **Transform3D** methods that set only one component of the transform are changing the transforms in the equation:

$$C = T * S * R$$

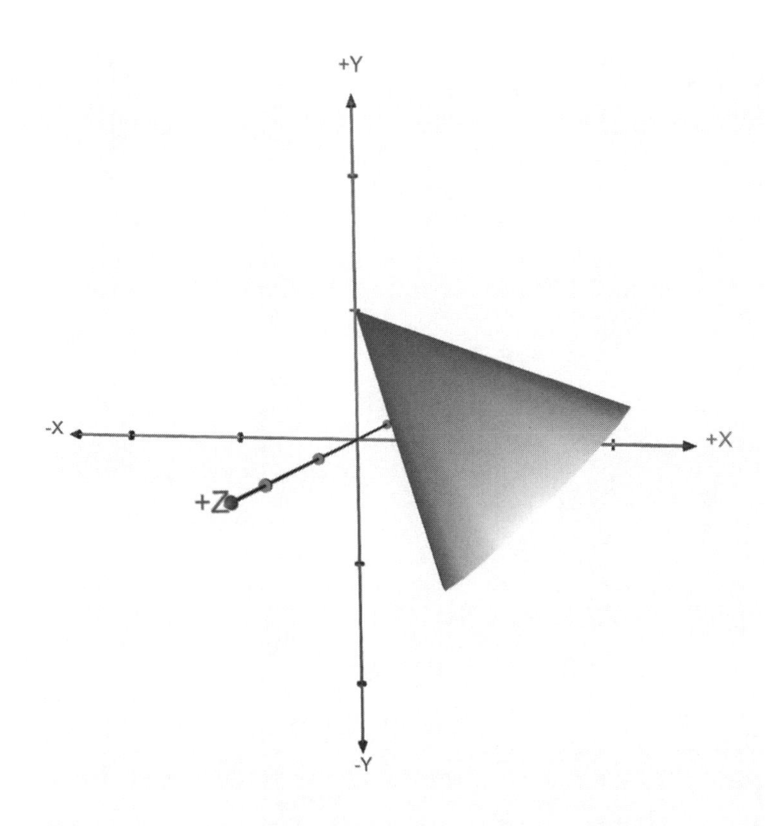

FIGURE 6–12 The cone, rotated around a reference point instead of [0, 0, 0].

where C, T, S, and R are the compound, translation, scaling, and rotation transforms. When transforms are multiplied, the result applies each transform from *right to left* (that is, the reverse of the left-to-right order we use for reading). In other words, this compound transformation applies the rotation transform to the points, followed by the scaling transform and then the translation transform.

The transform-scale methods described in the last section set up the compound transforms:

$$C = T * S$$
$$C = S * T$$

In the first case, the scale is applied and then the translation; in the second, the translation is applied and then the scale, resulting in the translation being scaled along with the coordinates.

Rotating an object around a reference point uses a slightly more complex transformation. First, the object is translated so that the reference point is at the origin, then the rotation is applied. This rotates the object around the origin, only the reference point is now at the origin, then the object is translated back to the reference point:

$$C = TrInv * R * Tr$$

Tr translates the object from the reference point to the origin, R does the rotation, and TrInv translates the object from the origin to the reference point (this is the opposite, or "inverse," of the Tr).

The transform explorer combines this transformation with the translation and scaling transforms:

$$C = T * S * TrInv * R * Tr$$

The transforms are combined using the Transform3D multiplication methods:

```
void mul(Transform3D t1, Transform3D t2);
void mul(Transform3D t1)
```

The first method sets the value of the transform to be the product of t1 and t2:

$$this = t1 * t2$$

The second sets the value of the transform to be the product of the current value of the transform and the t1:

$$this = this * t1$$

The Java 3D Explorer sets up the compound transformation by making transforms for the component transforms called `translateTrans`, `rotateTrans`, `scaleTrans`, `refPtTrans` (translate from ref point to origin), and `refPtInv` (translate from the origin to the ref point). The transforms are combined into the result transform, `tmpTrans`, using the calls:

```
tmpTrans.set(translateTrans);// C = T
tmpTrans.mul(scaleTrans);     // C = C * S = T * S
tmpTrans.mul(refPtInvTrans); // C = C * TrInv = T * S * TrInv
tmpTrans.mul(rotateTrans);    // C = C * R = T * S * TrInv * R
tmpTrans.mul(refPtTrans)// C = C * Tr = T * S * TrInv * R *Tr
```

Then the transform is copied to the **TransformGroup** for the cone to change the transformation:

```
coneTG.setTransform(tmpTrans);
```

Hierarchies

When a **TransformGroup** is the child of another **TransformGroup,** the effects of their **Transform3D** objects are multiplied so that all the children of the "child" **TransformGroup** are affected by both sets of transforms. For example, if a **TransformGroup** specifies a translation of [2, 17.5, 18], and has a child **TransformGroup** that specifies a translation of [3, 4.2, 27], their combined effect for the children of the child **TransformGroup** would be a translation of [5, 21.7, 45]. The transformation applied to a node is a combination of the transforms on the **TransformGroups** above the node.

Each **TransformGroup** defines a translation, rotation, and scaling relative to the next **TransformGroup** in the hierarchy. For example, Figure 6–13 shows an image of a simple model of a human body.

Each body part in the human is attached to the one above it: the elbow bone is connected to the shoulder bone, and the shoulder bone is connected to the body. In Java 3D the concept of being "connected to" another object is expressed by being a child of the corresponding grouping object. In other words, the shoulder joint is a **TransformGroup**; its children are a **Shape3D** node (for the geometry of the upper arm) and another **TransformGroup** for the elbow joint. The elbow joint has one child – a **Shape3D** object for the forearm. If we wanted to include the wrist and hand, it would also have another **TransformGroup** for the wrist joint. If you change the rotation of the shoulder joint by modifying the rotation value of the **Transform3D** and then writing it back into the **TransformGroup** for the shoulder joint, all the children of that **TransformGroup** will be rotated around that joint. This will not only change the orientation of the **Shape3D** object for the upper arm, it will also move the elbow, the forearm, the wrist, the hand, the fingers, and so on. When you rotate your shoulder, you find that your upper arm, lower arm, hands, and fingers all "come along for the ride." The same is true for our Java 3D model. Changing the shoulder rotation moves the entire arm (see Figure 6–14).

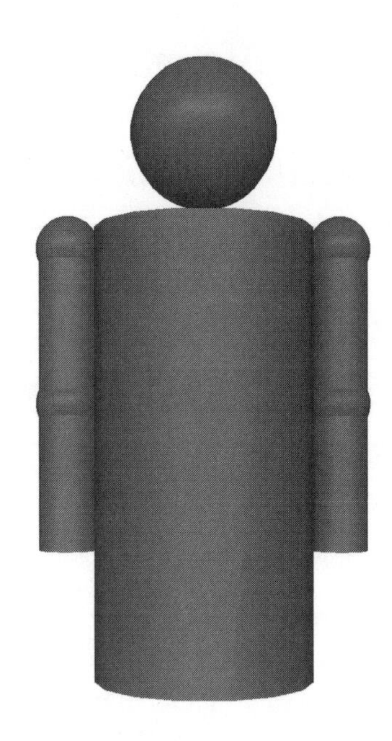

FIGURE 6–13 A Java 3D model of a human.

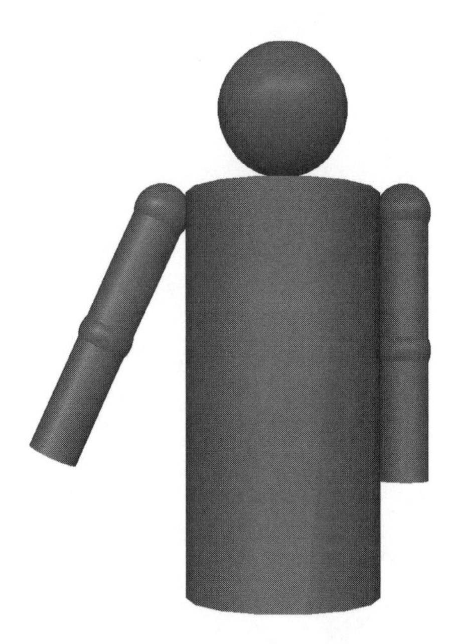

FIGURE 6–14 Changing the shoulder transform moves the whole arm.

Changing the elbow rotation just moves the wrist, as shown in Figure 6–15.

FIGURE 6–15 Changing the elbow transform moves the forearm.

The transformations for the limbs combine in the same way as multiplying transforms. If the shoulder transform is S and the elbow transform is E, the combined transform is:

$$C = S * E$$

So the transformation at the wrist is the elbow transform, E, followed by the shoulder transform, S.

Controlling Transforms with Mouse Behaviors

So far, we have been controlling transformations by making method calls on the **`Transform3D`** object, which we then copy to a **`TransformGroup`** to make a change to the scene graph. Java 3D provides behavior classes which make it easy to control transformations using the mouse. The subclasses of **`MouseBehavior`** change a transform for **`TransformGroup`** when the mouse is moved with a mouse button pressed. The subclasses are **`MouseRotate`**, **`MouseTranslate`**, and **`MouseZoom`**. They have similar interfaces. Let's look at **`MouseRotate`** in detail and then we'll look at the differences in the other classes.

The constructors for **MouseRotate** set up the association between a window that produces the mouse events and a **TransformGroup** that gets changed as the mouse moves:

```
MouseRotate();
MouseRotate(java.awt.Component c);
MouseRotate(java.awt.Component c, int flags);
MouseRotate(java.awt.Component c, TransformGroup tg);
MouseRotate(int flags);
MouseRotate(TransformGroup tg);
```

The constructors set the three basic pieces of data that affect the **MouseRotate** behavior. These are: the component to watch for mouse events, which defaults to the **Canvas3D** associated with your program; the **TransformGroup** to modify, which defaults to null (no transform to modify); and the flags that affect the way the mouse movements get translated into transform changes. We'll talk about the flag values later.

The target of the **MouseBehavior** can be set by calling:

```
void setTransformGroup(TransformGroup tg);
```

This will associate the **Behavior** with the TransformGroup.

For example, to make a **MouseRotate** control the rotation for an object:

```
MouseRotate behavior = new MouseRotate();
behavior.setTransformGroup(objTrans);
objTrans.addChild(behavior);
behavior.setSchedulingBounds(infiniteBounds);
```

This creates a **MouseRotate** behavior that changes the transform for `objTrans` when the mouse is dragged in the **Canvas3D** the scene graph is attached to. Notice that the behavior is made a child of `objTrans`. Like all Java 3D nodes, a **Behavior** must be attached to a live scene graph to be active. The **MouseRotate** behavior changes the transform when the primary mouse button is pressed and the mouse is dragged (the primary mouse button is usually the left mouse button). Dragging the mouse horizontally changes the X rotation of the transform; dragging the mouse vertically changes the Y rotation of the transform. This can make the mouse appear to "grab" the object and spin it around. The rate of rotation is controlled by the methods:

```
void setFactor(double factor);
void setFactor(double xFactor, double yFactor);
```

The scaling factors are expressed in radians of rotation per pixel of movement. See the previous note on radians versus degrees. The first method sets the X and Y scaling to the indicated factor, while the second sets each factor individually. The default factor is 0.03, which means that 50 pixels of mouse movement result in a rotation of 50 * 0.03 = 1.5 radians, or about 90 degrees of movement.

The flags passed to the constructor include the option:

```
INVERT_INPUT
```

The INVERT_INPUT flag indicates that the action of the behavior should be reversed. This is done when the **MouseRotate** behavior is used to move the **ViewPlatform** (we'll look at why moving the **ViewPlatform** is different later in this chapter). The other **MouseBehaviors** are **MouseTranslate** and **MouseZoom**.

MouseTranslate changes the X and Y translation for the **TransformGroup**. The transform changes when the mouse is dragged with the third mouse button pressed. For systems without three mouse buttons, holding down ALT while pressing the main mouse button has the same effect. The constructors and methods on this behavior are similar to **MouseRotate**, except that the scaling factor converts the mouse movement into translation instead of rotation. The default factor is 0.02. For example, 50 pixels of mouse movement equal 50 * 0.02 = 1.0 meters of translation.

MouseZoom changes the Z translation for the **TransformGroup** when the second mouse button is pressed (SHIFT/primary mouse button for single-button mice). The interface is the same, except that the default factor is 0.04, so 50 pixels of mouse movement equal 2 meters of translation.

Viewing

Viewing is closely related to transformations. Viewing is the process of turning the viewpoint of a viewer in the virtual world into an image on the screen. The **ViewPlatform** represents the viewpoint; it is associated with a **View**, which maps the viewpoint to a 2D image in a **Canvas3D**. In this section we'll look at how the transformation applied to the **ViewPlatform** changes the viewpoint, and then we'll look at the options on the **View** that specify how the viewpoint gets drawn on the **Canvas3D**.

Moving the ViewPlatform

The **ViewPlatform** is a node just like a shape or a light: it is made active by being part of a subgraph attached to a **VirtualUniverse** and it is moved around by changing transformation for the **TransformGroup** that holds it. Most programs use the **SimpleUniverse** utility to manage the **ViewPlatform**. **SimpleUniverse** creates the **ViewPlatform** along with a **TransformGroup**, **Locale**, and **VirtualUniverse**. A scene graph diagram for SimpleUniverse is shown in Figure 6–16.

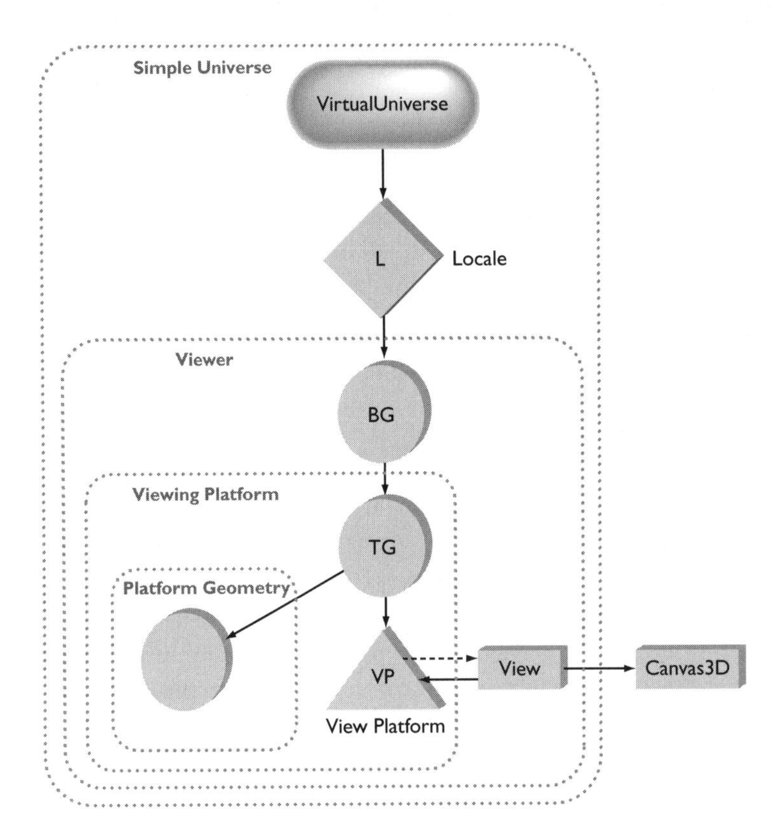

FIGURE 6–16 SimpleUniverse scene graph.

Changing the transformation for the **ViewPlatform** moves the viewpoint. The effect is similar to changing your own "transformation" in the real world. If you translate the **ViewPlatform** to the right, the scene shifts to the left. The same thing happens if you move your chair to the right: the "world" appears to move to the left. If you rotate the **ViewPlatform** to the right, the scene rotates to the left. This is the same as turning your head to the right: the world appears to rotate to the left. In general, changing the **ViewPlatform** transformation results in the inverse, or opposite, effect on the rendered image. What happens if you change the scaling for the **ViewPlatform**? The inverse effect is true again: if you scale the **ViewPlatform** by 2x, the shapes in the virtual world will appear to be ½ the size. Matching this effect in the real world is a bit more difficult, but you can imagine that if you were magically made twice as tall, everything in the world would appear to be half as big.

There is another way that changing the **ViewPlatform** transformation can change the scaling for shapes. The default **View** uses a "perspective projection." This means a shape will appear larger when it is close to the **ViewPlatform** than it does when it is far away from the **ViewPlatform**. This matches our experience in the real world. So if we move the **ViewPlatform** closer to a shape, it will appear larger; if we move further away, it will appear smaller. We'll look more at the perspective projection later when we look at the **View** object.

Basic Viewing: Finding a Good Vantage Point

Let's look at how this works in some real programs. When we looked at **HelloUniverse** back in Chapter 2, "Scene Graph Basics," we positioned the **ViewPlatform** using the method:

```
u.getViewingPlatform().setNominalViewingTransform();
```

This moves the **ViewPlatform** to make the area around [0, 0, 0] visible. Why was this necessary? The problem is that the spinning cube in **HelloUniverse** is located at [0, 0, 0]. The initial transformation for the **TransformGroup** that holds the **ViewPlatform** is the identity, which means that the **ViewPlatform** is also at [0, 0, 0]. In other words, the **ViewPlatform** is inside the spinning cube. Figure 6–17 shows an "overhead" view of the **ViewPlatform** and the cube after calling setNominalViewingPlatform().

The **ViewPlatform** is moved back so that the viewer can see the range –1 to +1 in X and Y at Z = 0.

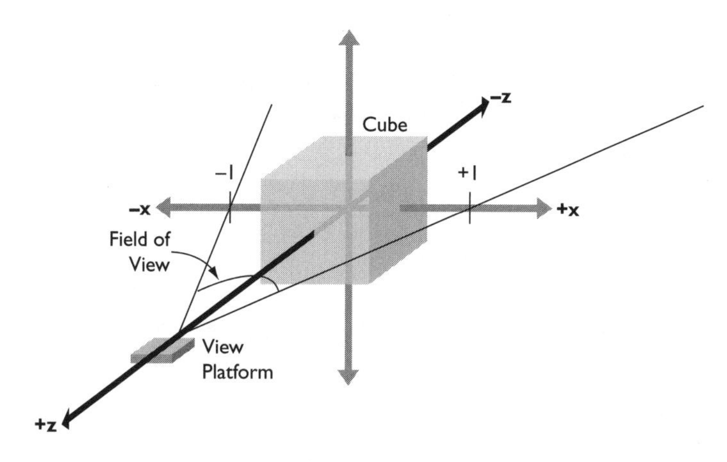

FIGURE 6–17 The effect of setNominalViewingTransform().

The setNominalViewingTransform() method looks at the *field of view* for the **View** to tell how much to move the **ViewPlatform**. The field of view is the range of angles that can be seen from the viewpoint; it is a bit like the lenses on a camera. A narrow field of view is like a telephoto lens; a wide field of view is like a fish-eye lens. The default field of view for Java 3D is about the same perception as our eyes.

Calling setNominalViewingTransform() moves the **ViewPlatform** to make the –1 to 1 range visible. As you can see in Figure 6–17, this is at about z = 2.4. This works well for objects that fit in the –1 to 1 range around the origin. What happens if the object we want to view is a different size?

When we looked at the **ObjectFile** loader back in Chapter 3, "Creating and Loading Geometry," we used the RESIZE flag on the loader to make sure that the loaded object was scaled to fit in the –1 to 1 range. Let's look at how we could move the **ViewPlatform** to view an object of any size. To do this, let's start by figuring out where in the world the scene is, and how big it is.

When we loaded the object, we got a **Scene** object, which we used to get a **BranchGroup** for the scene called sceneGroup. When the sceneGroup is made live, Java 3D will figure out a **BoundingSphere** for the scene. We can get the bounds to help position the **ViewPlatform**.

```
sceneGroup.setCapability(BranchGroup.ALLOW_BOUNDS_READ);
liveGroup.add(sceneGroup); // this makes the scene live
BoundingSphere sceneBounds =
      (BoundingSphere)sceneGroup.getBounds();
double radius = sceneBounds.getRadius();
Point3d center = new Point3d();
sceneBounds.getCenter(center);
```

Okay, so now we know the center and radius of a bounding sphere that just encloses the scene. Where do we put our **ViewPlatform**? First, we need to get the **View**:

```
SimpleUniverse u; // initialized by the earlier code.
View view = u.getViewer().getView();
```

We will position the **ViewPlatform** at the center of the bounds, and then move back in Z, far enough that the entire bound is in our field of view. First, we set up a vector to translate the ViewPlatform to the center of the bounds:

```
Vector3d viewVector = new Vector3d(center);
```

Then we use some simple trigonometry to figure out how far back to move the **ViewPlatform**:

```
double viewDistance = 1.4 * radius
            / Math.tan(view.getFieldOfView() / 2.0);
viewVector.z += viewDistance;
```

What does this do? The field of view is the viewing angle through which we see the scene, and we obtain it from our current **View**. We divide this angle by two to get the angle called alpha in Figure 6–18.

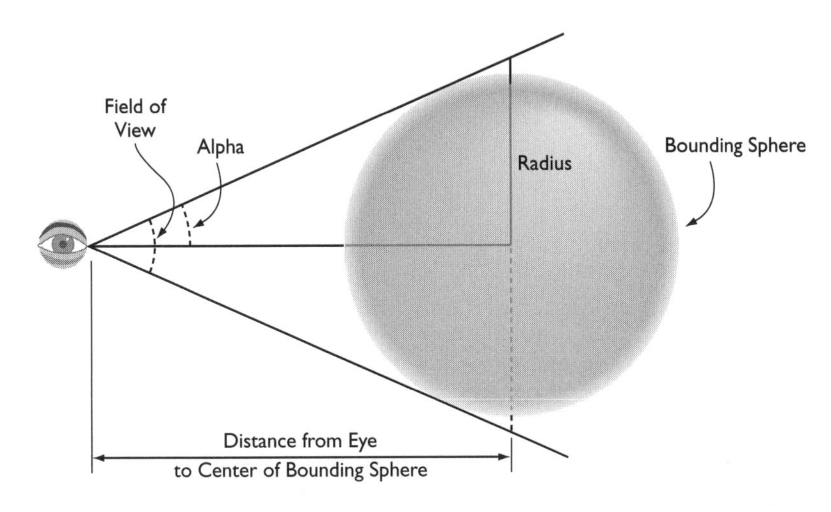

FIGURE 6–18 The alpha angle is obtained by dividing the viewing angle by two (view.getFieldOfView() / 2.0).

From the diagram, we can see that the radius of the bounding sphere divided by the distance from the viewpoint to the center of the bounding sphere is tan(alpha). Solving for the distance, we find it's just the radius divided by tan(alpha). We multiply by 1.4 to move us a little further back and make sure we have some space around the scene we're viewing, and add this distance to the Z location of the center of the bounding sphere. We leave X and Y unchanged, since we want the bounding sphere centered on our screen.

Now that we have this new viewpoint location, we set it into the viewing platform's **TransformGroup**:

```
SimpleUniverse u; // initialized above
Transform3D viewTransform = new Transform3D();
viewTransform.set(viewVector);
u.getViewPlatformTransform.setTransform(viewTransform);
```

This moves the view to point at the loaded scene.

Moving the ViewPlatform with the Mouse

In the Transformations section of this chapter, we looked at using the **MouseBehavior** classes to change the transformation for a **TransformGroup**. If we use `SimpleUniverse.setNominalViewingTransform()` to set up the initial **ViewPlatform** position, the **MouseBehaviors** can be used to move an object using the mouse. This works pretty well. The behaviors make the object rotate and translate in the direction of the mouse movement. There are problems with this approach, though. First, the transformations match the mouse movements only if the **ViewPlatform** is located along the +Z axis. Consider the case shown in Figure 6–19.

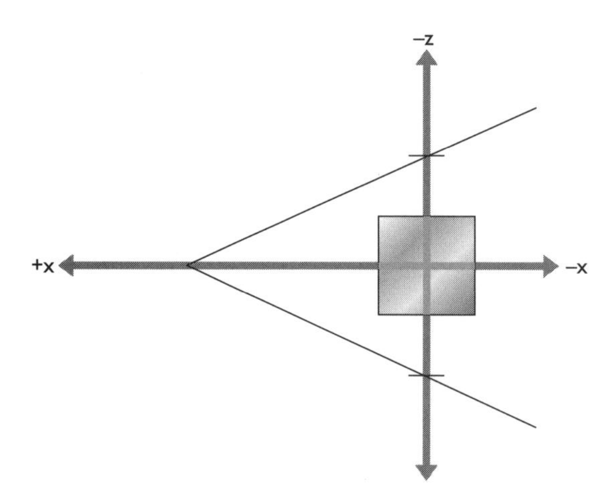

FIGURE 6–19 The ViewPlatform is positioned along +X axis.

The **ViewPlatform** has been moved so that it is located along the +X axis (see Figure 6–17 for the initial view along the +Z axis). Recall that the **MouseTranslate** behavior turns X and Y mouse movements into X and Y translations that are applied to the object. The problem is in this viewpoint, moving the mouse in the +X direction (to the right) is now indicating a movement in the –Z direction. Instead of moving the object in the –Z direction, **MouseTranslate** will move it in the +X direction, which is now toward the viewer.

The second problem is a bit subtler. Imagine yourself looking at a car in a parking lot. If you wanted to look all around the car, which would be easier: for you to walk around the car, or for you to remain stationary and have the car rotate? Having you walk around the car would be easier. There is a similar situation in

Java 3D. If the only object in your scene is a big, complicated model of a car, it is much less effort for Java 3D to move the **ViewPlatform** around the car than it is for Java 3D to rotate the car. From the program's perspective, changing the rotation for the **TransformGroup** that holds the car is all there is to rotating the car. However, inside of Java 3D there is lots of information about the car that Java 3D uses to optimize the rendering and other operations which have to be updated when the car is rotated. Moving the **ViewPlatform** involves a lot less overhead.

Java 3D 1.2.1 has a better alternative when you want to "spin" an object or scene: the **OrbitBehavior**. The basic action of **OrbitBehavior** is similar to using **MouseRotate**, **MouseTranslate,** and **MouseZoom** behaviors to control the transform for an object. The difference is that the **OrbitBehavior** moves the view platform around the object, "orbiting" around the object much like a satellite orbits the earth. The **OrbitBehavior** attaches to the **SimpleUniverse** to control the movement of the **ViewPlatform**.

The action of the **OrbitBehavior** is similar to the **MouseBehaviors**. Dragging the mouse while pressing the mouse buttons leads to different effects. Dragging while pressing the main mouse button makes the view orbit the center of rotation. This is called the ROTATE action in the flags below. The rotation appears to be the opposite direction of a **MouseRotate**, since the mouse is moving the **ViewPlatform** instead of the object. Dragging while pressing the second mouse button (or ALT-main mouse button) changes the distance from the center of rotation. This is called the ZOOM action in the flags. The third mouse button (or SHIFT-main mouse button) translates the **ViewPlatform** in the direction of the mouse movement. This is called the TRANSLATE action in the flags.

The constructors for **OrbitBehavior** take the canvas and flags for the behavior:

```
OrbitBehavior(Canvas3D canvas);
OrbitBehavior(Canvas3D canvas, int flags);
```

The flags that can be passed to the constructor are:

DISABLE_ROTATE
DISABLE_TRANSLATE
DISABLE_ZOOM
REVERSE_ALL
REVERSE_ROTATE
REVERSE_TRANSLATE
REVERSE_ZOOM
PROPORTIONAL_ZOOM
STOP_ZOOM

These allow the components of the behavior to be disabled or reversed. Reversing the actions makes the **OrbitBehavior** act more like the **MouseBehaviors** and may be more intuitive to users. The PROPORTIONAL_ZOOM flag indicates that the zoom (distance of orbit) action be proportional to distance to the center of rotation; that is, the mouse movement increases or decreases the orbit distance by a percentage of the current distance, instead of by a fixed amount. This mode is useful when the **ViewPlatform** is far away from the center of rotation. If this flag is not set, then the change in distance is proportional to the mouse movement. The STOP_ZOOM flag can be used to make sure the nonproportional zoom keeps the view radius larger than a minimum radius.

The scaling of the mouse actions is set by the methods:

```
void setRotateFactors(double xFactor, double yFactor);
void setRotXFactor(double xFactor);
void setRotYFactor(double yFactor);
void setTransFactors(double xFactor, double yFactor);
void setTransXFactor(double xFactor);
void setTransYFactor(double yFactor);
void setZoomFactor(double zFactor);
```

These methods scale the default actions. The defaults are to rotate 0.01 degrees per pixel of mouse movement for the ROTATE action, 0.01 units of translation for each pixel of mouse movement for the TRANSLATE and ZOOM actions, and to move the **ViewPlatform** 1% of the distance from the center of rotation for each pixel of mouse movement for the ZOOM action if PROPORTIONAL_ZOOM flag is set. For example, the default rotation action for a mouse movement of 100 pixels is to rotate by 100 * 0.01 = 1 radian = about 60 degrees. Calling

```
setRotateFactors(2.0, 2.0);
```

makes the rotation twice as sensitive, so that 100 pixels of movement lead to 100 * 0.01 * 2 = 2 radians = about 120 degrees of rotation.

The **OrbitBehavior** is attached to the **ViewingPlatform** for **SimpleUniverse** by calling the method on the **ViewingPlatform**:

```
void setViewPlatformBehavior(ViewPlatformBehavior b);
```

This attaches the **OrbitBehavior** to the **ViewingPlatform**. For example, to attach a **OrbitBehavior** to a **SimpleUniverse** called *u*, which is drawing to a **Canvas3D** called *canvas:*

```
OrbitBehavior orbit = new OrbitBehavior(canvas);
orbit.setSchedulingBounds(infiniteBounds);
```

```
u.getViewingPlatform().setViewPlatformBehavior(orbit);
```

More complex **ViewPlatform** behaviors can be implemented to make the viewer appear to walk or fly through a scene The Java 3D Fly Through package includes "fly," "hover," and "drive" behaviors, as well as collision detection to keep the viewer from moving through objects. See java.sun.com/products/java-media/ 3D for more information on Java 3D Fly Through.

Changing the View

While the **ViewPlatform** determines the location of the viewer in the virtual world, the **View** determines how the viewpoint gets made into a 2D image on the screen. Java 3D has a very rich viewing mechanism. We'll start by looking at the default viewing mechanism for Java 3D, called a perspective projection. Then we'll look at the options to the perspective projection, field of view, and clip distances. Next, we'll examine a different viewing mechanism, parallel projection. Finally, we'll investigate the more advanced viewing mechanisms that Java 3D supports.

Perspective Viewing

By default, Java 3D Views use *perspective projection*. The projection refers to how the 3D data gets turned into 2D shapes. For a perspective view, the 3D to 2D mapping is a bit like making a shadow on a wall using a point light source (see Figure 6–20).

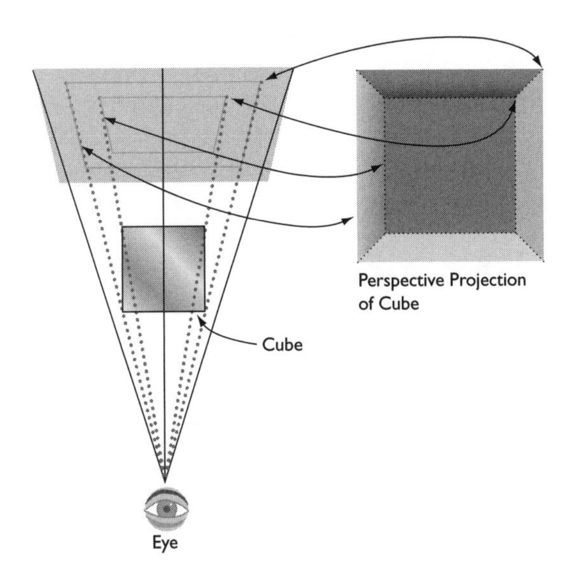

FIGURE 6–20 A perspective view is like a shadow cast from a point light source.

The left side of the figure shows an overhead view of the projection process. The eye is at the bottom, a cube to be viewed is in the middle, and the projected view of the cube is at the top. The resulting image is shown on the right. The image is like the shadow that would be cast if we put a light at the eye. Notice that the back part of the cube makes a smaller square than the front of the cube. This matches the way we view objects in the real world; an object appears smaller when it is farther away. Unlike a shadow, a projection preserves the colors of an object; only the appearance of the geometry is changed to give the illusion of depth.

Field of View

The field of view is the range of angles that can be seen from the eye. When a user looks at an image on the computer screen, the width of the screen and the viewer's distance from the screen create a natural field of view (see Figure 6–21).

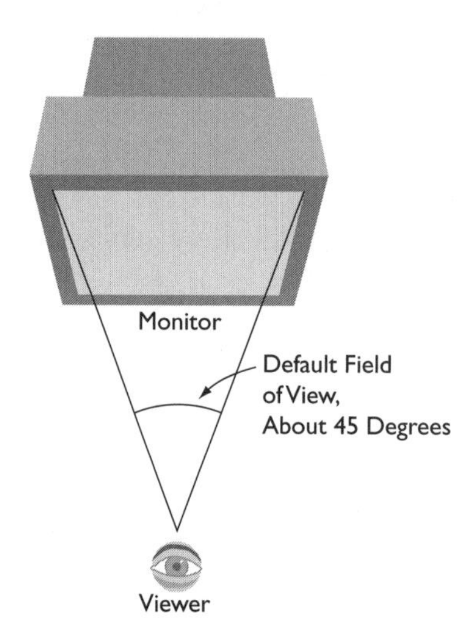

FIGURE 6–21 A viewer looking at a monitor creates a field of view.

The default field of view matches this angle, about 45 degrees. Using this field of view makes the view of the virtual world match what the viewer would see if the monitor were a window into the virtual world instead of an image of the real world.

Java 3D lets you change the field of view using the method on the View:

```
void setFieldOfView(double fov);
```

As usual, this method takes the angle in radians.

Using a narrower field of view simulates the effect of looking through a telescope or telephoto lens: distant objects appear larger and the scaling effect on distant objects is diminished. Using a wider field of view is more like a fish-eye lens. A wider range of angles is visible, but the scaling effect is increased, so that objects must be close to the eye to be visible without being made excessively smaller.

Clip Limits

The clip distances determine the closest and farthest objects that can be viewed in the **View**. In the real world, our eyes don't seem to have distance limitations: we can shift our gaze from a blade of grass to the stars above, an incredible range of distances. In practice, we do have limits on the distances we view. Our eyes can't focus on both the blade of grass and the stars at the same time. If one is in focus, the other is out of focus; this is called *depth of field*. It is possible to render scenes in computer graphics with depth of field effects, but only with some expensive calculations. Without special processing, computer graphics draw close and distant objects using a different mechanism. All of the objects in the scene are drawn in focus, but with a limited range of distances. The visible range is specified by the front and back clipping planes. Objects in front of the front clipping plane or in back of the back clipping plane are not visible.

The default clipping planes are defined in an interesting way. The clip limits are specified as distances in the real world viewer's space. That is, the clip limits are set up so that the front clip plane is 0.1 meters from the viewer's eyes, and the back clip plane is 10 meters from the viewer's eyes. This produces a good default, since it matches up with the practical limits of our eyes in the real world when focusing on a computer screen. On the other hand, it is difficult to figure out exactly what this translates into in the virtual world. Java 3D has an internal mapping between the physical world of the viewer and the virtual world of the **ViewPlatform** which it uses to translate the viewing distances. We'll look a little closer at this mapping soon.

The methods on the **View** for setting the clip distances are:

```
void setFrontClipDistance(double distance);
void setBackClipDistance(double distance);
void setFrontClipPolicy(int policy);
void setBackClipPolicy(int policy);
```

The first two methods specify the distances; the second two specify the place where the distance is measured. The clip policies are:

```
PHYSICAL_EYE
VIRTUAL_EYE
PHYSICAL_SCREEN
VIRTUAL_SCREEN
```

The PHYSICAL policies specify that the distance is measured in the physical (real) world; the VIRTUAL policies specify that the distance is measured in the virtual world. The EYE policies measure the distances from the eye (that is, from the **ViewPlatform** or the viewer), the SCREEN policies measure the distance from the screen. The default is PHYSICAL_EYE.

For now, let's consider how we could set the clip planes using distances in the virtual world so that the front and back clip distances are distances from the **ViewPlatform**. This is the VIRTUAL_EYE policy. Let's expand on our example above, where we have loaded a scene from a file so that the scene is centered at the origin, with a bounding sphere of radius meters. We figured out that we needed to move the **ViewPlatform** back by viewDistance meters to make the whole scene visible. We need to set the clipping limits so that the clip planes enclose the bounds for the scene. We can start by setting the back clip distance to be beyond the far edge of the scene. This is the view distance plus the radius of the scene. We'll multiply this by 2 to give us some room to move around and set the back clip policy to make the distance be measured from the **ViewPlatform**:

```
float backDistance = (viewDistance + radius) * 2.0;
view.setBackPlaneDistance(backDistance);
view.setBackClipPolicy(View.VIRTUAL_EYE);
```

The back clip distance can be overridden using the **Clip** node. If a **Clip** node is active, then the back clip distance comes from the **Clip** node. This is useful if you have an area of your world where the back distance should be closer than the **View** might set. For example, in an area with a **Fog** node active, shapes farther than the far distance for the **Fog** may be completely fogged. The **Clip** node can be used to clip those shapes to improve performance. See the discussion of **Fog** nodes in Chapter 4, "Appearances."

The front plane is a bit harder to place than the back clip plane. The simplest location would be right at the front edge of the extent of the scene, but that would make the scene clipped as soon as we move closer to the object. Instead, let's make the front clip distance as close to the viewer as possible so that we can move into the scene as much as possible without clipping. It is tempting to set the front clip distance to 0, so that everything is visible, right up to the eye. This doesn't work, however. Just as our eyes have a limited range of distances we can keep in focus, the perspective projection has a limited range of distances that can be represented without errors. This limitation is based on the ratio of the back clip distance over the front clip distance. In this case, let's use a ratio of 100:

```
float frontDistance = backDistance / 100.0;
view.setFrontPlaneDistance(frontDistance);
view.setFrontClipPolicy(View.VIRTUAL_EYE);
```

What happens if we set the front clip plane too close to the eye? Take a look at Figure 6–22.

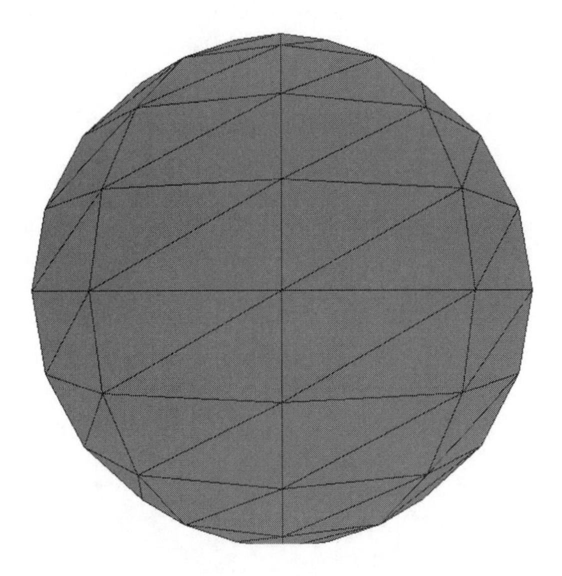

FIGURE 6–22 The inner sphere is not visible.

The figure shows a red sphere with white edges. The red sphere is actually enclosing a slightly smaller sphere that also has white edges. The inner sphere is not visible since it is inside the red sphere. Now look at Figure 6–23.

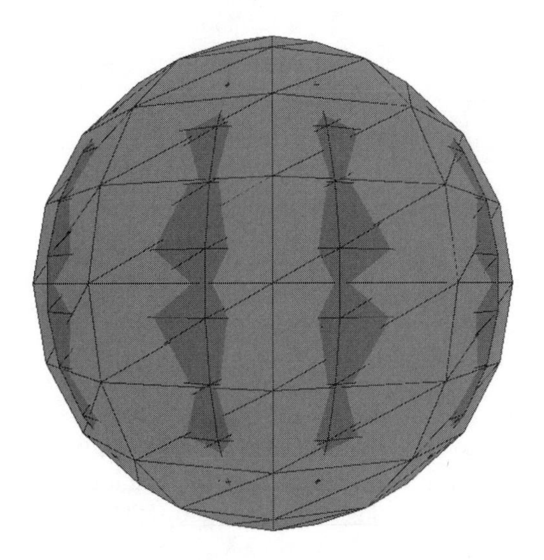

FIGURE 6–23 The inner sphere shows through.

Notice that the inner sphere is showing up through the red sphere. The difference is that the front clip plane has been moved to be too close to the eye, making the back/front ratio too large. The error happens because of the way the z values are transformed by the perspective transformation. Figure 6–24 shows what happens when we move the front clip plane closer to the eye.

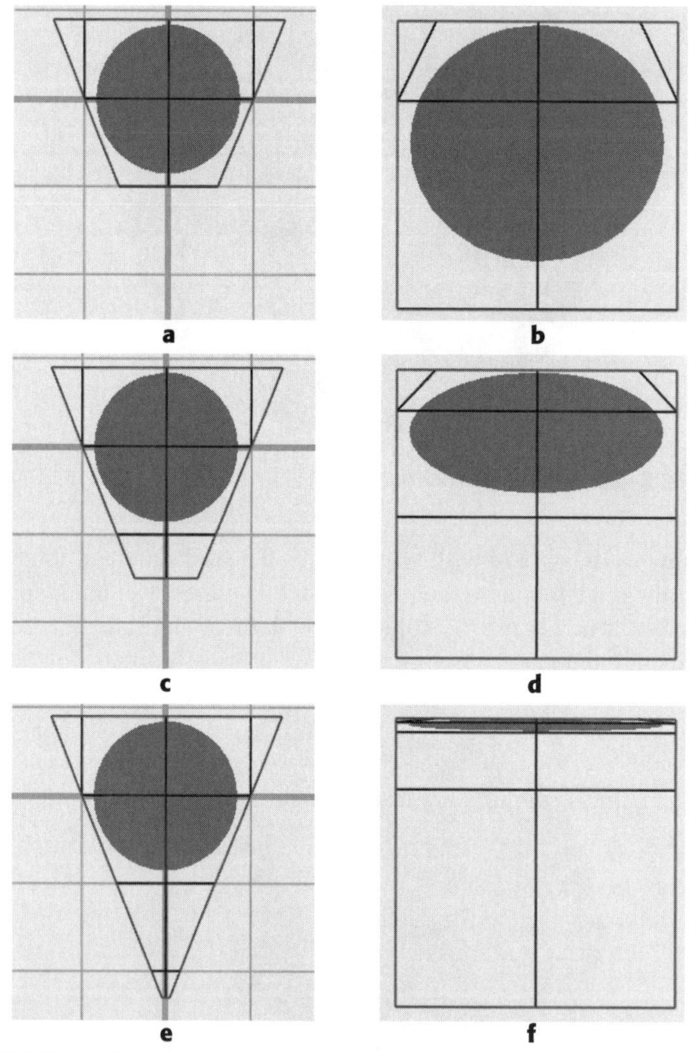

FIGURE 6–24 The effect of perspective for different back/front clip ratios. The images show an overhead view of the scene. The images on the left show the view in virtual world coordinates, and the images on the right show the same view after perspective projection. Images (a) and (b) show a ratio of 2.4; (c) and (d) show a ratio of 3.6; (e) and (f) show a ratio of 30.

The left side shows the view from overhead in virtual world coordinates. The right side shows the same view after the perspective projection. The "truncated pyramid" of the clip limits on the left becomes the square on the right. Notice that as the front plane gets closer to the eye, the sphere gets squished into the back of the projected space. When the back/front ratio gets too large, the sphere gets squished into such a small range of the depth buffer that the depth buffer stops working.

The problem with large back/front clip ratios concerns objects at the back of the depth range. The maximum ratio that can be used without a problem depends on the hardware: specifically, on the number of bits per pixel in the depth buffer. Older hardware tends to have only 16 bits per pixel and can show problems with the depth buffer for ratios as small as 100. Newer hardware tends to have more bits of resolution in the depth buffer, from 24 to 32 bits per pixel. At 32 bits per pixel, ratios up to 100,000 can be used. Since it is hard to know what resolution the end user will have, a maximum ratio of 3,000 is a good compromise, with 100 as a good conservative value.

Projection Policy

So far we have been looking at the perspective projection. It matches our perception of the world. However, there are cases where we want to draw the virtual world without any perspective effects. For example, Mechanical CAD (MCAD) displays are usually drawn without perspective. In these cases a parallel projection is used (see Figure 6–25).

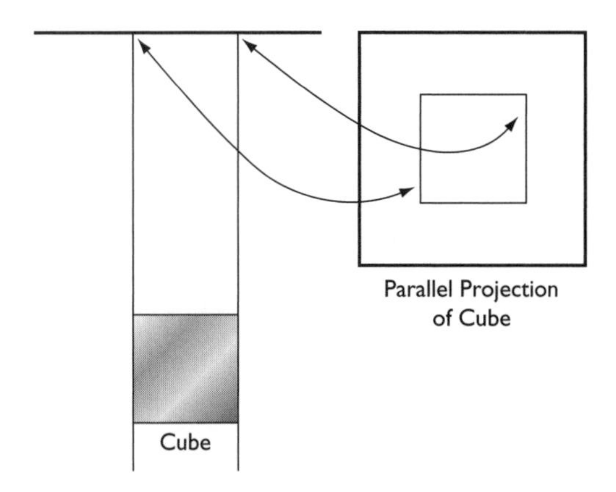

FIGURE 6–25 Parallel projection.

In a parallel projection, a shape has the same size whether it is close to the viewer or far away. The projection policy is set by the method:

```
void setProjectionPolicy(int policy);
```

The projection policy values are:

```
PERSPECTIVE_PROJECTION
PARALLEL_PROJECTION
```

When using a parallel projection, the front and back limits of the view come from the clip planes. The view is looking down the +Z axis, with the view extending through the rectangle limited by –1 and 1 in X and Y (see Figure 6–26).

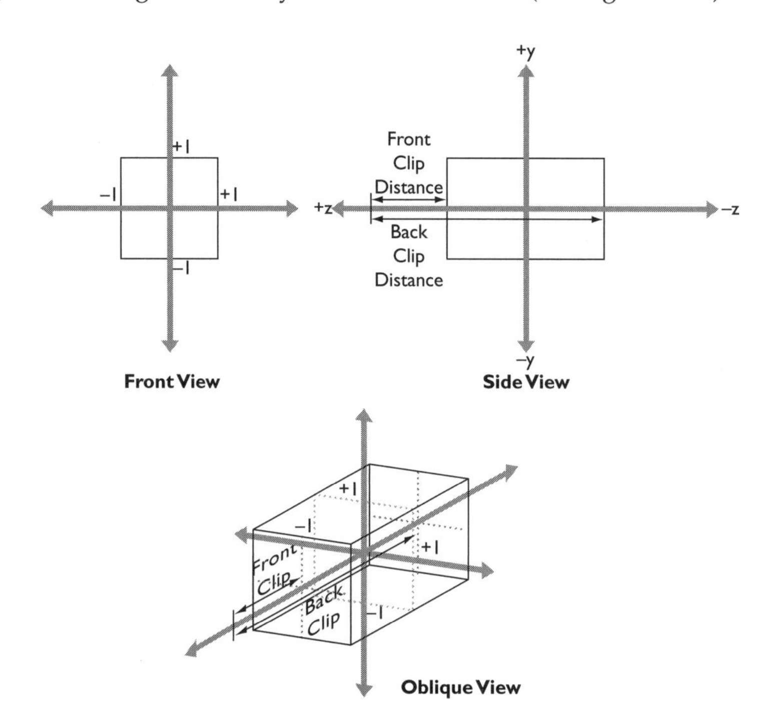

FIGURE 6–26 Parallel clip limits.

Change the scaling in the transformation for the **ViewPlatform** to change the clip limits. For example, scaling the **ViewPlatform** by 2x makes the X and Y clip limits the size, from [–0.5, –0.5] to [0.5, 0.5].

Advanced Viewing

Java 3D viewing is very versatile. We've looked at a single **ViewPlatform** connected to a **View** on a **Canvas3D**. There are many other ways to organize viewing in Java 3D. A program can switch between different viewpoints by having multiple **ViewPlatforms** and changing the **ViewPlatform** associated with the **View**. A program can have multiple views of the same virtual universe by having several **ViewPlatform-View-Canvas3D** combinations. Several **Canvas3D** can be associated with a **View**. The **Canvas3Ds** can be on different screens, making the **View** extend across the screens. The **Canvas3D** can be created with a graphics configuration that specifies stereo viewing, and Java 3D will create separate displays for the left and right eyes. See the javadoc for **View** and the Java 3D Specification for more details. Java 3D 1.3 is expected to have utilities similar to **SimpleUniverse** to make it easy to deal with these configurations.

Picking

Picking is sort of the opposite of viewing. Picking is the process of selecting shapes in the 3D virtual world using the 2D coordinates of the mouse on the **Canvas3D**. The **PickCanvas** class is used to turn the mouse location into an area of space, or **PickShape**, that projects from the viewer through the mouse location into the virtual world. **PickCanvas** extends the more general **PickTool** that defines the basic picking operations. When a pick is requested, Java 3D figures out the pickable shapes that intersect with the **PickShape**. The pick returns a list of **PickResult** objects, one for each shape that is intersected by the **PickShape**. Each **PickResult** can include one or more **PickIntersection** objects, which hold the data for each piece of the shape that intersects with the **PickShape**.

Each shape in the scene graph is pickable by default. The pickablity of shapes can be set using the following method on the **Node** base class:

```
void setPickable(boolean enable);
```

The children of a **Group** can be made unpickable by disabling picking on the **Group**.

PickTool

The **PickTool** class is the base class for picking operations. It defines the basic modes and methods for picking. The picking mode specifies the level of detail for the pick and intersection data. The picking mode is set using the method:

```
void setMode(int pickMode);
```

The modes are:

```
BOUNDS
GEOMETRY
GEOMETRY_INTERSECT_INFO
```

BOUNDS picking is the simplest mode. It returns the shapes with **Bounds** that intersect the **PickShape**. The **Bounds** are a simple representation of the geometric extent of the shape. Typically, the **Bounds** for a shape is a **BoundingSphere** that encloses the shape's geometry. Picking using bounds provides a quick intersection test, but the accuracy is not very good unless the bounds match the geometry closely. For example, the bounds for a sphere are a very tight match, since the shape of the geometry and the bounds match. On the other hand, the bounds for a single polygon are a loose fit, since the polygon is flat and the bounding sphere is round. Picking using bounds alone is effective if only a few, spatially distinct shapes are pickable, or if the shapes to be picked are spheres. The other picking modes use BOUNDS picking as a first pass, doing more exact intersection testing on the result of the BOUNDS pass.

GEOMETRY picking performs more accurate pick testing than the BOUNDS mode. It tests whether the geometry for the shape intersects the **PickShape**. To allow GEOMETRY mode picking the geometry for the shape must have the ALLOW_INTERSECT capability bit set. The **PickResult** for a GEOMETRY pick indicates the shape that was picked, but no more detailed information.

GEOMETRY_INTERSECT_INFO picking does the same pick test as the GEOMETRY mode, but it also saves information so that detailed information about the intersections can be inquired. The **PickResult** for a GEOMETRY_INTERSECT_INFO pick allows **PickInteresction** objects to be inquired for each intersection of the **PickShape** with the shape's geometry. The **PickIntersection** includes data on the subprimitive picked (the point, line, triangle, or quad), the closest vertex to the intersection, and geometric data at the intersection such as the coordinate, color, surface normal, and texture coordinates. The inquiries required to calculate the **PickIntersection** data require that the **Shape3D** to be picked has the ALLOW_GEOMETRY_READ capability bit set, and the **GeometryArrays** to be picked have the ALLOW_FORMAT_READ, ALLOW_COUNT_READ, and ALLOW_COORDINATE_READ capabilities set. If the geometry is indexed, the ALLOW_COORDINATE_INDEX capability must be set. To inquire the intersection color, normal, or texture coordinates, the corresponding READ capability bits must be set. The **PickTool** has a method that can be called on a **Shape3D** or **Morph** node to set the capability bits to allow GEOMETRY_INTERSECT_INFO picking:

```
static void setCapabilities(Node node, int level);
```

The level parameter indicates the level of picking to enable. The values are:

```
INTERSECT_TEST
INTERSECT_COORD
INTERSECT_FULL
```

INTERSECT_TEST sets the capability bits for GEOMETRY mode picking. INTERSECT_COORD sets the capability bits for GEOMETRY_INTERSECT_INFO picking to allow the inquiry of the coordinates of the intersections. INTERSECT_FULL sets the capability bits to allow all of the intersection information to be inquired.

The methods that perform the picks are:

```
PickResult[] pickAll();
PickResult[] pickAllSorted();
PickResult pickAny();
PickResult pickClosest();
```

All of these methods return null or a zero-sized array if no shape was picked. The `pickAll()` method returns an array of **PickResults**, indicating all of the shapes which intersect with the **PickShape**. The `pickAllSorted()` method returns the same array as `pickAll()`, with the **PickResults** sorted by distance from the viewer; the closest picks are returned first in the array. The `pickAny()` method returns a single, arbitrarily chosen **PickResult**; this method may be faster than `pickAll()` if several shapes are picked, since the picking method will return as soon as a valid pick is found. The `pickClosest()` method will return the first **PickResult** that would have been returned by `pickAllClosest()`.

The **PickShape** is usually set using the **PickCanvas** class. When using the **PickTool** directly, the **PickShape** can be specified using the method:

```
void setShape(PickShape ps, Point3d startPt);
```

This method sets the **PickShape**. The distance to the start point is used for the picking methods that sort by distance. There are several variations on this method which allow the **PickShape** to be specified as a bounds, ray, segment, cone, or cylinder. See the javadocs for **PickShape** and **PickTool** for more details.

PickCanvas

The **PickShape** for the **PickTool** is usually set using a **PickCanvas**. **PickCanvas** extends **PickTool** to make it simple to pick using mouse events on a **Canvas3D**. The **PickCanvas** constructors take the **Canvas3D** and **BranchGroup** or **Locale** to be picked:

```
PickCanvas(Canvas3D c, BranchGroup b);
PickCanvas(Canvas3D c, Locale l);
```

The **PickShape** is specified using the methods:

```
void setShapeLocation(int xpos, int ypos);
void setShapeLocation(java.awt.event.MouseEvent mevent);
void setTolerance(float t);
```

The `setShapeLocation()` methods set the **PickShape** to center on the location of the mouse. The **PickShape** extends from the viewer, or *eye point*, through the mouse location and into the virtual world. The setTolerance() method specifies the radius of the **PickShape** around the mouse location. It indicates how close the picked shape has to be to the mouse location to be pickable. The eye point and pick tolerance create a cone that extends from the eye into the scene (a cylinder for a parallel view—see Figure 6–27).

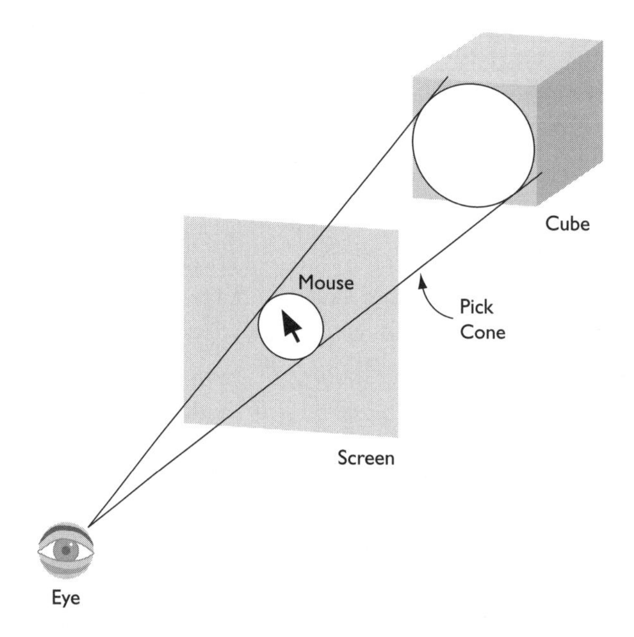

FIGURE 6–27 Picking in a perspective view uses a cone from the eye around the mouse point.

A pick tolerance of 0.0 indicates that the cone should have a radius of 0.0 around the mouse point. This makes the **PickShape** a line that extends from the eye through the mouse point. Using a "zero tolerance" may speed up the picking slightly, since it is simpler to calculate the pick intersection with a line instead of a cone, but picking points and lines is almost impossible using a tolerance of 0.0. Use a non-zero value like 0.5 or more if you want to pick points and lines. A pick tolerance of 2–4 pixels works well, making it easy to pick shapes without getting the mouse exactly on top of the shape to be picked.

PickCanvas extends **PickTool**, so the methods to set the pick mode and make the pick are the same as for **PickTool**. For example, to initialize picking on a **Canvas3D** called `canvas` and a **BranchGroup** called `scene`, a program can call:

```
PickCanvas PickCanvas = new PickCanvas(canvas, scene);
pickCanvas.setPickMode(PickTool.GEOMETRY_INTERSECT_INFO);
pickCanvas.setTolerance(4.0f);
```

Then for each mouse event, the program sets the **PickShape** and does the pick by calling:

```
pickCanvas.setShapeLocation(mouseEvent);
PickResult[] results = PickCanvas.pickAll();
```

This returns the set of picks within 4 pixels of the mouse event, with complete intersection information available.

PickResult

A **PickResult** holds the pick information for a shape that intersects the **PickShape**. The **PickResult** indicates the shape that was picked, information about the scene graph that holds the shape, and information about the individual intersections of the **PickShape** with the geometry in the shape.

The picked shape can be inquired from the **PickResult** using the method:

```
Node getObject();
```

This will return the picked shape, which will be a **Shape3D**, **OrientedShape3D,** or **Morph**.

The **PickResult** also indicates the parent nodes that hold the shape. The complete set of ancestors can be inquired by calling:

```
SceneGraphPath getSceneGraphPath();
```

The **SceneGraphPath** indicates the path from the **Locale** to the picked node, including any **Link-SharedGroup** connections. You can search the **SceneGraphPath** for a specific node type using the method:

```
Node getNode(int nodeType);
```

Where the nodeType is:

```
SHAPE3D
MORPH
PRIMITIVE
GROUP
TRANSFORM_GROUP
SWITCH
```

```
LINK
BRANCH_GROUP
```

The closest ancestor of the indicated node type is returned.

If `GEOMETRY_INTERSECT_INFO` mode picking is used, the specific intersections can be inquired from the **PickResult** using the methods:

```
int getNumIntersections()
PickIntersection getIntersection(int index);
```

These return the number of intersections and information on a specific intersection.

PickIntersection

A **PickIntersection** holds the information about a single intersection of a **PickShape** with a shape node. The intersection point is the location on the geometry which is closest to the center of the **PickShape**. When the pick is made, the **PickIntersection** records the **GeometryArray** that was intersected; the subprimitive that was intersected, that is, the point, line, triangle, or quad that was intersected; and the VWorld coordinate of the intersection point. Additional information can be inquired from the **PickIntersection**, such as the closest vertex to the intersection point, the local coordinates, color, surface normal, or texture coordinates at the intersection point.

Other Uses for Picking

Picking can also be used for collision avoidance, keeping the **ViewPlatform** from moving into objects in the scene. To do this, a **PickShape** is constructed that encloses the current and new locations of the **ViewPlatform**. Then a pick is done. If the pick returns any hits, an object obstructs the movement of the **ViewPlatform**.

Summary

This chapter covered three basic tools: transformations, viewing, and picking. The basic transformation operations are translation, scaling, and rotation. **Transform3D** supports methods that set the transform to have these operations, or to change only that component of the transformation. Multiplying simple transformations can form more complex transformations. Hierarchies of objects can be formed in which objects further down the hierarchy combine their transformation with the higher-level objects. The mouse can control transformations using **MouseBehaviors**.

Viewing is the mapping of a viewpoint in the 3D virtual universe to a 2D window on the screen. Transforming the **ViewPlatform** can change the viewpoint. The mouse can control the transformation for the **ViewPlatform** using an **OrbitBehavior**. The **View** controls the mapping of the viewpoint to the **Canvas3D**. Options on the **View** include the projection mode, field of view, and clipping limits.

Picking returns the shapes in the virtual world using the mouse to specify points on the **Canvas3D**. Picking returns **PickResult** objects for each shape that is selected. Information on the individual intersections can be inquired from the **PickResult**.

APPENDIX

A Transformation Details

You can use **Transform3D** objects without understanding exactly how they work, but a bit of background is useful. A transformation turns the X, Y, and Z coordinates of a point into a new set of coordinates:

$$x' = m00 * x + m01 * y + m02 * z + m03$$
$$y' = m10 * x + m11 * y + m12 * z + m13$$
$$z' = m20 * x + m21 * y + m22 * z + m23$$

where [x, y, z] are the original coordinates, [x', y', z'] are the transformed coordinates, and m00, m01, and so on are the variables that produce the desired transformation. A "matrix" is a compact representation of the following numbers:

m00 m01 m02 m03
m10 m11 m12 m13
m20 m21 m22 m23
m30 m31 m32 m33

Note that there is a fourth row of coefficients. We won't cover these values here, but they are part of the general "4x4" matrix used for 3D transformations (they are used for some viewing operations).

The simplest matrix is the "identity matrix":

1 0 0 0
0 1 0 0
0 0 1 0
0 0 0 1

This is the equivalent of the equations:

$$x' = x$$
$$y' = y$$
$$z' = z$$

In other words, an identity matrix does not change the coordinates that pass through it; it has no translation, scale, or rotation. Next, consider a matrix that has values in the right column:

1 0 0 5
0 1 0 3
0 0 1 1
0 0 0 1

This is the equivalent of the equations:

$$x' = x + 5$$
$$y' = y + 3$$
$$z' = z + 1$$

This matrix specifies a translation of [5, 3, 1]. What happens if you want to scale the point, instead of translate it? You change the diagonal coefficients instead of the right column, as follows:

7 0 0 0
0 7 0 0
0 0 7 0
0 0 0 1

If you plug those matrix values into the equations above, you get:

$$x' = 7 * x$$
$$y' = 7 * y$$
$$z' = 7 * z$$

This produces a uniform scaling, as expected. Of course, the scaling can be non-uniform. To scale a sphere into a horizontal ellipsoid, you might use the following:

7 0 0 0
0 3 0 0
0 0 3 0
0 0 0 1

This would multiply Y and Z by 3, but X by 7, which would stretch the sphere more along the horizontal axis than the other axes.

Rotations are more complex, and are based on the sine and cosine values for the angles of rotation. The details are beyond the scope of this book, but can be found in any good graphics textbook. Here is a simple example. A rotation of 90 degrees around the X axis is represented by the matrix:

$$\begin{matrix} 1 & 0 & 0 & 0 \\ 0 & 0 & -1 & 0 \\ 0 & 1 & 0 & 0 \\ 0 & 0 & 0 & 1 \end{matrix}$$

This is the equivalent of the equations:

$$x' = x$$
$$y' = -z$$
$$z' = y$$

You can see this using the Java 3D Explorer with the rotation [1, 0, 0, 90]. Before the transformation, the top of the cone is at 0, 1, 0. After, it is at 0, 0, 1; this is the same result we get by plugging 0, 1, 0 into the equations.

Other rotations produce much more complex matrices. The main thing you need to know is that a rotation will change the values in the upper left 3x3 submatrix of a Transform3D object.

This introduces an interesting problem—since the same part of the matrix is used to store both the scaling and the rotation, how does that work? The answer is that a matrix that has both scaling and rotation has those values combined in the upper left 3x3 submatrix. In fact, a `Transform3D` can hold the result of many operations joined together.

Index

A

B

F

G

H

I

J

L

M

N

O

P

Q

R

S

W

X

Y